FAMILY PRACTICE LIBRARY

BIOFEEDBACK: BEHAVIORAL MEDICINE

Seminars in Psychiatry

BIOFEEDBACK: BEHAVIORAL MEDICINE

Edited by

Lee Birk, M.D.
Assistant Clinical Professor of Psychiatry
Harvard Medical School
Clinical and Research Director
Boston Area Associates for Learning Therapies, Inc.
Newton, Massachusetts

GRUNE & STRATTON
A Subsidiary of Harcourt Brace Jovanovich, Publishers
New York   San Francisco   London

The chapters of this book originally appeared in the November, 1973 issue (Volume V, Number 4) of *Seminars in Psychiatry,* a quarterly journal published by Grune & Stratton, Inc. and edited by Milton Greenblatt, M.D. and Ernest Hartmann, M.D.

Library of Congress Cataloging in Publication Data

Main entry under title:

Biofeedback: behavioral medicine.

"The chapters of this book originally appeared in the November, 1973, issue (volume V, number 4) of Seminars in psychiatry."
   Includes bibliographies.
   1. Biofeedback training. 2. Medicine, Psychosomatic. 3. Psychotherapy. I. Birk, Lee, ed.
II. Seminars in psychiatry. [DNLM; 1. Feedback.
2. Psychophysiology. WL102 B6145   1973]
BF319.5.B5B56   615.8   73-19707
ISBN 0-8089-0832-4

© 1973 by Grune & Stratton, Inc.

All rights reserved. No part of this publication may be reproduced or transmitted in any form or by any means, electronic or mechanical, including photocopy, recording, or any information storage and retrieval system, without permission in writing from the publisher.

Grune & Stratton, Inc.
111 Fifth Avenue New York, New York 10003

Library of Congress Catalog Card Number 73-19707
International Standard Book Number 0-8089-0832-4

Printed in the United States of America

Contributors

Adler, Charles S., M.D., Co-Director, Applied Biofeedback Institute, Denver, Colo.

Birk, Lee, M.D., Assistant Clinical Professor of Psychiatry, Harvard Medical School, Boston, Mass.; and Clinical and Research Director, Boston Area Associates for Learning Therapies, Inc., Newton, Mass.

Bleecker, Eugene R., M.D., Research Fellow, Cardiovascular Research Institute, University of California Medical Center, San Francisco, Calif.

Brady, Joseph V., Ph.D., Professor of Behavioral Biology, Department of Psychiatry and Behavioral Sciences, Johns Hopkins University School of Medicine, Baltimore, Md.

Budzynski, Thomas H., Ph.D., Assistant Professor of Clinical Psychology, University of Colorado Medical Center, and Co-Director, Applied Biofeedback Institute, Denver, Colo.

Engel, Bernard T., Ph.D., Chief, Laboratory of Behavioral Sciences, Gerontology Research Center, National Institute of Child Health and Human Development, and Associate Professor of Behavioral Biology, Johns Hopkins University School of Medicine, Baltimore, Md.

Glueck, Bernard C., M.D., Director of Research, Institute of Living Hospital, Hartford, Conn.

Green, Elmer E., Ph.D., Director of Voluntary Controls Project, Research Department, Menninger Foundation, Topeka, Kans.

Harris, Alan H., Ph.D., Assistant Professor of Behavioral Biology, Department of Psychiatry and Behavioral Sciences, Johns Hopkins University School of Medicine, Baltimore, Md.

Legalos, Charles N., M.A., Staff Member, Boston Area Associates for Learning Therapies, Inc., Newton, Mass.; and Ph.D. Candidate, York University, Toronto, Canada.

Lynch, James J., Ph.D., Director, Behavioral Laboratories, Department of Psychiatry, University of Maryland Medical School, Baltimore, Md.

Mullaney, Daniel J., Ph.D., Research Assistant, Department of Neuropsychiatric Research, U.S. Naval Hospital, San Diego, Calif.

Sargent, Joseph D., M.D., Chief of Internal Medicine, Department of Neurology, Neurosurgery and Internal Medicine, Menninger Foundation, Topeka, Kans.

Schwartz, Gary E., Ph.D., Assistant Professor of Personality Psychology, Department of Psychology and Social Relations, Harvard University, Cambridge, Mass.; and Chief of Psychophysiology, Erich Lindemann Mental Health Center, Boston, Mass.

Shapiro, David, Ph.D., Senior Associate in Psychiatry (Psychology), Harvard Medical School, Massachusetts Mental Health Center, Boston, Mass.

Sterman, M. B., Ph.D., Chief, Neuropsychology Research, Veterans Administration Hospital, Sepulveda, Calif.; and Associate Professor of Anatomy and Psychiatry, University of California at Los Angeles, Los Angeles, Calif.

Stoyva, Johann M., Ph.D., Associate Professor of Psychology, University of Colorado Medical Center, Denver, Colo.

Stroebel, Charles F., Ph.D., M.D., Director, Laboratories for Experimental Psychophysiology, Institute of Living, and Research Professor of Psychology, University of Hartford, Hartford, Conn.

Surwit, Richard S., Ph.D., Research Fellow in Psychology, Department of Psychiatry, Harvard Medical School, Massachusetts Mental Health Center, Boston, Mass.

Walters, E. Dale, M.A., Associate Research Psychologist, Research Department, Menninger Foundation, Topeka, Kans.

Weiss, Theodore, M.D., Assistant Professor, Department of Psychiatry, University of Pennsylvania School of Medicine, Philadelphia, Pa.

Contents

I. INTRODUCTION AND SCIENTIFIC OVERVIEW

Chapter 1
Biofeedback—*Furor Therapeuticus* .... *Lee Birk*   1

Chapter 2: Basic Science Foundations of Biofeedback and Autonomic Learning
Introduction...*Lee Birk*   5
Instrumental (Operant) Conditioning of Visceral and Autonomic Functions...................................*Alan H. Harris and Joseph V. Brady*   9

Chapter 3: Biofeedback—Specific Learning Component vs Nonspecific Learning Component (Placebo Effect)
Introduction...*Lee Birk*   17
Biofeedback Treatment in Medicine and Psychiatry: An Ultimate Placebo? ....*Charles F. Stroebel and Bernard C. Glueck*   19

II. CLINICAL APPLICATIONS

Chapter 4: Tension Headache
Introduction...*Lee Birk*   35
EMG Biofeedback and Tension Headache: A Controlled Outcome Study
    Thomas H. Budzynski, Johann M. Stoyva, Charles S. Adler, and Daniel J. Mullaney   37

Chapter 5: Migraine Headache
Introduction...*Lee Birk*   51
Psychosomatic Self-regulation of Migraine Headache
    Joseph D. Sargent, E. Dale Walters, and Elmer E. Green   55

Chapter 6: Cardiac Arrhythmias
Introduction...*Lee Birk*   69

Part I
Clinical Applications of Operant Conditioning Techniques in the Control of the Cardiac Arrhythmias............................*Bernard T. Engel*   73

Part II
Operant Conditioning of Heart Rate in Patients With Premature Ventricular Contractions ....*Theodore Weiss and Bernard T. Engel*   79

Part III
Learned Control of Ventricular Rate in Patients With Atrial Fibrillation
    Eugene R. Bleecker and Bernard T. Engel   101

Part IV
Learned Control of Cardiac Rate and Cardiac Conduction in the Wolff–Parkinson–White Syndrome .... *Eugene R. Bleecker and Bernard T. Engel* 115

Chapter 7: Raynaud's Disease
Introduction .... *Lee Birk* 121
Biofeedback: A Possible Treatment for Raynaud's Disease
Richard S. Surwit 123

Chapter 8: Hypertension
Introduction .... *Lee Birk* 131
Biofeedback and Essential Hypertension: Current Findings and Theoretical Concerns .... *Gary E. Schwartz and David Shapiro* 133

Chapter 9: Epilepsy
Introduction .... *Lee Birk* 145
Neurophysiologic and Clinical Studies of Sensorimotor EEG Biofeedback Training: Some Effects on Epilepsy .... *M. B. Sterman* 147

III. THE STATE OF THE ART: GENERAL REMARKS

Chapter 10: Biofeedback and Psychotherapy
Introduction .... *Lee Birk* 167
Biofeedback and Psychotherapy .... *Charles N. Legalos* 169

Chapter 11: Biofeedback Procedures in the Clinic
Introduction .... *Lee Birk* 175
Biofeedback Procedures in the Clinic .... *Thomas H. Budzynski* 177

Chapter 12: Furor Therapeuticus *Revisited*
Introduction .... *Lee Birk* 189
Biofeedback: Some Reflections on Modern Behavioral Science
James J. Lynch 191

IV. CONCLUSION

Chapter 13
Biofeedback: A Clinician's Overview .... *Lee Birk* 203

Index 207

I. Introduction and Scientific Overview

Chapter 1

Biofeedback—*Furor Therapeuticus*

Lee Birk, M.D.

ON A PANORAMIC HILLTOP one rainy afternoon in colonial America, about 200 years ago, perhaps during one of the dread yellow fever epidemics, Benjamin Rush, signer of the Declaration of Independence, framer of the Constitution, and "Father of American Psychiatry" is said to have emerged inexplicably from his horse-drawn carriage, suddenly overcome with a sense of his healing mission and his therapeutic method; in this mood, with a burst of zealotry, he is said to have shaked his cane at the city below while uttering the words: "Bleed and purge all the city!" This done, he got back in the carriage and drove on to see his next case.

Benjamin Rush was far from a stupid man—with very little scientific knowledge to go on he had correctly divined genuinely useful hygienic principles for the soldiers in the Revolutionary War. These were first published by the Army in 1778, and were republished again in 1808, again twice during the Civil War, and again for a fifth time in 1908. And, on the subject of bloodletting, Rush had rightly observed that it "raised the pulse rate when it was depressed, (and) that it also reduced its force . . . ; (that it) checked vomiting, removed delirium. coma and obstinate wakefulness, checked or prevented hemorrhages . . . , and caused redness of the eyes to disappear . . . ."[1]

Therapeutic purging and bleeding have passed from this scene (in the civilized medical world), but there still is a lesson for us in the anecdote: It can be all too easy to become fervently fascinated with a treatment method, caught up in a kind of *furor therapeuticus,* the practice and technology of which leaves little time and energy either for careful empirical evaluation of therapeutic efficacy, or for the analysis of underlying pathophysiology.

Biofeedback is now the subject of articles in *Science* and *Playboy* and is being used as treatment for insomnia, headache, irregular heartbeat, circulatory problems, backache, anxiety, strokes, epilepsy, asthma, reading disability, and high blood pressure. More recently, there was even a report on biofeedback as a contraceptive method, and a book just published as a paperback earlier this year asserts: "Biofeedback is

—an extraordinary technique which allows you to control the

©*1973 by Grune & Stratton, Inc.*

state of your health, happiness and well-being solely through the power of your mind.
—a spectacular scientific theory which has become fact in hospitals and laboratories across the country.
—a revolutionary method of getting quickly in touch with the inner self.
—something Yogis and Zen masters have been doing for centuries to achieve inner peace and joy.
—a visonary technology which places the power for change and control in the hands of the individual and allows him to control his own destiny."[2]

While this paperback description is both utopian and sensationalistic, it is perhaps not an exaggeration to point out that a new "behavioral medicine," biofeedback, now still in its infancy, may in fact represent a major new developing frontier of clinical medicine and psychiatry. Medicine, of course, for centuries has relied on only four major curative mechanisms: aiding and potentiating the body's (or "the mind's") natural recuperative powers; pharmacologic mechanisms; surgical interventions; and the effect of person,[3] from "bedside manner" to transference. Now, with the development of behaviorally derived techniques of demonstrated effectiveness, capable of bringing previously involuntary bodily functions under voluntary control, it appears we have in hand the makings of a fifth major mechanism for psychiatry and medicine, a behavioral control mechanism, in which the patient can, for the first time, take a fully active and direct role in literally learning not to be sick.

The purpose of this seminar is to take a hard critical look from an evidence-oriented point of view at biofeedback and especially at the manifold medical and psychiatric claims being made for it. Each major chapter is written by an eminent research person in a particular area, and the emphasis throughout is on looking both at research data bearing on the physiology underlying various applications, and at whatever empirical data is available bearing on clinical outcome.

As the collector and editor of these separate contributions, in this introductory chapter I will make some general orienting remarks that I hope will be of help to nonspecialized readers. Since the field derives conceptually from the experimental psychology of learning, is technologically implemented through electrical engineering, and deals with part of the subject matter of medicine, psychiatry and neurology, and since most of us are nonspecialized in one or more of these areas, it seems wise to emphasize general principles and not to take necessary technical background for granted. With this in mind, each chapter is prefaced with an Introduction by the editor.

Biofeedback can be defined as the use of monitoring instruments (usually electrical) to detect and amplify internal physiologic processes within the body, in order to make this ordinarily unavailable internal information available to the individual and literally to feed it back to him in some form. Thus for example, through biofeedback, a patient with a tension headache (caused by abnormal levels of tension or contraction in the frontalis or occipitalis muscles of the head) ordinarily knows only that the front or the back of his head hurts or doesn't hurt. With biofeedback he can know precisely from moment to moment what is the level of tension (contraction) in his frontalis and occipitalis muscles, through the use of an electromyogram to detect activity in those muscles, and through an amplification and display system by means of which he can "hear" the level of muscular activity as a series of small clicks that are spaced in time as a function of the level of tension, and/or he can "see" the level of tension by reading a dial.

Similarly, without biofeedback, patients with labile hypertension have no way of knowing when their blood pressure is elevated. For this disorder, of course, the monitoring instrument must be a sphygomanometer of some type, measuring blood pressure, not an electromyogram measuring muscle tension.

The clinical importance of this is that, utilizing such organ-specific artificial feedback, with continued exposure and practice (biofeedback training) there is evidence that individuals can learn to bring under partial conscious control particular bodily functions that ordinarily are not subject to conscious control (like heart rate and blood pressure, for example) or which ordinarily are under only minimal conscious control, like tension in the frontalis and occipitalis muscles.

The general term feedback was coined by the mathematician Norbert Weiner and concisely defined by him as "a method of controlling the system by reinserting into it the results of its past performance."[3] Biofeedback, then, is a special case of this, where the system is a biologic system and where the feedback is artificial, mediated by man-made detection, amplification, and display instruments, rather than being present as an inborn feedback loop inherent within the biologic system. Biologically, then, one should not be so surprised at the efficacy of biofeedback, since, as one reviewer put it, "every animal is a self-regulated system owing its existence, its stability and most of its behavior to feedback controls."[4] Every infant, for example, learns hand–eye coordination, (and even the whole concept of space and distance) by means of "visual proprioceptive feedback." By repeated trial-and-error learning, through feedback, eventually the infant comes to be able to control his arm and hand muscles quite precisely, and to reach accurately toward where things are in space, choosing the right direction, distance, angle of approach, and width of grasp on the basis of prior feedback-gained experience.[5] In a way then, the real surprising thing is not that biofeedback should work at all, but that it was not experimentally looked for and so "discovered" earlier than it actually was.

Its relatively late discovery is at least partially attributable to the existence of a prevailing bias in the history of the experimental psychology of learning—a bias that has tended somewhat artificially to divide processes of learning into Pavlovian or respondent conditioning applying to autonomic and visceral learning, and governing the functioning of the organs and glands inside the body, vs. Skinnerian, "operant," or instrumental conditioning, previously thought to apply only to the learning of external behaviors mediated by skeletal muscles.

This dichotomy has now been proven to be somewhat artificial and at least partially erroneous. In retrospect, it can be seen as deriving in part from the fact that Pavlov and his followers—Pavlov was a physiologist—interested themselves heavily in the study of autonomic learning processes, whereas Skinner and his followers, all psychologists, have consciously and explicitly eschewed interest in the "black box" of the brain and in internal physiology generally.

Analogously, they limited themselves primarily to using the operant model for studying learning processes. And so the legend arose and was mistakenly codified not only as theory but as fact that the processes of operant conditioning apply only to external behaviors mediated by skeletal muscle, and not to internal autonomic behaviors. During the 1960s, this factually unfounded assumption began to be eroded by early experimental work.

To sum up then, it seems accurate to say that before about 1960 this field was undiscovered, because of the paralytic effects of rigidly held but untested theories. During the 1960s the field began to be scientifically explored by experimental study and pilot clinical study. In 1973, the public is being urged by the zealots and the entrepreneurs who are now claiming this whole field as their own to enjoy a euphoric ride on the crest of a wave of therapeutic ebullience that sometimes borders on mindless omnipotence.

The aim of this seminar is to provide a balanced factual presentation of each major area of biofeedback research and practice, to permit a sober, accurate, and research-inducing assessment of its achievement and its potential. It is my own belief that biofeedback has already been proven to have very considerable clinical value in certain clinical situations (see Chapter 13) and that it seems also to have great promise in some other areas, but that it is in clear danger of being oversold, to the point of counter-movement revulsion, unless balance can be reintroduced. Dr. Lynch in Chapter 12 presents a possible view of the broader social processes that may in part determine the drift toward wild hopes and spectacular claims in this field. Chapter 2, by Drs. Alan Harris and Joseph Brady, amounts to a recapitulation of the basic science underpinnings of these new treatment techniques. Chapter 3 deals with the crucially important matter of the placebo component in all biofeedback procedures. Chapters 4 through 9 each deal with one major area within the field as a whole.

Chapter 10, on biofeedback and psychotherapy, gives some flavor of how the new Behavioral Medicine can be usefully combined even with more traditional medical treatment, even in the case of combination with its most distant medical cousin, psychotherapy. Chapter 11, entitled "Biofeedback Procedures in the Clinic," is a collection of early clinical experience on the therapeutic use of biofeedback for a variety of conditions. Its author, Dr. Budzynski, is both the major developer of biofeedback for tension headache—he also is the author of the chapter (Chapter 4) that deals with this subject—and one of the most widely experienced and versatile psychosomatic and psychiatric clinicians using biofeedback.

In the last chapter, the editor attempts to give a very brief summation of the achievements of biofeedback to date, in terms of clinical techniques of established practical value.

REFERENCES

1. Binger C: Revolutionary Doctor: Benjamin Rush. 1746–1813. New York, Norton 1966
2. Karlins M, Andrews LM: Biofeedback: Turning on the Power of Your Mind. New York, Warner Books, 1972
3. Birk L, Stolz S, Brady JP, et al: American Psychiatric Association Task Force Report: Behavior Therapy in Psychiatry, June 1973
4. Wiener N: Cybernetics. Cambridge, MIT Press, 1961
5. Mayr O: The origins of feedback control. Sci Am 223:111, 1970
6. Taylor JG: The Behavioral Basis of Perception. New Haven, Yale Univ Pr, 1962

Chapter 2: Basic Science Foundations of Biofeedback and Autonomic Learning

Introduction

THIS CHAPTER is the most important one in this seminar because it constitutes a review of the basic science foundations of biofeedback; these underlie all the endless variations in technique as they can be devised to ameliorate various psychosomatic conditions. The material in this chapter is excerpted* from a longer review article dealing with the whole broad field of Visceral and Autonomic Conditioning. Only material directly relevant to clinical biofeedback is included.

As Drs. Harris and Brady explain:

> [Visceral and autonomic conditioning is] . . . concerned with the effects of behavioral conditioning procedures, both classical and instrumental, upon physiological response measures commonly referred to as "visceral" and/or autonomic (e.g., heart rate, blood pressure, gastric motility). Within this general framework, the laboratory animal research to be reviewed can be divided into three broad investigative categories based upon the relationship between the physiological measures and the conditioning procedures. In the first *Classical Autonomic Conditioning* category, the physiological event which is conditioned appears initially as an unconditioned response (e.g., salivation) to an unconditioned stimulus (e.g., food) and is subsequently observed to occur (though not necessarily in identical form) during presentation of a conditioned stimulus (e.g., bell) which has been paired repeatedly with the unconditioned stimulus. The second *Concurrent Autonomic Conditioning* category is defined by experimental approaches which depend primarily upon operant conditioning procedures to establish and maintain ongoing performances (e.g., lever pressing) while concurrently measuring physiological changes (e.g., hormone elevations) which show systematic relationships to the conditioned instrumental behavior. And in the third *Instrumental Autonomic Conditioning* category, an essential feature of the procedure emphasizes a contingency relationship between antecedent physiological changes (e.g., heart rate increase) and experimentally programmed environmental consequences (e.g., food delivery and/or shock avoidance).

It is this third category, Instrumental Autonomic Conditioning, that is crucial for biofeedback, because all biofeedback procedures follow the operant or instrumental paradigm of learning:†

criterion (autonomic) response → reinforcing stimulus.

This is a contingency relationship because the reinforcing stimulus (S) occurs precisely when and only if the criterion response (R) occurs. The reinforcing stimulus can be a primary reinforcer, like water for water-deprived animals,

---

*Reproduced with the kind permission of the Editors of the *Annual Review of Psychology*. The full review article, covering Classical Autonomic Conditioning and Concurrent Autonomic Conditioning, is to be published in February 1974 by the *Annual Review of Psychology*. Only Instrumental Autonomic Conditioning is reviewed here, because of its immediate relevancy to clinical biofeedback work.

†The operant paradigm, remember, was falsely thought not to apply to autonomic learning at all until about 1960, because of an historical accident in the development of experimental psychology and physiology. (See pages 3–4 of Chapter 1).

© 1973 by Grune & Stratton, Inc.

or it can be a progress–information or "feedback" type of reinforcer for humans who want to learn control of the response system and thus are reinforced by the cues about progress toward that goal.

The autonomic (or autonomically mediated) responses reinforced in biofeedback procedures are as diverse as warming of the hands, in migraine (see Chapter 5); changing the rate or rhythm of the heart, as in work with cardiac arrhythmias (see Chapter 6); to changing even the activity of the brain itself,* as in pilot work with epileptic patients (see Chapter 9).

The reinforcing stimulus in these disparate applications may be a light, a tone, or a reading on a dial, but it is always some sensory signal or stimulus that provides information to the patient about "how he is doing" in attempting to learn to bring this function under voluntary control, by indicating to him minute quanta of early success in changing a bodily function in a desired direction.

This whole chapter on the basic science foundations of biofeedback deals only with animal studies; obviously, then, it is important to remember that cats and rabbits, for example, who do not "know" what they are trying to achieve by biofeedback, are also able to be influenced by these same kinds of learning processes, through the use of primary reinforcing stimuli.

With or without instruction, cognitive awareness or conscious intention to change a particular bodily function, the fundamental and irreducible paradigm of biofeedback is the operant conditioning of bodily responses that usually are largely out of awareness.

Careful reading of this chapter will make it clear that most of the very powerful specific effects in studies on biofeedback in animals have been obtained through the use of primary reinforcement. That is, the reinforcement used has been not just a simple sensory stimulus, as in most human studies, but a primary reinforcing stimulus. For example, water is used to reinforce water-deprived animals (see page 9) or electrical brain stimulation in the "reward area" of the brain is used (see page 11).

In animals the use of "feedback" as such thus has assumed a much lesser importance than in the human work; here feedback, when used at all, typically is used as a bridging stimulus between fixed ratio reinforcements. One illustrative example of this is the study of Hothersall and Brener.[1] Working with curarized rats, with the goal of producing heart rate changes, they presented a light flash each time the heart rate met a prescribed criterion level. Then, for every 25 successive heart beats successfully meeting the criterion level, the primary reinforcer of electric brain stimulation was applied. The feedback lights are used as bridging stimuli which, stated anthropomorphically, "tell the animal he is doing all right" and that a primary reinforcement is on the way. Or, to state this in the more precise and useful scientific language of operant conditioning, the feedback lights are bridging stimuli that function as discriminitive stimuli preceding the availability of the primary reinforcer.

The emphasis on pure feedback in human work is probably due in part to the

---

*Actually, strictly speaking this particular application deals not with an ANS-R (autonomic nervous system response), but with a CNS-R (central nervous system response).

verbal reinforcement provided by enthusiastic experimental subjects and patients to experimenters and clinicians.

The use of primary reinforcing stimuli should be much more carefully explored in future human studies. This might strengthen the effects produced quite considerably, because in effect most human biofeedback work uses the weakest element in the procedures that have been developed with animals. There are, of course, some considerable practical problems, in that it is cumbersome and awkward, even with cooperation and consent, to deprive human patients of water, for example, in order to use the availability of water as a reinforcer. And it would certainly be unethically radical in most clinical cases to resort to electrical brain stimulation in humans, except perhaps under very special and life-threatening circumstances.

Lee Birk, M.D.

REFERENCE

1. Hothersall D, Brener J: Operant conditioning of changes in heart rate in curarized rats. J Comp Physiol Pyschol 68:338–342, 1969

Instrumental (Operant) Conditioning of Visceral and Autonomic Functions

Alan H. Harris, Ph.D., and Joseph V. Brady, Ph.D.

ANIMAL STUDIES concerned with the experimental analysis of instrumental autonomic conditioning represent a relatively recent development in the visceral learning field with laboratory roots originating in the work of Neal Miller and his students at Yale in the mid-1960s. Indeed, several earlier reports with human subjects[15,29,35,40,42,45,55,61,63] had foretold of such "operant" learning effects involving visceral and autonomic processes, and an extensive literature on "voluntary" physiologic control by Yoga meditation and breathing techniques[1-3,68,69] has long been available. However, the experimental analysis of such instrumental autonomic conditioning effects in the animal laboratory has clearly activated a new research era in the investigation and application of such "visceral learning" phenomena.

The earliest reported animal learning experiments on instrumental autonomic conditioning involved an attempt by Miller and Carmona[49] to change the rate of *salivation* in a water-deprived dog by operantly reinforcing both increases and decreases in this antecedent autonomic response with a contingent environmental consequence (i.e., water reward). Although the results of this study showed clearly that such autonomic responses could be operantly controlled, attention was focused upon the possible role of skeletal muscle activity as a "mediator" of the observed visceral changes. Since the curarization technique used to control such skeletal muscle mediation produced direct effects upon salivation, an experiment by Trowill[67] explored the operant control of *heart rate* in curarized laboratory rats using rewarding electrical brain stimulation (medial forebrain bundle at the level of the posterior hypothalamus) as a contingent reinforcing consequence. Although the actual changes were small, both increases and decreases in heart rate were successfully conditioned. A subsequent study by Miller and DiCara[50] showed that the magnitude of the instrumentally conditioned heart rate response could be influenced dramatically (producing changes approximating 20% of basal values) by a "shaping" procedure that required the animals to meet a progressively more difficult criterion in order to obtain the rewarding brain stimulation. In addition, this experiment also demonstrated that such operantly conditioned autonomic changes could be brought under discriminative control of the specific stimulus complex that provided the occasion for reinforcement of either the heart-rate-raising or lowering response. In a further confirmation of this instrumental heart rate conditioning effect, Hothersall and Brener,[34] using curarized rats and electrical brain stimulation reward, incorporated a feedback light whenever the prescribed criterion was met, and extended their investigation to include a demonstration of operant

---

Excerpts from "Animal Learning—Visceral and Autonomic Conditioning," by Alan H. Harris and Joseph V. Brady, Annual Review of Psychology, Vol. 25. © 1974 by Annual Reviews Inc. All rights reserved.

© *1973 by Grune & Stratton, Inc.*

extinction when the instrumentally conditioned heart rate response was no longer reinforced with brain stimulation.

Persistent concern with the degree of skeletal involvement in such instrumental autonomic conditioning was reflected in a series of experiments by Black[6] with dogs initially trained on a lever-pressing shock–avoidance task and subsequently curarized for operant conditioning of either *electromyographic* or heart rate responses. The level of curarization insured little or no overt movement but did not completely eliminate the EMG response. The results showed that the instrumentally conditioned heart rate changes were closely associated with the conditioned EMG changes, which readily transferred to affect the performance in the noncurarized state. In a later report, however, Black[8] concluded that the heart rate response could be conditioned independently of overt movement, without conceding that the operantly controlled autonomic changes occurred in the absence of some central events related to the initiation and performance of skeletal motor responses. DiCara and Miller[18] had in fact hypothesized that such central activity (e.g., motor cortex impulses) classically conditioned to elicit heart rate changes might account for the demonstrated autonomic effects but argued on the basis of an experiment with curarized rats using a tail-shock control that such indirect skeletal motor influences could not provide a sufficient account of the instrumentally conditioned heart rate change. They further showed[18] that the completely curarized rat (i.e., no EMG responses from the gastrocnemius muscle) could learn to both increase and decrease heart rate as an operant shock–avoidance response, thus establishing that the instrumental autonomic conditioning effect was not an artifact of the electrical brain stimulation reinforcer. The results of this study also showed that discriminative control over the conditioned heart rate change could be developed and maintained by a stimulus that always preceded shock presentation. Such instrumentally learned heart rate changes have also been shown to persist in the absence of reinforced practice trials over extended periods (e.g., 3-mo retention tests) and to be relearned after extinction.[21]

Transfer of learning effects have also been demonstrated in a series of studies by DiCara and Miller,[22,23] in which heart rate changes instrumentally conditioned under curare were subsequently (1 wk later) observed in free-moving rats, and additional training in the noncurarized state was shown to produce changes of even greater magnitude. Similar transfer was also demonstrated from the noncurarized to the curarized state, and the differences in respiration and gross movement were found to decrease as the differences in heart rate increased. This emergent response specificity has also been documented in an experiment by Miller and Banuazizi,[48] in which independent operant control of both heart rate changes and *intestinal contractions* was demonstrated, and Fields[27] has subsequently demonstrated the remarkable specificity of such conditioning effects by producing instrumentally learned increases or decreases in the *P-R interval of the EKG* independently of changes in the P-P interval. However, that the issues related to a linkage between somato-motor and cardiovascular activities in the instrumental autonomic conditioning process have not been definitively settled is clearly evident in a recent report by Goesling and Brener,[30] which showed that two different training procedures (i.e., immobility training vs. activity training) can have a greater effect upon heart rate changes in curarized rats than the reinforcement contingencies per se. Prior discrimination training, however, appears to have no effect upon the magnitude of the changes produced by subsequent instrumental heart rate conditioning in curarized animals.[64]

Interaction effects involving operant heart rate conditioning and other related psychophysiologic processes have been investigated in a number of animal learning studies. Curarized rats operantly pretrained to decrease heart rate have, for example, been shown to subsequently acquire (in the noncurarized state) shuttle-box escape–avoidance behavior more readily than rats similarly pretrained to increase their heart rate.[25] It has also been reported[26] that blood pressure changes were positively correlated significantly with heart rate decreases instrumentally conditioned as an avoidance response in rhesus monkeys, but such blood pressure effects were uncorrelated with instrumentally conditioned heart rate increases in the same animals. Differences in the opposite direction have been reported with respect to epinephrine and noreprinephrine by DiCara and Stone[24] who found higher endogenous cardiac and brainstem catecholamine levels in rats operantly trained to increase heart rate as compared to rats instrumentally conditioned to decrease heart rate. Cardiac H^3-norepinephrine retention studies by these same authors, however, suggested that rats trained to decrease heart rate under curare were subjected to greater stress than rats trained to increase heart rate. Of additional interest in this regard is the finding by DiCara et al.[17] that an intact neocortex is essential for instrumental autonomic conditioning, although this appears not to be the case with respect to the classical conditioning of the same heart rate and gastrointestinal responses.

The instrumental conditioning of *blood pressure* in the curarized rat was convincingly demonstrated by DiCara and Miller[19] using a shock–avoidance procedure to reinforce both increases and decreases in systolic pressure levels independently of changes in heart rate and rectal temperature. In a subsequent study, these same investigators[20] using electrical brain stimulation as a reinforcer with the curarized rat dramatically confirmed the specificity of such instrumental autonomic learning by selectively conditioning vasomotor tone increases in one ear and vasomotor tone decreases in the other ear of the same animal. Significantly, these conditioned *blood flow* changes were not correlated with heart rate, rectal temperature, or vasomotor tone in the tail, suggesting a remarkable and previously unrecognized localization of sympathetic action. Following a replication of these[19] findings, Pappas et al.[53] further demonstrated that instrumentally conditioned systolic blood pressure increases and decreases in noncurarized rats did not transfer to the curarized state, but that retraining the same animals after curarization produced even larger magnitude pressure changes than in the noncurarized state. Similar observations with respect to the specificity of instrumentally conditioned cardiovascular changes previously reported by DiCara and Miller[19,22] received additional support from the Pappas et al.[53] finding that the operantly conditioned blood pressure effects were independent of heart rate and gross skeletal activity.

Diastolic blood pressure elevations of large magnitude (50–60 mm Hg) conditioned instrumentally as a shock avoidance response in the rhesus monkey were first reported by Plumlee,[54] although the relatively short duration of the changes and the observed postural effects suggested mediation by a Valsalva maneuver (i.e., alteration of intrathoracic pressure by abdominal muscle contraction). Somewhat more modest elevations in mean arterial pressure (e.g., 25 mm Hg) were maintained in squirrel monkeys by Benson et al. (18) for periods of 20 min or longer as a result of an operant reinforcement contingency arrangement that required the indicated pressure change as a shock–avoidance response. And Harris et al.[31] have also shown that substantial elevations in both systolic and diastolic blood pressure (e.g., 50–60 mm Hg) could be established and maintained in dog-faced baboons by an operant conditioning procedure that provided for food delivery and shock avoidance programmed as environmental consequences contingent upon prescribed increases in diastolic pressure levels. The instrumentally conditioned blood pressure changes were sustained for intervals up to and exceeding 5 min and appeared to bear somewhat systematic but complex temporal relationships to variations in heart rate. More recently, these same authors[32] have extended this basic instrumental autonomic conditioning procedure with the baboon to produce more sustained and clinically relevant increases (30–40 mm Hg) in both systolic and diastolic blood pressure throughout daily 12-hr experimental sessions. Significantly, the maintained, instrumentally conditioned blood pressure increases were accompanied by elevated but progressively decreasing heart rate levels.

Instrumentally conditioned *glandular response* changes have also been demonstrated in an experiment with curarized rats rewarded by electrical brain stimulation for both increases and decreases in the rate of *urine formation* by the kidney.[51] Using inulin-^{14}C and tritiated p-aminohippuric acid (PAH), it was also determined that both *glomerular filtration* rate and *renal blood flow* were systematically altered by the operant conditioning procedure, though heart rate, blood pressure, and peripheral blood flow were not, confirming the high degree of specificity and localization of action emphasized in previous reports.[19,20,27,48] More recently, Banuazizi[4] has extended the experimental analysis of selectively conditioned intestinal contractions in the curarized rat by demonstrating discriminative stimulus control of both short- and long-duration intestinal responses operantly reinforced by shock avoidance. Significantly, the study also included a control for the unconditioned effects of the electric shock as a possible "state-dependent" influence upon the contractile response and confirmed the instrumental intestinal conditioning under even these more stringent requirements.

The role of *feedback* stimulation in the establishment and maintenance of instrumentally conditioned visceral and autonomic response changes has been emphasized in several recent studies[31,32,34,44] despite the somewhat equivocal status of the "interoceptive discrimination" issue as reflected in the literature of the past decade.[36,37,46,65,66] The early and more recent studies of Miller and his students as reviewed previously involved reinforcing stimulus changes (e.g., electric brain stimulation) that provided immediate feedback following visceral or autonomic response variations. As more extended-duration instrumental autonomic conditioning effects have been investigated, however, exteroceptive stimuli (e.g., lights, tones) linked with the internal environment by advanced electrophysiologic recording and amplification techniques[12,13,33,43] have provided both digital and analogue representations of critical interoceptive events and processes. In addition, such feedback stimuli serve as conditioned reinforcers bridging the temporal gap between the visceral response and its maintaining environmental consequences. The effectiveness of such stimulus feedback applications has been convincingly demonstrated in the instrumental heart rate conditioning studies of Hothersall and Brener[34] with curarized rats, and the operant blood pressure conditioning experiments of Harris et al.[31,32] with laboratory baboons.

Despite this emergent operational orientation, *interpretive* and *theoretical accounts* of instrumental autonomic conditioning procedures and results continue to focus upon "mediational" issues as these have been reviewed and discussed at length in several recent reports.[14,38,39,41,57,58] As fruitless as the resulting regress to "pure" operant status may now appear, the controversies surrounding experimental attempts to control such "voluntary mediators" in instrumental autonomic conditioning studies have at least emphasized the need to reexamine some basic formulations regarding conventional distinctions between "the two types" of learning.[56,59] With respect to more focused concern involving the interrelationship between autonomic–visceral and somato–motor activity, two more or less distinguishable points of view can be identified. Miller, DiCara, and associates,[16,18-20,47,48,53,67] on the one hand, have appeared to take the position that evidence from their own experiments and those of others[60,62] supports the independence of somato-motor and autonomic-visceral control. Black,[6-8] Brenner, and Goesling,[11] and Obrist et al.,[52] on the other hand, prefer to represent autonomic–visceral and somato–motor activities as two components of a more general, centrally controlled response process. That the dividing line between the two formulations may not be too firmly drawn, however, would seem to be indicated by the fact that virtually all the adherents to the latter school of thought[9,30,52] appear willing to concede that the postulated "normal" linkage between the two systems may be modified in a variety of ways. Indeed, a more moderate "separable but interacting" formulation[10] of the observed psychophysiologic relationships may better serve the purposes of both clinical and experimental investigators concerned with the conditions under which dissociation or decoupling of the two systems can and do occur in the course of ongoing behavioral transactions between organism and environment.

Be all this as it may, the fact remains that the field of animal learning appears now to be extending the horizons of conditioning to probe the depths of "inner space"[28] with the same incisive methodologic approach that has proven so productive in analyzing more conventional behavioral interactions with the external environment. The potential of this investigative endeavor to provide new insights into the behavioral control of physiologic processes holds the promise of an active participatory role for man in learning to deal effectively with his proverbial "worst enemy."

LITERATURE CITED

1. Anand B, Chhina G: Investigations on yogis claiming to stop their heart beats. Indian J Med Res 49:90–94, 1961
2. Anand BK, Chhina GS, Singh B: Some aspects of electroencephalographic studies of Yogi. Electroencephalogr Clin Neurophysiol 13:452–56, 1961
3. Bagchi BK, Wenger MA: Electrophysiological correlates of some Yoga exercises. Presented at the First International Congress of Neurological Sciences, Brussels 3, 1957
4. Banuazizi A: Discriminative shock avoidance learning of an autonomic response under curare. J Comp Physiol Psychol 80:236–46, 1972
5. Benson H, Herd JA, Morse WH, et al: Behavioral inductions of arterial hypertension and its reversal. Am J Physiol 217:30–34, 1969
6. Black AH: Operant conditioning in curarized dogs. Cond Reflex 2:158, 1967
7. Black AH: Transfer following operant conditioning in the curarized dog. Science 155:201–3, 1967
8. Black AH: Operant conditioning of autonomic responses. Cond Reflex 3(2):130, 1968
9. Black AH: Autonomic aversive conditioning in infrahuman subjects, in Brush FR (ed): Aversive Conditioning and Learning 3–104. New York, Academic Press, 1971, pp 3–104
10. Brady JV: Emotion: Some conceptual problems and psychophysiological experiments, in Singh D, Morgan CT (eds): Current Status of Physiologic Psychology: A Book of Readings 63–78. Monterey, Calif, Brooks, Cole, 1972, pp 63–78
11. Brener JM, Goesling WJ: Heart rate and conditioned activity. Presented at The Society for Psychophysiological Research Meeting, Washington, DC, 1968
12. Brown C, Thorne P: An instrument for signaling heart rate to unrestrained human subjects. Psychophysiology 1(2):192–94, 1964
13. Budzynski TH, Stoyva JM: An instrument for producing deep muscle relaxation by means of analog information feedback. J Appl Behav Anal 2:231–37, 1969
14. Crider A, Schwartz GE, Shnidman S: On the criteria for instrumental autonomic conditioning: A reply to Katkin and Murray. Psychol Bull 71(6):455–61, 1969
15. Crider A, Shapiro D, Tursky B: Reinforcement of spontaneous electrodermal activity. J Comp Physiol Psychol 61:20–27, 1966
16. DiCara LV: Learning in the autonomic nervous system. Sci Am 222(1):30–39, 1970
17. DiCara LV, Braun JJ, Pappas BA: Classical conditioning and instrumental learning of cardiac and gastrointestinal responses following removal of neocortex in the rat. J Comp Physiol Psychol 73(2):208–16, 1970
18. DiCara L, Miller NE: Changes in heart rate instrumentally learned by curarized rats as avoidance responses. J Comp Physiol Psychol 65:1–7, 1968
19. DiCara L, Miller NE: Instrumental learning of systolic blood pressure responses by curarized rats: Dissociation of cardiac and vascular changes. Psychosom Med 30(5, Pt 1):489–94, 1968
20. DiCara L, Miller NE: Instrumental learning of vasomotor responses by rats: learning to respond differentially in the two ears. Science 159:1485–86, 1968
21. DiCara LV, Miller NE: Long-term retention of instrumentally learned heart-rate changes in the curarized rat. Commun Behav Biol 2(Pt A):19–23, 1968
22. DiCara LV, Miller NE: Heart-rate learning in the noncurarized state, transfer to the curarized state, and subsequent retraining in the noncurarized state. Physiol Behav 4:621–24, 1969
23. DiCara LV, Miller NE: Transfer of instrumentally learned heart-rate changes from curarized to noncurarized state: Implications for a mediational hypothesis. J Comp Physiol Psychol 68(2, Pt 1):159–62, 1969
24. DiCara LV, Stone EA: Effect of instrumental heart-rate training on rat cardiac and brain catecholamines. Psychosom Med 32(4):359–68, 1970
25. DiCara LV, Weiss JM: Effect of heart-rate learning under curare on subsequent noncurarized avoidance learning. J Comp Physiol Psychol 69:368–74, 1969
26. Engel BT, Gottlieb SH: Differential operant conditioning of heart rate in the restrained monkey. J Comp Physiol Psychol 73(2):217–25, 1970
27. Fields C: Instrumental conditioning of the rat cardiac control systems. Proc Natl Acad Sci USA 65(2):293–99, 1970
28. Fischer R: A cartography of the ecstatic and meditative states. Science 174:897–904, 1971
29. Fowler RL, Kimmel HD: Operant conditioning of the GSR. J Exp Psychol 63:563–67, 1962
30. Goesling WJ, Brener J: Effects of activity

and immobility conditioning upon subsequent heart-rate conditioning in curarized rats. J Comp Physiol Psychol 81:311–17, 1972

31. Harris AH, Findley JD, Brady JV: Instrumental conditioning of blood pressure elevations in the baboon. Cond Reflex 6:215–26, 1971

32. Harris AH, Gilliam WJ, Findley JD, et al: Instrumental conditioning of large magnitude daily 12-hour blood pressure elevations in the baboon. Science (in press)

33. Hefferline RF, Keenan B: Amplitude-induction gradient of a small-scale (covert) operant. J Exp Anal Behav 6:307–15, 1963

34. Hothersall D, Brener J: Operant conditioning of changes in heart rate in curarized rats. J Comp Physiol Psychol 68(3):338–342, 1969

35. Johnson RJ: Operant reinforcement of an automatic response. Dissert Abstr 24:1255–56, 1963

36. Kadden RM, Schoenfeld WN, Snapper AG: Cardiac pacing in the rhesus monkey: A technique and some behavioral data. Proceedings of the 78th Annual Convention of the American Psychological Association, 1970

37. Kadden RM, Snapper, AG, Schoenfeld WN, et al: Transvenous intracardiac pacing in the rhesus monkey. Commun Behav Biol 5:255–58, 1970

38. Katkin ES, Murray EN: Instrumental conditioning of autonomically mediated behavior: theoretical and methodological issues. Psychol Bull 70(1):52–68, 1968

39. Katkin ES, Murray EN, Lachman R: Concerning instrumental autonomic conditioning: A rejoiner. Psychol Bull 71(6):462–66, 1969

40. Kimmel E, Kimmel HD: Replication of operant conditioning of the GSR. J Exp Psychol 65:212–13, 1963

41. Kimmel HD: Instrumental conditioning of autonomically mediated behavior. Psychol Bull 67(5):337–345, 1967

42. Kimmel HD, Hill FA: Operant conditioning of the GSR. Psychol Rep 7:555–62, 1960

43. Krausman DT: A system for providing an on-line analogue display of beat-by-beat cardiac output. Med Biol Eng 10:81–88, 1972

44. Lang PJ: Autonomic control or learning to play the internal organs. Psychology Today (Oct)

45. Lisina MI: The role of orientation in the transformation of involuntary reactions into voluntary ones, in Voronin LG, Leontiev AN, Luris AR, et al (eds): Orienting Reflex and Exploratory Behavior, Washington DC, American Institute of Biological Sciences, 1958, pp 339–44

46. Mandler G, Kahn M: Discrimination of changes in heart rate: Two unsuccessful attempts. J Exp Anal Behav 3(1):21–26, 1960

47. Miller NE: Learning of visceral and glandular responses. Science 163:434–45, 1969

48. Miller NE, Banuazizi A: Instrumental learning by curarized rats of a specific visceral response, intestinal or cardiac. J Comp Physiol Psychol 65:1–7, 1968

49. Miller NE, Carmona A: Modification of a visceral response, salivation in thirsty dogs, by instrumental training with water reward. J Comp Physiol Psychol 63:1–6, 1967

50. Miller NE, DiCara L: Instrumental learning of heart rate changes in curarized rats: Shaping and specificity to discriminative stimulus. J Comp Physiol Psychol 63:12–19, 1967

51. Miller NE, DiCara L: Instrumental learning of urine formation by rats; changes in renal blood flow. Am J Physiol 215:677–83, 1968

52. Obrist PA, Webb RA, Sutterer JR, et al: The cardiac–somatic relationship: Some reformulations. Psychophysiology 6(5):569–87, 1970

53. Pappas BA, DiCara LV, Miller NE: Learning of blood pressure responses in the noncurarized rat: Transfer to the curarized state. Physiol Behav 5(9):1029–32, 1970

54. Plumlee LA: Operant conditioning of increases in blood pressure. Psychophysiology 6:283–90, 1969

55. Razran G: The observable unconscious and the inferable conscious in current Soviet psychophysiology: Interoceptive conditioning, semantic conditioning, and the orienting reflex. Psychol Rev 68:81–147, 1961

56. Schoenfeld WN: Some old work for modern conditioning theory. Cond Reflex 1:219–23, 1966

57. Schoenfeld WN: Oyepk on mediating mechanisms of the conditioned reflex. Cond Reflex 5:165–70, 1970

58. Schoenfeld WN: Conditioning the whole organism. Cond Reflex 6:125–28, 1971

59. Schoenfeld WN: Problems of modern behavior theory. Cond Reflex 7:33–65, 1972

60. Schwartz GE, Shapiro D, Tursky B: Learned control of cardiovascular integration in man through operant conditioning. Psychosom Med 33 (4):57–62, 1971

61. Shapiro D, Crider AB, Tursky B: Differentiation of an autonomic response through operant conditioning. Psychonom Sci 1:147–48, 1964

62. Shapiro D, Tursky B, Schwartz GE: Differentiation of heart rate and systolic blood pressure in man by operant conditioning. Psychosom Med 32 (4):417–23, 1970

63. Shearn DW: Operant conditioning of heart rate. Science 137:530–31, 1962

64. Slaughter J, Hahn W, Rinaldi P: Instrumental conditioning of heart rate in the curarized rat with varied amounts of pretraining. J Comp Physiol Psychol 72 (3):356–59, 1970

65. Slucki H, Adam G, Porter RW: Operant discrimination of an interoceptive stimulus in rhesus monkeys. J Exp Anal Behav 8 (6):405–14, 1965

66. Slucki H, McCoy FB, Porter RW: Interoceptive SD of the large intestine established by mechanical stimulation. Psychol Rep 24 (1):35–42, 1969

67. Trowill JA: Instrumental conditioning of the heart rate in the curarized rat. J Comp Physiol Psychol 63 (1):7–11, 1967

68. Wenger MA, Bagchi BK: Studies of autonomic functions in practitioners of yoga in India. Behav Sci 6:312–23, 1961

69. Wenger MA, Bagchi BK, Anand BK: Experiments in India on "voluntary" control of the heart and pulse. Circulation 24:1319–25, 1900

Chapter 3: Biofeedback—Specific Learning Component versus Nonspecific Learning Component (Placebo Effect)

Introduction

THIS CHAPTER, like the last one, is of crucial importance to the whole field of biofeedback, because it deals with the important and pervasive phenomenon of "placebo effects" as they interdigitate with effects of specific autonomic learning.

On a theoretical level, one can think of all placebo effects as being determined by the cumulative vector sum of all previous learning with people, and especially learning with respect to care-givers. Thus, a man conditioned early by his experiences with warm parents and a warm helpful family doctor would be likely to evince a more positive placebo effect than a man conditioned by negative experiences with destructive parents and negative experiences with doctors who were brusque, caused pain, and did not bring help or comfort.

In laboratory work with animals, reviewed by Drs. Harris and Brady in Chapter 2, one assumes the absence of placebo effects, but in work with humans these are very important. Animals given ipecac quite uniformly vomit as a result, as do humans, under most circumstances. In humans, however, systematic manipulation of placebo effects can actually alter the effects of administering this normally emetic drug. In one classic study done with patients suffering from hyperemesis gravidarum (nausea and vomiting), placebo effects were manipulated so successfully that giving ipecac actually *alleviated* nausea and vomiting! Such strong placebo effects, long known to be pervasive throughout psychiatry and medicine, simply cannot be ignored. Nor can they appropriately be merely "controlled for," as has been done effectively in many excellent studies of the effects of psychotropic drugs. This is not appropriate for biofeedback research, because the effects of suggestion, for human subjects, are intimately intertwined with direct autonomic learning effects; suggestion—i.e., positive or negative expectation—either potentiates the direct learning effects or significantly reduces their impact.

Dr. Stroebel has done the scientifically commendable and courageous thing—he has taken on placebo effects "head on" and has developed measures of their direction and magnitude. This has enabled him to study what effects on outcome are produced by various clinical configurations, like strong specific learning component/weak placebo effect, or weak specific learning effects/strong placebo effect (see pages 26–28).

This has great practical importance because, as Dr. Stroebel's chapter indicates (see page 26), there can be crucial differences in clinical outcome that result if care is not taken to manipulate the size and direction of these two separate forces for change.

Lee Birk, M.D.

REFERENCE

1. Wolf S: Effects of suggestion and conditioning on the action of chemical agents in human subjects. J Clin Invest 29:100–109, 1950

Biofeedback Treatment in Medicine and Psychiatry: An Ultimate Placebo?

Charles F. Stroebel, Ph.D., M.D., and Bernard C. Glueck, M.D.

SPECULATION about the potentials of biofeedback in the treatment of psychiatric, psychosomatic, and somatopsychic disorders is widespread. Enthusiasts view biofeedback as an objective scientific means for achieving control of neural and visceral processes that are normally outside the range of conscious awareness, even though they are also associated with attention, perception, emotions, and feelings. A subjective parallel is an apparently comparable degree of control reportedly achieved through inner suggestion by practitioners of various yogic techniques.

Biofeedback actually has both objective and subjective components. The participant is placed in a closed feedback loop where information about one or more of his normally unconscious physiologic processes is made available to him as a visual, auditory, or tactile signal. The subject's progress in controlling the process (e.g., density of EEG alpha, muscle tension, or blood pressure) can be monitored objectively with a polygraph. His subjective mental state in achieving such control and his interpretation of it cannot be monitored, except by introspective report.

At present, adequate psychophysiologic data to substantiate clinical expectations for biofeedback are scarce. Because of increasing concern with issues of deception and informed consent, most present and future clinical studies will be of the demonstration type, where controls necessarily will be inadequate. The critical question of a subjective placebo effect will be raised for most of these studies, as will a variety of corollary issues, such as cotreatment contaminants, suggestion, autohypnosis, etc. Debate among experimentalists will center on this issue: Is the subject really learning biofeedback control, is he merely altering his cognitive set, or is he responding to a suggestion-placebo effect by whatever means?[6,12,14]

As clinicians, we have wondered if it ever will be possible to separate out the "real" vs. the placebo effects of biofeedback in human subjects. Probably not, much to the anguish of our scientific side, which demands objectivity, experimental precision, and epistemologic surety in our quest for a scientific understanding of man and his problems.

On the other hand, the perplexing objective–subjective mix that characterizes biofeedback may force us to recognize the existence of a "soft" clinical issue that has eluded attempts at clarification by many psychologists and physicians in the post-Watsonian era of scientific medicine. Recognition that the placebo effect, per se, is inextricably interwoven with the illness onset and illness recovery process is long overdue. The "contaminating" placebo effect may be a

---

Reprint requests should be addressed to Dr. Charles F. Stroebel, Institute of Living Hospital, 400 Washington Street, Hartford, Conn. 06106.
 © 1973 by Grune & Stratton, Inc.

crucial clinical variable of utmost importance that we have minimized in our zeal for a scientific medicine.

Of course, placebo effects have not escaped scientific scrutiny. Observe the classic studies of its profound effects on pathologic pain by Beecher[2] and numerous controlled drug and psychophysiologic studies.[13,21-23,26] However, routine clinical application of our knowledge about placebos varies from disdainful neglect by "scientific" doctors, who ignore the effect, to "shamed" discomfort on the part of "unscientific" general practitioners, who recognize its influence.

This paper will explore the possibility that biofeedback procedures may prove to be an "ultimate placebo" by squarely placing both the placebo effect and the patient himself in a position of importance in the prevention and treatment of illness. Seen in this light, the placebo component of a biofeedback procedure may assume an importance greater than its potentially active component, particularly in transfer of the active psychophysiologic principle of biofeedback out of the laboratory into daily life, and in eventual persistence of its effects.

A placebo has been defined as "any medication [treatment] used to alleviate symptoms, not by reasons of specific pharmacologic action, but solely by reinforcing the patient's favorable expectancies from treatment."[10]

Placebo procedures have been used by psychophysiologists to resolve those effects of treatment that are primary, i.e., produced by the active treatment principle, from effects that may result from implicit or explicit response predispositions on the part of the subject–patient and/or experimenter–clinician. Increasing concern with the issues of deception and informed consent in research with human subjects will significantly restrict use of such placebo procedures in future clinical research. Experimental studies with normal volunteer or paid subjects and contrived instruction procedures will likely not solve the problem, since the implicit expectations of such subjects, now almost universally high with regard to biofeedback, are hardly neutral or random.

An "ultimate placebo" might be defined as a procedure that provides the patient with an effective means of preventing illness and/or potentially curing himself by helping him regulate the pace of his daily life-style, of his thought patterns, of his body processes, his habits, and his perceptual style, hopefully reducing susceptibility to pathologic levels of hyperactivation when faced with stressful life events. Suggesting that biofeedback may serve as "an ultimate placebo" does not imply that it will be universally effective, just as drug placebos vary in effectiveness with a variety of individual perceptual–coping styles (field dependence–independence, kinesthetic enhancing or reducing, intolerance of sensory isolation), which have been measured to place a patient somewhere on a continuum of placebo reactors–nonreactors.[22] Just as physicians identify the personality styles and defense mechanisms of patients to be able to optimally interact with them clinically,[11,19] biofeedback procedures should permit patients to use trial and error experience to personally optimize their own perceptual and coping styles in dealing with daily stress. Hence, usage here of the word "ultimate" implies a self-individualized path with many different options, where the person himself senses responsibility for achieving the goal of therapy.

Suggesting that biofeedback may serve as an ultimate placebo does not minimize its potential as an active therapeutic principle. Rather, it shifts the focus in a positive direction toward clinical pragmatism away from an experimental impasse with human subjects, which may never be solved with satisfaction by the rigorous standards of modern science.

BIOFEEDBACK AS A REAL EFFECT

Impressive evidence for the active therapeutic principle of biofeedback does exist in animals, where the question of a subjective placebo response is minimized. Of special interest is the fact that most of these data were acquired while the animals were curarized, minimizing the possibility of feedback control via effects from setting, tensing, or manipulating of skeletal musculature. The variety of autonomic responses controlled (both decreased and increased) through instrumental feedback during the 1960s is impressive, including heart rate, intestinal contractions, kidney function, hyperemia of stomach mucosa, blood flow in specific regions of the skin, blood pressure independent of heart rate, as well as control of brain wave activity.[16] Professor Neal Miller, a leader in this effort, has speculated (1969), that "Biofeedback should be well worth trying on any symptom, functional or organic, that is under neural control, that can be continuously monitored by modern instrumentation, and for which a given direction of change is clearly indicated medically... for example, cardiac arrhythmias, spastic colitis, and asthma, and those cases of high blood pressure that are not essential compensation for kidney damage."[16]

Miller's stature as a leading psychobiologist gave credibility to biofeedback and its medical potential. The mass media, and not a few scientists, began to serve biofeedback up as the "new magic bullet-cure for all ills." Dozens of firms began to capitalize on this publicity by producing inexpensive over-the-counter feedback boxes. However, unpredictably, reports began emanating from Miller's laboratory that the exciting early work with operant autonomic control under curare could not be replicated. Whereas the earlier studies actually demonstrated faster acquisition of control under the curare state (explanation: muscle movement apparently interfered with visceral learning) and transfer of control to the noncurare state, studies since 1970 have demonstrated very little acquired control of variables, such as heart rate, under the curare condition. A number of explanations for the replication failure have been advanced, e.g., the usual pharmaceutical supplier of curare changed sources in 1969. It is conceivable that the curare agent available since then is less pure with some antihomeostatic effect that alters learning.

Despite the replication failure under curare, evidence for the active principle of biofeedback (i.e., acquiring voluntary control of autonomic and neural responses) remains convincing in animal studies without curare, and is affirmative, although not conclusive, in human studies.[5,9,20]

RESULTS WITH BIOFEEDBACK AS A PLACEBO EFFECT

The previous section concluded that a substantive data base now exists to assume that the active principle of biofeedback can work. However, if the active principle really were not effective, could placebo effects conceivably account for the physiologic changes that actually have been observed in human subjects? Data from a number of nonbiofeedback studies confirm this possibility. For example, Franks explored the potential role of suggestion in psychotherapy and concluded that even death was not immune from psychologic influence (voodoo death).[7] Shapiro has widely reviewed the placebo literature and cites data to support the potential of this effect in virtually every therapeutic area, including "incurable malignancies."[18]

Uncertainty about the degree of physiologic specificity obtained with placebo phenomena has been clarified in an experiment by Sternbach.[21] He gave three sets of instructions in a "drug" experiment stating that one kind of pill would relax the stomach, that a second was a placebo pill having no effect, and that the third was a stimulant to the stomach. In actuality, all three pills were identical plastic-coated magnets used to monitor gastrointestinal activity. In most subjects, the stomach motility responded in accordance with the anticipated effect of the drug.

Graham and colleagues have studied the attitudes of patients suffering from 13 different psychosomatic conditions; subsequently they suggested three specific attitudes to healthy subjects under hypnosis and observed physiologic changes partially mimicking the associated psychosomatic disorders.[8] Barber has argued that hypnosis, per se, is not needed to obtain such results, and documents numerous case studies where suggestion alone could be used to elicit and dissipate various psychosomatic disorders.[1]

If animal studies documenting the active principle of biofeedback were not available, the foregoing evidence would probably be sufficient to conclude that all of the human results with biofeedback could be explained by invoking a subjective–placebo, cognitive, expectancy, suggestion-type rationale.

SUBJECTIVE INTERPRETATION OF ALTERED STATES

A distinction should be made between the foregoing physiologic changes as opposed to psychologic concomitants of the placebo effect. Once an altered physiologic state has been achieved (via active principle or placebo effect), psychologic factors again come into operation to determine how the altered physiologic state is subjectively interpreted. Orne has described these psychologic factors as the "demand characteristics" of the situation;[17] e.g., the subject-patient's expectations of a possible alteration in mood or "high" from the experience, or implicit/explicit suggestions or cues provided by the experimenter-physician. This rationale may explain the variety and range of subjective reports obtained by Brown and others when feedback is provided within specific EEG frequency bands.[4] Figure 1 summarizes these date from several sources, including our own experience using the Clyde Mood Scale as a rating device.

It is a distinct possibility that certain of the EEG states (theta and alpha) may make subjects especially prone to suggestion and/or uncritical of primary process thoughts, conceivably enhancing hypnotic phenomena and/or free association in psychoanalytic psychotherapy.

An alternative explanation for variations in subjects' mood reports correlated with a specific band of EEG activity would be the dissociation of EEG and behavioral arousal that has been demonstrated pharmacologically and in sen-

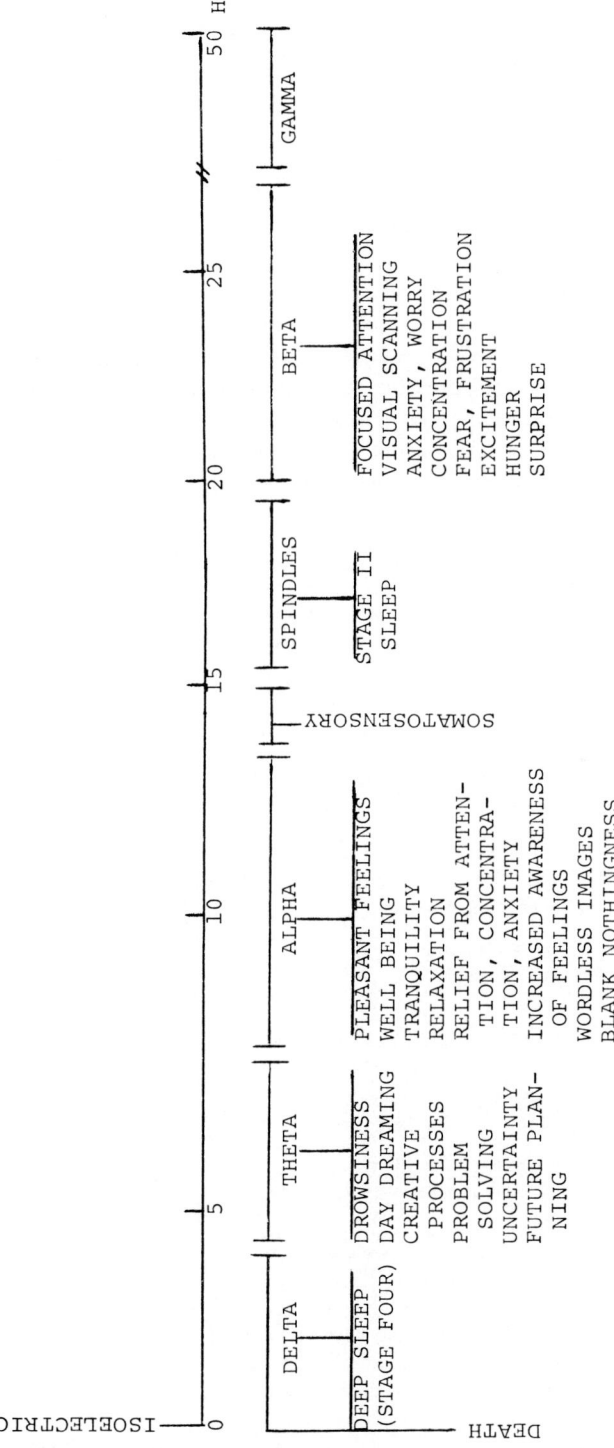

Fig. 1. Moods and psychophysiologic states associated with various bands within the spectrum of EEG activity.

sory deprivation experiments.[3,15,27] For example, Lynch and Paskewitz have suggested that alpha biofeedback has certain similarities to sensory deprivation, including elimination of patterned external stimulation and unfocusing of attention.[14]

EFFECTIVENESS OF BIOFEEDBACK AS A BALANCE OF ACTIVE AND INACTIVE PRINCIPLES

For didactic purposes, the preceeding sections examined biofeedback separately as primarily an active or a placebo process. In reality, the two principles operate simultaneously in varying proportions. The problem is, what proportions? Obviously, some index of the interaction and balance between inactive (placebo) and active (voluntary control) components is needed for meaningful evaluation of (1) current effectiveness at any point during training and (2) prediction of long-range effectiveness.

Evaluation of the active component is straightforward, essentially being derived from a subject's "learning curve." An example would be measuring the

Table 1. Placebo-Active Therapeutic Index (PATI) Procedure

Step 1: Obtain two pieces of information from each training trial as follows:
  (1) *Active Control Score:* Estimate the degree of voluntary control achieved by the subject–patient. This estimate, easily obtained from a cumulative learning curve, is made to the nearest quartile and is assigned a score value from the following chart:

Quartile	Per cent Control	Score
Q_4	75%–100%	+2
Q_3	50%–74%	+1
Q_2	25%–49%	−1
Q_1	0%–24%	−2

  (2) *Expectancy Score:* The subject–patient is asked to rate the degree of expectancy, enthusiasm, and confidence which he has in the treatment procedure on a 3 x 5 card after each trial. The rating scale and its assigned score values are as follows:

Expectancy Rating	Score
Very High	+2
High	+1
Moderate	−1
Low	−2

Step 2: Calculate two indices as follows:
  (1) Current PATI = Active control score + Expectancy score

  (2) Prognostic PATI = $\sum_{A=0}^{A=75} \frac{\text{Active Score}}{\text{Expectancy Score}}$

   = Cumulative algebraic sign (plus, zero, minus) of the ratio $\frac{\text{Active control score}}{\text{Expectancy score}}$ summed over trials until the active score exceeds 75% (where the curve becomes assymptotic and nonlinear).

Step 3: (A) Obtain an adjective estimate of *Current Effectiveness of Treatment* by entering Table 2 with the current PATI (range of +4− −4).

  (B) Obtain an adjective estimate predicting *Long-term Effectiveness of Treatment* by entering Table 2 with the cumulative algebraic sign of the prognostic PATI (plus or zero v. negative).

per cent of time that alpha density is above criterion during an alpha enhancement session.

Unfortunately, there has not been any description of the means for evaluating the placebo component and its interaction with the active principle in determining effectiveness of treatment. Understandably, most of us find even semiquantitative assessment of placebo effects notoriously difficult, a fact that may account for their neglect by scientific medicine.

Impressed as we are by the significant role of placebo effects in evaluating biofeedback, we have placed high priority on developing tentative models that could aid in better understanding the successes and failures with biofeedback that we have observed in our patients and subjects. It is our hope that these efforts will help overcome the previously noted experimental impasse regarding placebo effects and permit clinically effective application of biofeedback techniques; conceivably these models may advance our treatment rationale with other placebo-sensitive medical therapies.

PLACEBO–ACTIVE THERAPY INDEX MODEL

The model that we propose, called the Placebo–Active Therapeutic Index (PATI), requires the input of two easily obtained pieces of information, and calculation of two indices (Current PATI and a Prognostic PATI index) that are used to enter a table to obtain an objective estimate of (1) current effectiveness and (2) prediction of long-term effectiveness of treatment. A step-by-step procedure for using the PATI model is presented in Tables 1 and 2.

Figure 2 schematically illustrates the rationale behind the PATI model. Balanced against one another are two opposing but independent sigmoid curves representing cumulative distributions of active (on the left) and placebo (on the right) components of treatment. Once the active control and expectancy scores have been obtained (steps 1 through 3 in Table 1), each can be marked at the appropriate point on its respective sigmoid curve. Their combined (interaction) effect can be visualized as a single line connecting the two points for each trial. This line represents "current effectiveness" and indicates the degree of

Table 2. Current and Long-range Effectiveness of Therapy

Current PATI	Current Effectiveness	Long-term Effectiveness	
		Sign of Prognostic PATI	
		Plus or Zero	Negative
+4	Very High	Excellent	Questionable
+3			
+2	High	Good	Poor
+1			
0	Moderate	Questionable	Poor
−1			
−2	Low	Poor	Very Poor
−3			
−4	Very Low	Very Poor	Very Poor

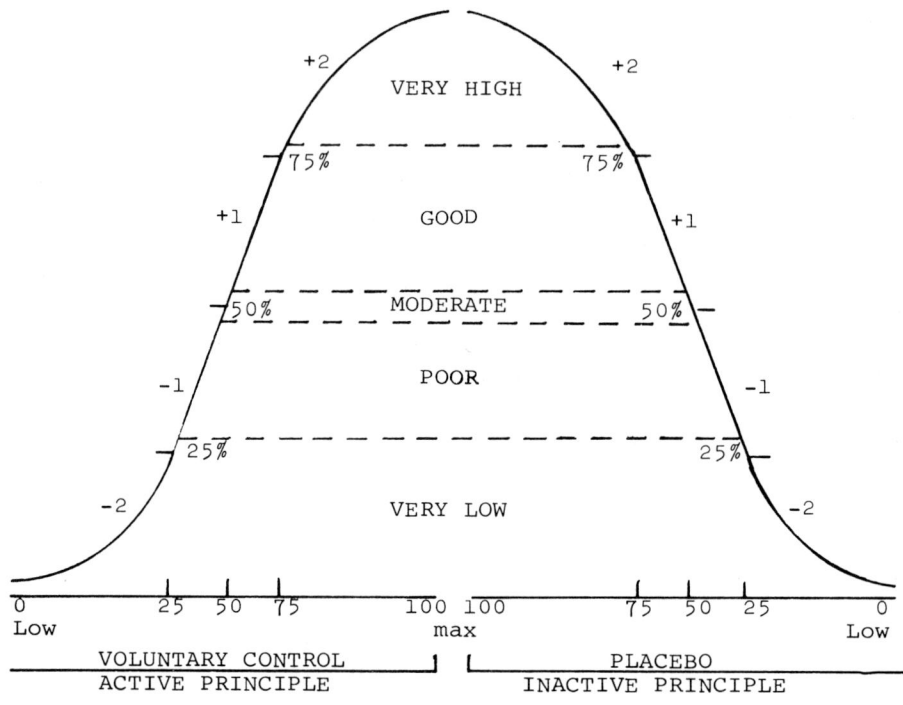

Fig. 2. Schematic representation of the Placebo-Active Therapeutic Index model (PATI). Dotted lines indicating balance of a variety of active and expectancy scores are included to demonstrate the basis for the "current effectiveness" scoring scale.

balance and relative elevation of placebo and active components on their respective cumulative curves.

Unbalanced conditions (high active, low placebo, or low active, high placebo) counterbalance one another to contribute to current effectiveness, but tend to be unstable, carrying an unfavorable prognosis. These occur when a subject's expectations (overly enthusiastic) consistently exceed his actual success at active control, or when his expectations (overly pessimistic) are consistently less than his degree of voluntary control. In other words, a cumulative active/expectancy ratio that is negative implies that the subject is generally unrealistic in coupling his expectancies with his degree of active control. If his expectancies have been too high, he will very likely discontinue practice of his biofeedback technique when he is not immersed in the demand characteristics surrounding his training sessions. If his expectations are consistently too low, his motivation for continuation away from the demand characteristics of the laboratory will be even lower.

The PATI model implies that biofeedback training can be optimized by maintaining a relative balance between active control and placebo expectancies. If expectations by the subject are too high or too low over the course of training sessions, the eventual long-term effectiveness (transfer out of the laboratory and persistence) is likely to be low, even though the subject apparently performs well in the laboratory setting.

SPECIFIC AND NONSPECIFIC LEARNING COMPONENTS (PLACEBO EFFECT)

DATA TO SUPPORT THE PATI MODEL

General support for the PATI model is provided by data obtained in our laboratory in studying 50 normal and 25 psychiatric in-patient subjects in 2150 sessions of alpha training with auditory feedback when alpha density exceeded 25% of that in an eyes-closed, control session. The data for all subjects who eventually achieved a high degree of discriminative control of alpha density can be partitioned into three groups: Group A, low expectancy; Group B, moderate expectancy; and Group C, high expectancy.

Group A subjects with consistently low expectancies generally reported that the alpha "on" condition was a "nothing" state, their minds being blank of images and words. These subjects were ambivalent, frequently missed scheduled sessions, felt that they had received very little benefit from their training experience and stated that they did not plan to continue practicing the alpha technique when they finished training. Retests 1 mo later demonstrated a significant loss of ability to achieve previous alpha densities under feedback and no feedback conditions. This outcome was predicted by mean PATI scores for the final training session as follows: active score = +2; expectancy score = −2; current PATI = 0; prognostic PATI = (−); current effectiveness = moderate; long-term effectiveness = poor. Lines A and B in Fig. 3 represent this group on the final training session (A) and 1 mo later (B).

Group B subjects tended to consistently balance moderate expectancies with

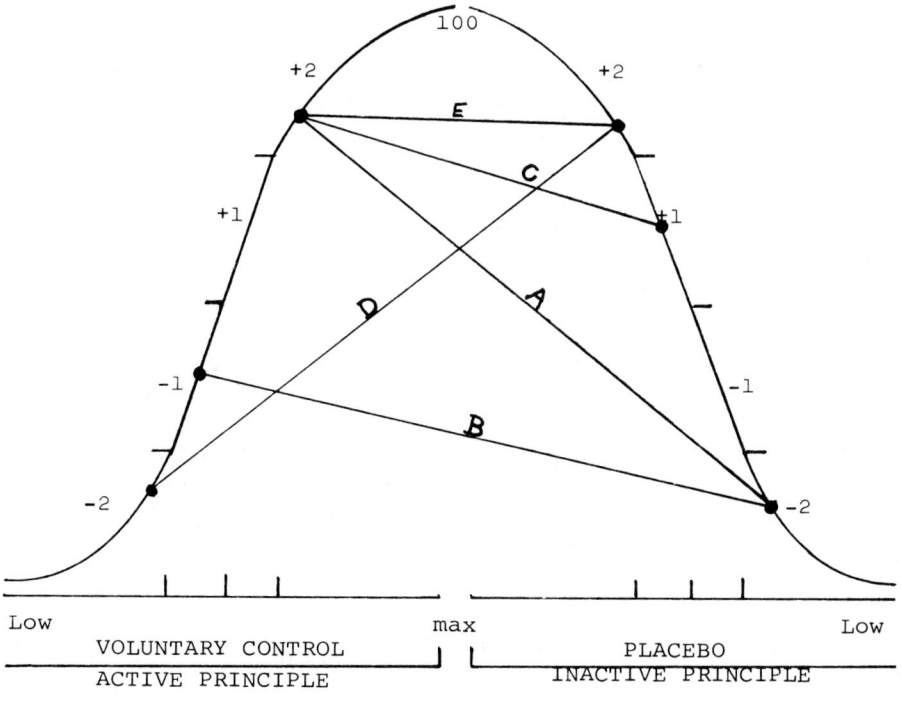

Fig. 3. Illustration of five possible outcomes (A through E) for the PATI model for specific cases discussed in the text.

success at active control. They generally interpreted the alpha "on" condition as a kind of "inner calmness" that helped them regulate the style and pace of their daily lives. At 1 and 3 mo after training, they maintained their ability to control alpha and reported that they practiced alpha control daily to give perspective to their previously "rushed" daily schedule. Mean PATI scores for the last training session predicted this apparently successful outcome as follows: active = +2; expectancy = +1; current PATI = +3; prognostic PATI = 0; current effectiveness = high; long-term effectiveness = excellent; line C in Fig. 3 represents this group on the final training session and at 3 mo.

Group C subjects, those consistently expressing very high expectancies, tended to be evangelistic, seeking extra sessions for themselves and recruited friends for training; they reported pleasant, tranquil, relaxed, and frequent "high" feelings during the alpha "on" condition. Retest at 1 mo showed no loss of their ability to control alpha and a continuing degree of enthusiasm. While at 3 mo these same subjects retained their ability to control alpha (active principle), all but two had lost their enthusiasm, reporting that they seldom had time to practice except as a means for inducing sleep. The placebo component of their training had apparently dissipated. Mean PATI scores at the last training session were consistent with this outcome: active = +2; expectancy = +2; current PATI = +4; prognostic PATI = (−); current effectiveness = very high; long-term effectiveness = questionable. In Fig. 3, line D represents this group during early training; line E represents the end of training and at 1 mo; line A demonstrates the loss of expectancy at 3 mo.

The PATI model and data supporting it suggest that biofeedback results can be optimized if active control and expectancies of outcome are maintained in relative balance during the course of training sessions. In subsequent applications of EEG alpha and EMG as relaxation techniques, and with patients receiving differential temperature and EMG training for migraine and tension headaches, we seek to adjust a subject's expectancies to keep pace with his degree of active control. Subjects are told that their biofeedback training will be effective only to the extent that they use it to gain perspective in regulating the pace of their lives on a daily basis. They acquire their training with the expectation that the experience should be used as something more than a novel, quick "high" or as an occasional "stop-gap" self-therapy.

Regular practice and body awareness are also encouraged by daily completion of the *Psychophysiological Diary*,[24] a computer-scored record of moods, body changes, and life events. While the *Diary* does provide a continuing link with the demand characteristics of the laboratory, it also encourages the subject to view himself as the responsible agent in regulating his life-style and health. He becomes the crucial link in maintaining his own placebo–expectancy response.

This transformation in the old adage of "Physician, heal [by] thyself," to "Patient, heal thyself," has promising potential for reasonably intelligent, middle-class patients.

FURTHER IMPLICATIONS OF THE PATI MODEL

Examination of the time-course of active/expectancy ratios during training for a variety of biofeedback procedures reveals a differentiating principle that

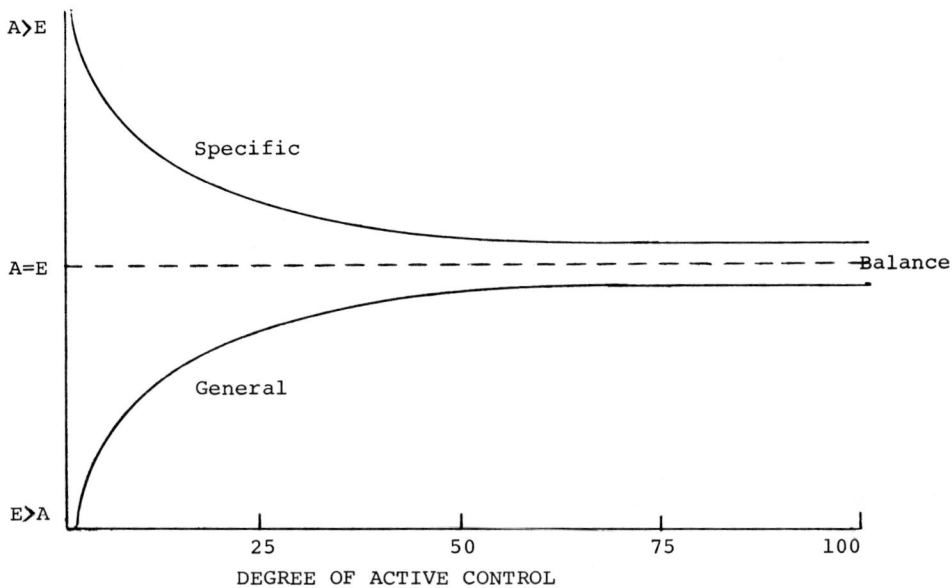

Fig. 4. Biofeedback procedures can be differentiated into general and specific types based on study of relative predominance of active (A) or expectancy (E) scores over the course of training (see Table 3).

is a useful guideline for the experimenter–clinician in regulating his own role as a placebo agent in optimizing long-term effectiveness. This principle, which emerges from analysis of Fig. 4, suggests that biofeedback procedures can be categorized into one of two types, general or specific, as listed in Table 3.

"General-type" biofeedback procedures, including EEG alpha and theta enhancement and frontalis muscle EMG reduction, require what has been described as "passive volition" or defocusing of attention for achieving relaxation and lower levels of general arousal, external attention, and tension, states

Table 3. Types of Biofeedback

General*	Specific†
EEG Alpha	Thermal
	Migrane headache
	Raynaud's disease
EEG Theta	Neck EMG
	Tension headache
Frontalis EMG	Back EMG
	Muscular back pain
	pH
	Gastric ulcer
	Pressure
	Irritable colon
	Blood pressure
	Ulcerative colitis
	EKG
	Cardiac dysrhythmias

*Objective: relaxation and lowering of tension.
†Objective: to regulate or lower the activation of a target organ system.

thought to be imcompatible with a flight or fight response to stress. For these procedures, the expectancy score tends to be significantly greater than the active score, particularly during early training, as shown in Fig. 4.

"Specific-type" biofeedback techniques include a variety of procedures used to regulate or lower the activation of a target organ system that presents clinically as a psychosomatic symptom. Like the general type, voluntary control in the specific situation also involves a kind of passive volition, but also permits a much greater degree of mental activity and attention to external cues. Hence, these procedures can more easily be incorporated into a behavioral therapy desensitization framework. For specific-type procedures, the active control score usually exceeds the expectancy score until the subject begins to experience symptom relief from his training (see Fig. 4).

These derivations of the PATI model predict that long-term effectiveness of training can be optimized through regular use of PATI ratings, permitting the experimenter–clinician as a placebo agent to verbally suppress a subject's tendencies toward high expectancies during early trials in general-type training; in contrast, low expectancies should be actively boosted during early phases of specific types of training.

The PATI model may prove useful in predicting current and long-term effectiveness of any procedure or treatment that is placebo sensitive. Two examples will be cited.

An incredible range of benefits (improved memory and concentration, controlled headaches, solved problems, sleep without drugs, complete relaxation, improved school work, controlled bad habits, development of your intuition and ESP) is being advertised nationally for several varieties of nonbiofeedback "alpha–theta mind control," which are taught as intensive courses lasting 30–40 hr. Testimonials and high-pressured confrontation apparently are used to create exceedingly high expectancies and a heightened state of auto-suggestibility in participants. The actual degree of alpha or theta control achieved is not routinely measured, and has been quite low in several ex-participants who requested postcourse testing in a biofeedback laboratory. Given the conditions of very high expectancy and very low active control (see line D, Fig. 3), the PATI model would predict that these techniques for achieving advertised benefits will be moderately effective during the course, but will possess very poor long-term effectiveness when participants are no longer immersed in the demand characteristics of the course itself, including social interaction with other participants and the instructor.

A second extension of the PATI model can be made into a nonbiofeedback technique for achieving deep relaxation: Transcendental Meditation (TM). Traditionally, TM training involves 4 hr of lectures, during which the instructor seeks to create very high expectancies about potential benefits from learning the technique ("creative intelligence;" "unstressing the nervous system") followed by 1 hr of actual meditation instruction and 3 hr of group discussion and meditation. While Wallace[25] has demonstrated that experienced meditators do achieve a state of deep relaxation by psychophysiologic criteria, the percentage of new meditators rapidly achieving a significant degree of relaxation ("active control") is not routinely measured and is uncertain. For subjects who are slow in achieving active control, the PATI model would predict a moderate degree of current effectiveness during training succeeded by very poor long-term effectiveness. In fact, a significant attrition rate has been observed 2–3 mo after training. The PATI model suggests several ways TM training could be optimized. First, instructors should be moderate in creating high expectancies during initial lectures before the actual technique for achieving active control is provided; second, active contact should be continued with the initiate to maintain his expectancies until it is reasonably certain that he can consistently achieve a degree of active control-relaxation equivalent to his expectations. A number of TM instructors have reportedly begun incorporating a program of continuing contact into their training procedure with significant reduction of the attrition rate.

DISCUSSION

Experience with a variety of biofeedback techniques with normal subjects and patients led us to the conclusion that exclusive consideration of the active component of biofeedback, without consideration of the placebo-expectancy component, was an inadequate basis for meaningful clinical application of the procedures. Persistence and transfer of training to real-life situations outside the laboratory on a continuing basis apparently require consideration of additional factors in the form of a self-reinforcing placebo effect or other type of reward.

A simple model called the Placebo-Active Therapeutic Index (PATI) was developed to incorporate and legitimate placebo-expectancy effects as an important component of biofeedback training to be evaluated and manipulated, rather than ignored or neglected.

The model, which has proved useful with a variety of general and specific biofeedback procedures, emphasizes the need for achieving a relative balance of active and expectancy factors to optimize long-term effectiveness of training. Improvements and potential correlates (e.g., personality style) of the model and its relatively crude scoring scheme (to the nearest quartile) are under continuing investigation.

Analysis of the model lends support to the concept of biofeedback procedures as an "ultimate placebo." For example, the successes of modern scientific medicine have been widely impressed upon the populace by the mass media in various forms: Medical soap operas, documentaries, and commercials for patent medicines. The public has come to expect a "magic-bullet" pill or a "sixty-minute TV-doctor cure" by an omnipotent physician who allegedly possesses a vast armamentarium of infallible cures. So well has this message been received that physicians are no longer expected nor permitted to make occasional mistakes. According to this modern prescription, the doctor has become solely responsible for the cure, not the patient.

It is true that once tissue pathology has occurred, whether through infection, trauma, poison, congenital defect, or tumor, external intervention by modern medicine to patch the defect is often impressive and largely beyond the subjective control of the patient. However, the vast majority of ills and the illness-onset situation itself,[18] are clearly not beyond subjective control. These cannot be the private domain of the doctor–scientist, but are a matter of responsibility for each individual.

Modern medicine probably does not sufficiently emphasize this need for individual responsibility. Acclimated as he is to be a recipient rather than a participant in treatment, modern man may require personal demonstration through a structured period of self-learning to incorporate the concept of individual responsibility into his daily life-style in times of both health and illness. Biofeedback may serve as an optimal procedure for a structured self-learning experience, since individuals can learn first-hand about regulating the effects of daily stress on body functioning.

Many scientist-physicians wonder "what is missing" and become defeatists when they observe widespread lack of compliance by patients in taking prescribed medications, in following dietary restrictions, and in regulating their pace of life. The "something" that is missing may be the more active involvement of the patient himself in the prevention-treatment process. Balanced recognition and application of both active and expectancy factors in biofeedback may provide a meaningful basis for helping man acquire this involvement, becoming, in essence, his own ultimate placebo.

ACKNOWLEDGMENT

The authors are indebted to the following for assistance: Jane Archer, Laverne Barbagallo, R.N., Brooke Craven, Charles Glueck, and Michael Scammon. We are also grateful to Erik Peper and Gay Luce for their advice at the early stages of our work with biofeedback.

REFERENCES

1. Barber TX: LSD, Marihuana, Yoga and Hypnosis. Chicago, Aldine, 1970
2. Beecher HA: Pain: One mystery solved. Science 151:840, 1966
3. Bradley PB: Central action of certain drugs in relation to the reticular formation of the brain, in Japser HH (ed): The Reticular Formation of the Brain. Boston, Little, Brown, 1958
4. Brown B: Recognition of aspects of consciousness through association with EEG alpha activity represented by a light signal. Psychophysiology 6:442, 1970
5. Budzynski T, Stoyva J, Adler C: Feedback-induced muscle relaxation: Application to tension headache. J Behav Exp Psychiatry 1:205, 1970
6. Crider A, Schwartz GE, Shnidman SR: On the criteria for instrumental autonomic conditioning: A reply to Katkin and Murray. Psychol Bull 71:455, 1969
7. Franks JD: Persuasion and Healing. Baltimore, Johns Hopkins Pr, 1961
8. Graham DT, Kabler JD, Graham FK: Physiological response to the suggestion of attitudes specific for hives and hypertension. Psychosom Med 24:159, 1962
9. Green EE, Green AM, Walters ED: Voluntary control of inner states: Psychological and physiological. J Transper Psychol 2:1, 1970
10. Hirsie LE, Campbell RJ: Psychiatric Dictionary (ed 3). New York, Oxford Univ Pr, 1960
11. Kahana RJ, Bibring GL: Personality types in medical management in Zinberg N (ed): Psychiatry and Medical Practice. New York, International Univ Pr, 1964, pp 108-123
12. Katkin KE, Murray EN: Instrumental conditioning of autonomically mediated behavior: Theoretical and methodological issues. Psychol Bull 70:52, 1968
13. Lasagna L, Mosteller F, von Felsinger J, et al: A study of the placebo response. Am J Med 16:770, 1954
14. Lynch JJ, Paskewitz DA: On the Mechanisms of the Feedback Control of Human Brain Wave Activity. Biofeedback and Self Control. Chicago, Aldine, 1971
15. Mathews AM: Psychophysiological approaches to the investigation of desensitization and related procedures. Psychol Bull 76:73, 1971
16. Miller NE: Learning of visceral and glandular responses. Science 163:434, 1969
17. Orne MT: On the social psychology of the psychological experiment: With particular reference to demand characteristics and their implications. Am Psychol 17:776, 1962
18. Shapiro AK: Factors contributing to the placebo effect: Their implications for psychotherapy. Am J Psychother (Suppl):73, 1964

19. Shapiro D: Neurotic Styles. New York, Basic Books, 1965

20. Shapiro D, Schwartz GE: Biofeedback and visceral learning clinical applications. Semin Psychiatry 4:171–184, 1972

21. Sternbach RA: The effects of instructional sets on autonomic responsivity. Psychophysiology 1:67, 1964

22. Sternbach RA: Pain: A Psychophysiological Analysis. New York, Academic Press, 1968

23. Stroebel CF: Psychophysiological pharmacology, in Greenfield NS, Sternbach RA (eds): Handbook of Psychophysiology. New York, Holt Rinehart & Winston, 1972

24. Stroebel CF, Luce GG, Glueck BC: Psychophysiological Diary: A Computer Scored Daily Record of Moods, Body Changes and Life Events. Hartford, Institute of Living, 1971

25. Wallace RK: Physiological effects of transcendental meditation. Science 167:1751, 1970

26. Wolf S, Doering C, Clark M, et al: Chance distribution and the placebo "reactor." J Lab Clin Med 49:837, 1957

27. Zubek JP: Physiological and biochemical effects in sensory deprivation, in Zubek JP (ed): Sensory Deprivation: Fifteen Years of Research. New York, Appleton-Century, 1969

II. Clinical Applications

Chapter 4: Tension Headache

Introduction

TENSION headache, or "muscle-contraction headache," is an extremely common condition; it can be described as a

> ... steady, nonpulsatile ache, unilateral or bilateral, in the temporal, occipital, parietal or frontal regions ... [of the head] ... ; pain [may be described as] ... tightness ... , bandlike sensations, as a viselike ache ... or as ... cramplike head pains.... Pain may be fleeting ... or the headache may last for weeks, months or even years....[1]

The pathogenesis of pain is due to "long-sustained contraction of skeletal muscle about the face, scalp and neck."[1] In spite of the fact that the mechanism is well understood, traditional medical management, frustratingly enough, has notoriously little to offer:

> Reassurance, massage, manipulation and manual stretching of the nuchal (neck) and occipital muscles, aspirin and phenobarbital (30 mg three times a day) reduce the intensity of most such headaches.... Bed rest, local heat, warm baths and the passage of time (!) are important adjuvants ... , (but) headaches associated with life stress and emotional tension are only temporarily modified....[1]

In the application of biofeedback to tension headache, then, the target physical symptom is pain in the head secondary to high levels of tension in the frontalis and/or occipitalis muscles. The physiologic instrument used is an electromyogram or EMG, measuring muscle tension; the criterion response is relaxation of the frontalis/occipitalis muscles; the reinforcement is auditory feedback, in the form of reduction in the frequency of clicks paralleling same-sized reductions in muscle tension.

This chapter is placed first among all the chapters on clinical applications of biofeedback for two major reasons. (1) The usefulness of biofeedback for headache in general and for tension headache in particular has been particularly well established. (2) The psychophysiologic mechanism of tension headache, and of its treatment by biofeedback is especially clear, simple, and direct. The underlying physiology is, for example, much more complex in Wolff–Parkinson–White syndrome (Chapter 6, Part 4) or in epilepsy (Chapter 9).

Like other psychosomatic disorders, tension headache begins with life stress and touches upon unsolved inner conflicts: the familiar psychophysiologic paradigm is:

life stress, unsolved inner conflicts → physical symptoms.

For psychophysiologic headache syndromes—including both tension headache (Chapter 4) and migraine headache (Chapter 5)—suppressed or poorly recognized anger (latent anger responses) are typically at the heart of the matter. Psychotherapy, emphasizing insight and the cognitive uncovering of such anger and the reasons for it, can deal with one part of the problem. The behavior therapy procedure, assertive training, in which the patient learns to

© *1973 by Grune & Stratton, Inc.*

express his angry feelings more directly and effectively (once he recognizes them!) can also help. These measures are ways of dealing with the left or input side of the psychophysiologic paradigm; biofeedback is a way of dealing with the right or output side of that paradigm, the side which, for tension headache patients, means that they have increased levels of tension in the occipitalis and/or frontalis muscles, and resultant pain. Whatever may be the external life stress or the inner conflict, this phenomenon of increased occipitalis/frontalis muscle tension, for tension headache patients, is the final common pathway of life stress.

Dr. Budzynski's outcome data (see especially Figs. 3 and 4, pages 42 and 43, and Table 2, page 46) show that through biofeedback, the patient can learn to become aware of what is the level of tension in the muscles of his head *and can learn to reduce the level of muscular tension, in order to relieve the pain of headache, or to abort a headache in the making.*

It is also worth noting here that biofeedback training can facilitate cognitive learning about the triggering stimuli for such psychosomatic reactions;* thus, biofeedback can facilitate the work of concomitant psychotherapy and assertive training, as they are used in an attempt to deal with the input side of the psychophysiologic equation.

Lee Birk, M.D.

REFERENCE

1. Beeson PB, McDermott W (eds): Cecil-Loeb Textbook of Medicine (ed 12). Philadelphia, Saunders, 1967, pp 1477–78

---

*For a detailed case report illustrating this phenomenon of clinical synergism between biofeedback and psychotherapy, see Chapter 10.

EMG Biofeedback and Tension Headache: A Controlled Outcome Study

Thomas H. Budzynski, Ph.D., Johann M. Stoyva, Ph.D., Charles S. Adler, M.D., and Daniel J. Mullaney, M.A.

A significant reduction in muscle contraction headache activity was observed in patients trained in the relaxation of the forehead musculature through EMG biofeedback. Training consisted of 16 semiweekly, 20-min EMG feedback sessions augmented by daily home practice. A pseudofeedback control group and a no-treatment control group failed to show significant reductions. A 3-mo follow-up questionnaire revealed a greatly decreased medication usage in the experimental group.

IN THE LATE 1950s, two British researchers[1] employed a then unique electromyographic (EMG) integration circuit to show that the resting level of frontalis EMG activity was higher in tension headache patients than normals. Since the immediate cause of pain associated with this common type of headache (more properly called muscle contraction headache) is usually due to a sustained contraction of the scalp and neck muscles,[2-4] we hypothesized that if patients could be taught to relax these muscles, the pain would be alleviated.

A previous study in our laboratory has indicated that individuals can be trained to lower frontalis tension levels through EMG biofeedback.[5] Subjects in this study reported that there was a generalization of the relaxation to other muscle groups especially in the head and neck area. In view of these observations and the results of the British study, we decided to apply EMG feedback from the frontalis to tension headache.

The results of a pilot study with five patients[6] revealed that the EMG feedback training appeared to be effective in reducing the frequency and severity of tension headaches. However, to rule out the possibility that these results were mainly attributable to either placebo or suggestion effects, we initiated the present study, which employed two control groups in addition to the experimental group.

METHOD

Patients

Advertisements were placed in a local paper asking for individuals afflicted with frequent tension headaches to participate in a study at the University of Colorado Medical Center. The applicants were not offered pay. A 22-item telephone questionnaire was used to screen out applicants who appeared to have other than muscle contraction headaches. Those who passed the telephone

---

Reprint requests should be addressed to Dr. Thomas H. Budzynski, University of Colorado Medical Center, 4200 E. Ninth Avenue, Box 2621, Denver, Colo. 80220.

Republished by permission of Psychosomatic Medicine (in press).

Supported by NIMH Grant MH-15596 and Research Scientist Development Award KO1-MH-43361.

© *1973 by Grune & Stratton, Inc.*

interview next underwent a thorough medical and psychiatric examination in order to rule out the possibility of neurologic and other organic disorders and to confirm the diagnosis of tension headache. Typically, this type of headache is characterized by a dull "band-like" pain located bi-laterally in the occipital region, although it is often felt in the forehead region as well. It is gradual in onset and may last for hours, weeks, even months.

Following the examination patients were asked to begin daily charting of their headache activity. The purpose of this charting was to provide us with quantitative data on headache levels for the entire course of the study. As shown in Fig. 1 (a hypothetical patient), the charts were 3″ × 5″ cards with the vertical scale representing headache intensity from 0–5, with "5" indicating an intense, incapacitating headache. A "4" represented a very severe headache that made concentration difficult, but the patient could perform tasks of an undemanding nature. A "3" headache was painful, but the patient would be able to continue at his job. The "2" level represented a headache pain level that could be ignored at times. A level "1" headache was a very low-level type that entered awareness only at times when attention was devoted to it.

The patient plotted one point for each waking hour, and the headache data were averaged to obtain a weekly score. For example, in Fig. 1, the hourly average for this day would be computed in this fashion:

$$H_D = \frac{(1 \times 3) + (2 \times 4) + (3 \times 3) + (4 \times 4) + (5 \times 2)}{24} = 1.92$$

The weekly score would be the simple average of the seven H_D scores for that patient. An average of 1.92 for a week would indicate an extremely high level of headache activity.

In order to establish a base-line level of headache activity, all patients charted headaches for 2 wk prior to any training. Data from the pilot study indicated that an average of 0.3 was a moderate level of headache activity. Those patients

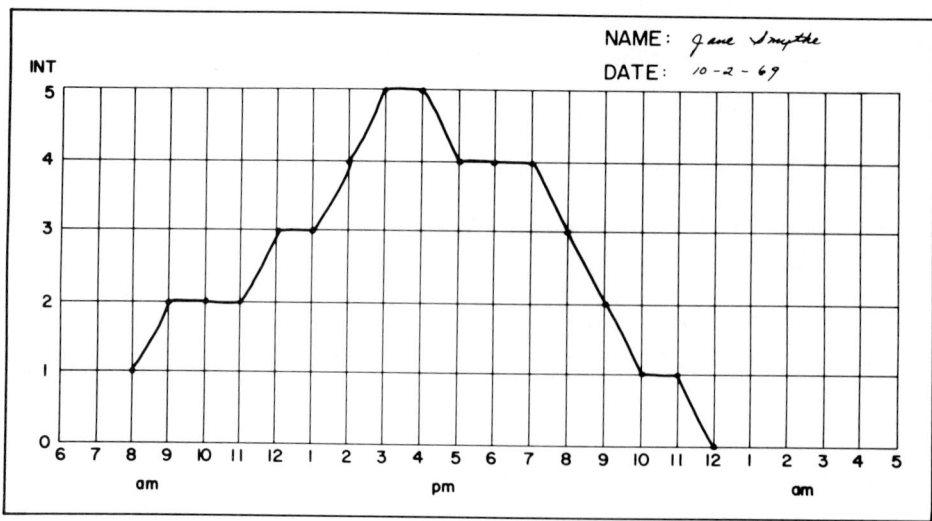

Fig. 1. Headache rating chart.

who scored below this average (approximately 25%) for the 2-wk base line were not included in the main study but were assigned to a "case study" group. These "case study" patients were not used in the main study, but they were given EMG feedback training. Almost all of these individuals reported a sudden disappearance or decline of headaches soon after their acceptance into the study. However, their headaches usually returned after 5-12 days. This placebo or suggestion response produced genuine wonderment in most of these patients.

All patients who passed the physical and psychiatric interview screen were given the Minnesota Multiphasic Personality Inventory (MMPI). This test was again administered at the end of the training period. Those patients who showed evidence of severe psychologic problems as detected by the MMPI were eliminated from the main study, although they were allowed to continue training. Dropouts were replaced with patients who answered the second advertisement placed in the paper. Of the 18 patients selected for the study, two were male and 16 were female. The mean age was 36 yr, with a range of 22-44 yr. The mean duration of severe headache activity for groups A, B, and C was 9.6, 6.8, and 6.7 yr, respectively. Occupations included secretaries, teachers, housewives, graduate students, nurses, and a writer.

Experimental Design

After the 2-wk base-line period, during which two no-feedback sessions were used to assess pre-training EMG levels, 18 patients were randomly assigned to one of three groups for a total of six in each group. Group A patients received the EMG biofeedback training (the experimental condition). Group B patients also received the "feedback," except that it was tape recorded from Group A (the "pseudofeedback" condition), i.e., the feedback signal produced and heard by the experimental patients was tape recorded and then played back to the Group B patients. Thus, they received noncontingent feedback. Group C did not receive training, but the patients were asked to keep track of their headaches on the daily charts (no-treatment condition).

After the 2-wk base line, Groups A and B received 16 sessions of training (ideally, two sessions per week) followed by a 3-mo follow-up period. During this time the patients charted their daily headache activity. At the end of the 3-mo follow-up, patients from Groups A and B were brought back for three no-feedback sessions to assess their ability to produce low EMG levels. A questionnaire was also administered to Groups A and B at the end of the 3-mo follow-up. The questionnaire was particularly designed to assess evidence of symptom substitution and levels of medication usage.

Upon completion of 16 sessions by Groups A and B, Group C patients were allowed to begin feedback training. Similarly, after the 3-mo follow-up, Group B patients were told that they could, if they so desired, receive additional training of a slightly different sort (real feedback).

Instructions to the Patients

The instructions to Group A patients were as follows:

> Tension headaches are primarily due to sustained contraction or tightness in the muscles of the scalp and neck.

> The goal of this study is to learn to relax your muscles so that the tension level never gets too high, and you no longer get headaches. This will involve a great deal of work on your part, both here in the lab, and also at home.
>
> In order to help you learn, we are going to provide you with information as to the level of muscle tension in your forehead region. You will hear a series of clicks in the headphones. The click rate will be proportional to your forehead tension; that is, the higher the tension, the faster the click rate. Your job will be to find out what makes the click rate slow down, because this means lower muscle tension. Try to eliminate those things that make the click rate go faster. Do not try *too* hard, or this will defeat your goal of deep relaxation. Remember to keep your attention focused on the clicks—do not let your mind wander.
>
> This session will last about 30 min.
>
> Remember—do not go to sleep.
>
> Any questions?

The instructions to Group B patients were as follows:

> Tension headaches are primarily due to sustained contraction or tightness in the muscles of the scalp and neck.
>
> The goal of this study is to learn to relax your muscles so that the tension level never gets too high, and you no longer get headaches. This will involve a great deal of work on your part, both here in the lab, and also at home.
>
> As you relax, it is important to keep out intruding thoughts. The varying click rate you will hear in the headphones will help you to keep out these thoughts. It is very important to keep your attention focused on the varying rate of clicks. Do not let your mind wander.
>
> This session will last about 30 min.
>
> Remember—do not go to sleep.
>
> Any questions?

Patients in this control group were *not* told that the feedback reflected tension levels in their forehead musculature because they could easily have determined that this was not true.

Group C patients were told that they were to chart their headache activity each day and that training would begin after a 2-mo base-line period. These patients were brought to the laboratory several times during this period for full instrumentation, no-feedback sessions in order to encourage them to remain in the study.

Home Practice

Since our pilot study results had indicated the critical importance of daily practice outside the laboratory setting, patients in Groups A and B were told to practice relaxation outside of the laboratory for two 15–20-min periods every day. No specific relaxation instructions were given for the home practice except that the patients were told to relax in the same way they had in the laboratory—but, of course, without the aid of any instruments.

Instrumentation and Laboratory Procedure

The "BIFS" EMG feedback system (Bio-Feedback Systems, Inc., Boulder, Colo.) was designed to assist individuals in reaching a condition of thorough muscle relaxation by means of information feedback. The unit was able to provide several types of auditory feedback as well as visual feedback. However, for this study, only auditory feedback in the form of a series of click sounds was employed. The frequency of the clicks was proportional to the integrated

EMG level. A high EMG level produced a high click rate. As the EMG level declined, the click frequency decreased. The patient, who had EMG electrodes applied to the skin surface over the frontalis muscle, attempted to lower the click rate by progressively relaxing the muscle.

The electrodes ($\frac{1}{2}$ inch in diameter; silver, silver-chloride) were placed 1 inch above each eyebrow and spaced 4 inches apart on the patient's forehead. One reference electrode was located in the center of the forehead. Electrode resistances were less than 10,000 ohms. The patient reclined on a couch, in a dimly lighted, electrically shielded room, and kept his eyes closed.

The EMG feedback unit functions as diagrammed in Fig. 2. An ac differential preamplifier with a bandwidth of 120–1000 Hz is used to amplify (gain = 1000) the bioelectric signal generated by the muscle. The amplified EMG signal is then both quantified and converted into a feedback signal by the BIFS. The fluctuating EMG level is changed into a varying click rate. Thus, the patient can "hear" his own muscle activity. The quantification of the EMG is such that a digital readout, available each minute, represents the average level of EMG activity in microvolts (μV) peak-to-peak (p–p) for that minute.

A cassette tape recorder was used to present the feedback clicks, as recorded from experimental patients, to the pseudofeedback control patients.

RESULTS

EMG Levels

In this carefully selected group of tension headache patients, the level of frontalis EMG during the 2 base-line wk averaged slightly over 10 μV (p–p) for

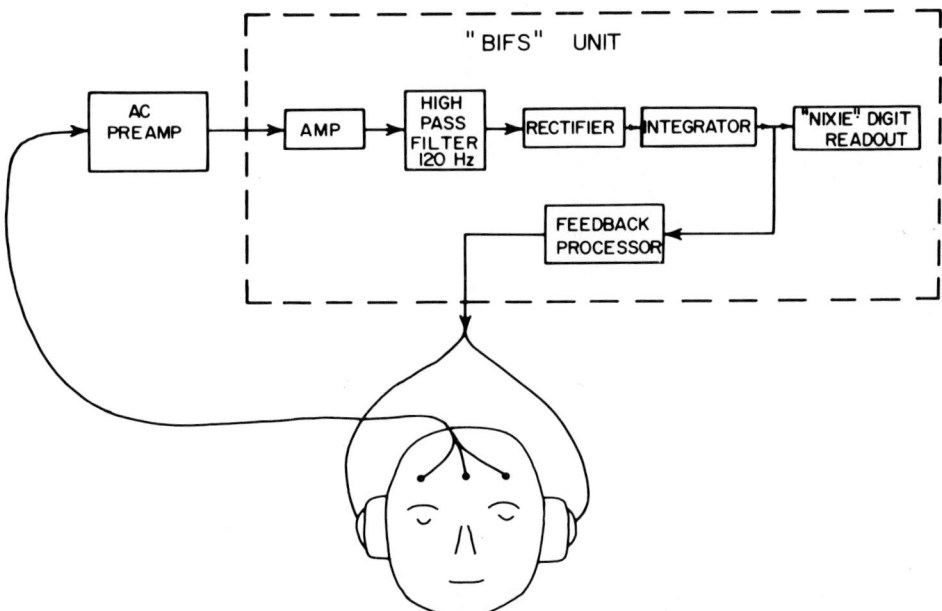

Fig. 2. Functional diagram of the EMG feedback system.

each group. These values are at least double those shown by young normal subjects in our laboratory. These readings are also a considerable increase over the 6 μV p–p base-line level for the five patients in the pilot study[6] and probably reflect the more stringent selection criteria used in the present study. It is evident from Fig. 3 that the mean EMG level for Group A showed a considerable decrease from the base-line level in the first feedback sessions. The mean EMG level of the Group B patients also dropped somewhat after the base-line sessions; however, the mean value of Group B remained at a higher level than the mean of Group A. The Group B curve also showed a great deal more variation than did that of the feedback group, perhaps not a surprising result since it is characteristic of feedback to decrease the variance of the response.

It was expected that the pseudofeedback Group B patients would show some decrease in EMG level as a result of the focusing of attention on a meaningless and comparatively monotonous stimulus (the "feedback" clicks). Furthermore, the shifting of attention from troublesome, anxiety-evoking thoughts to a relatively neutral stimulus probably also contributed to the lowered EMG level. Interestingly, it may be noted that the focusing of attention on a neutral, meaningless thought or word, to the exclusion of other thoughts, is an essential characteristic of many meditative disciplines.

Although all three groups did not show differences in base-line EMG levels, there was a significant difference ($p < 0.05$, one-tailed) between Groups A and B during the last 2 wk of training (Group C did not receive any training).

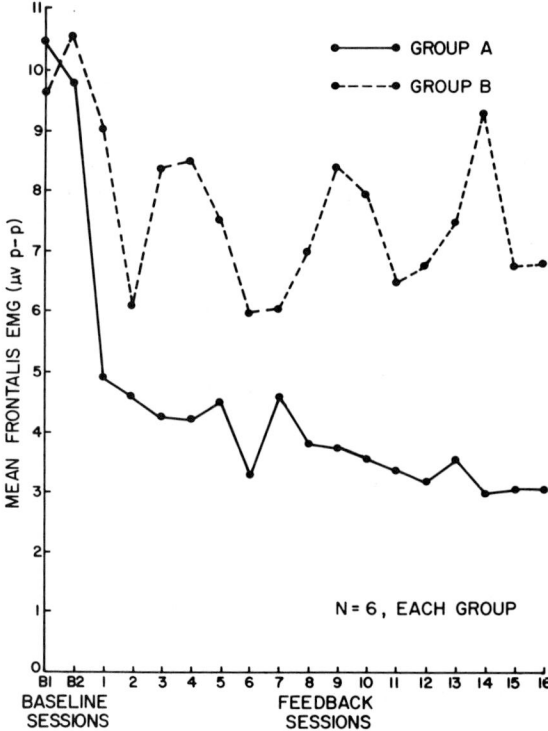

Fig. 3. Mean frontalis EMG levels across sessions. Group A, true feedback; Group B, pseudofeedback.

After the 3-mo follow-up period, the patients from Groups A and B were tested for three sessions with no feedback. The mean frontalis EMG levels were 3.92 and 8.43 μV p–p for A and B, respectively, and again represented a significant difference ($p < 0.01$, one-tailed) between the groups. Apparently the trained group had retained the learning over the 3-mo period.

Headache Activity

As expected, the averaged headache rating scores for both Groups A and B declined over time (see Fig. 4). However, as Fig. 4 indicates, *base-line* levels of headache activity had been somewhat lower in Group A than in Group B or C. Therefore, a Kruskal-Wallis analysis of variance by ranks was first applied to the base-line headache data. This test showed that the starting levels of the three groups were not significantly different from each other.

Additionally, in order to eliminate the possibility that different base-line levels were contributing to a significant difference between groups, we performed a slope analysis for each group.[7] Only Group A produced a statistically significant decline ($p < 0.001$ when the regression coefficient was tested against the null hypothesis of zero slope).

The headache data for *individual* patients in each group were also analyzed in this fashion. The analysis revealed that four out of six patients in Group A showed significant declines ($p < 0.05$) in headache activity, while in the pseudofeedback control group, only one of six showed a significant decline. None of the Group C patients showed a significant decline below base-line levels.

Finally, the Kruskal-Wallis analysis of variance by ranks, which had been applied to the base-line headache activity, was also used to test differences among the three groups at the end of the training period (weeks 8 and 9). At this time, there were significant differences in headache activity among the groups ($p < 0.001$).

Correlation Between EMG Levels and Headache Activity

When weekly headache activity during the base-line and training weeks was correlated with weekly frontalis EMG levels, the Group A data showed a +0.90

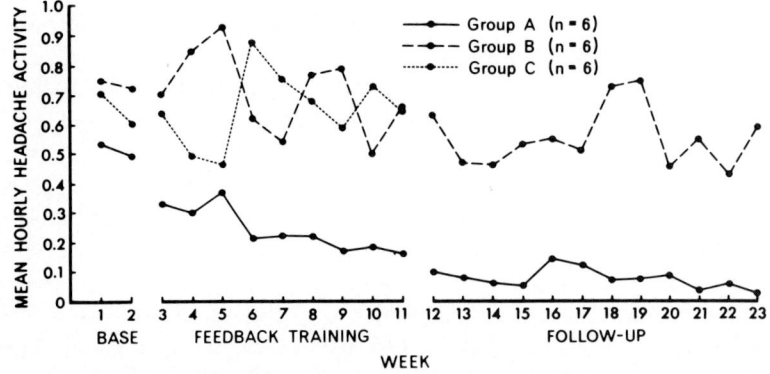

Fig. 4. Headache activity during feedback training (all 3 groups) and during the 3-mo follow-up (A and B only). Group A, true feedback; Group B, pseudofeedback; Group C, no treatment.

correlation while the Group B showed only −0.05, or essentially no correlation. This result may be due to the fact that the patients receiving the real feedback were indeed learning to relax in the laboratory and were able to apply this learning outside the laboratory, whereas the pseudofeedback patients generally were not able to do so.

The 3-mo follow-up data (see Fig. 4) indicated that the Group B patients appeared to have stabilized at a mean headache level of about 0.53, whereas Group A was producing very little in the way of headache activity during the last month.

Dropouts

It should be noted that there were four dropouts from the original Group B. These were patients who felt that the training was not having any effect on their headaches. All of them were experiencing high levels of headache activity when they retired from the study. However, the Group B patients who remained felt that the training was helpful. There were also two dropouts in Group C, but none in Group A. All dropouts were replaced with new patients.

Subjective Reports

While being instrumented prior to the sessions as well as just after the sessions, the patients would often volunteer comments as to their success or lack of it with the training. These comments were later entered into a log book by the technicians. On the basis of these comments, it soon became apparent that in this study, as well as the prior pilot study, the patients passed through several discrete stages in terms of their ability to use a "cultivated" relaxation response to reduce headache activity.

Stage 1: Patient is unable to prevent or abort headaches.

Stage 2: Patient becomes more aware of the tension preceding the headaches and can relax to some degree with a conscious effort. However, he cannot abort headaches.

Stage 3: Patient shows an increasing awareness of the tension, plus he is better able to relax consciously and abort light-to-moderate headaches. The frequency and intensity of headaches is now diminishing.

Stage 4: Patient now seems to relax automatically in the face of stress and does not have to make a conscious effort to do so. The headache activity is now appreciably reduced or even eliminated.

The last stage would seem to indicate that the ability to relax in the face of stress eventually becomes an overlearned habit resulting in a change in life style.

MMPI Results

All the patients were given the Minnesota Multiphasic Personality Inventory (MMPI) before and after the training period. In general, the "before" profile of scores showed that the Hs (hysteria), D (depression), and Hy (hypochondriasis) scales were somewhat elevated (the means for all three groups were in the low 60s). The "after" profiles of all three groups showed reductions in these three scales; however, the only statistically significant mean before–after change occurred in the Hy score of Group A ($p < 0.05$, two-tailed).

Table 1. Number of Patients in Each Group Showing Declines of
Ten or More Points on Three MMPI Scales

	Hs	D	Hy
Group A	3	3	4
Group B	2	1	1
Group C	1	1	1

Table 1 lists the number of patients in each group who showed declines of 10 points or more on these three scales. Group A produced a total of 10 change-scores equal to or greater than 10 points, while Group B showed four, and Group C a total of three. A chi-square test performed with the data from this table showed that the three groups were significantly different ($p < 0.01$) in the number of negative change-scores greater than 10.

The "before" profile showing the elevated triad of hysteria, depression and hypochondriasis is in general agreement with Martin,[4] who found the same elevations in a large group of tension headache patients.

Follow-up Data

A four-page post-training questionnaire was used to assess drug usage, evidence of symptom substitution, mood and behavior changes, and interpersonal relationships. All the patients in Groups A and B received this questionnaire after the 3-mo follow-up period. The patients were asked to rate the severity or frequency of symptoms on a scale of 0–3. Ratings were made for four periods: before training, first half of training, second half of training, and after training.

In Group A, decreasing severity or frequency was seen in 27 of 28 items. Group B patients rated themselves as decreasing on 23 of 28 items. In both groups the items showing the greatest decreases were depression, tension, anxiety, insomnia, fast heart beat, irritability, persistent thoughts, sexual disinterest, and fear of driving. Lesser decreases in both groups included chest pain, use of alcohol, sweating, and sexual anxieties. In addition, the Group A patients registered large decreases in tiredness, apathy, fear of crowds, and compulsive behavior. Patients in both groups saw themselves as improved in relationships with spouses and/or friends.

Although, generally, there was no evidence of symptom substitution, one patient in Group A did report a certain amount of stomach distress as she proceeded through training in deep relaxation. This phenomenon appears to be related to the sudden shift from a predominantly sympathetic autonomic state towards a parasympathetically dominant pattern. This transition does seem to produce an increase in stomach acidity in some individuals. As the patient continues the daily relaxation practice this reaction tends to disappear.

Drug usage decreased dramatically in Group A patients. As seen in Table 2, four of six went from a rate of 3–4 capsules of prescription tranquilizers and pain killers (typically, Valium, Librium, Fiorinal, and Darvon) per day to only occasional use of the tranquilizer. Another patient in Group A decreased his intake of aspirin from up to ten per day to two per week. The final patient in this group did not take medication for his headaches (and did not show a significant decrease in headache activity).

Table 2. Drug Usage in Group A (Experimental)

Patient	Before Study	First Half of Training	Second Half of Training	After Training
1	Fiorinal, Valium 3–4 daily	Fiorinal, Valium 3–4 daily	Librium 3–4 daily	Librium 3/wk
2	Darvon, Equagesic (all day)	Darvon, Equagesic (all day)	Darvon, Equagesic Seldom	Darvon Seldom
3	Valium 4/day	Valium 1/day	None	None
4	Anacin 10/day	Anacin 4/day	Anacin 2/wk	Anacin 2/wk
5	Darvon 4/day	Darvon 4/day	Darvon 2/day	None
6	None	None	None	None

Two of the Group B patients (see Table 3) reported decreases in medication, while three did not change in their usage. One patient switched from a Fiorinal-by-day, Librium-by-night schedule to Librium day and night. Interestingly, one patient from this group who showed *no* decrease in drug usage had reported a decrease in headache activity.

The questionnaire also required patients to rate their level of headache activity before, during, and after the training. In Group A, five of six rated their headaches as decreasing. One patient indicated no change. Three of the Group B patients rated themselves as decreasing in headache activity, while three others saw no change. One of those who rated her headaches as decreasing did now show a decrease in her daily charting of the headache activity.

Eighteen-month follow-up. Approximately 1½ yr after the completion of

Table 3. Drug Usage in Group B (Pseudofeedback Control)

Patient	Before Study	First Half of Training	Second Half of Training	After Training
1	Fiorinal 2/day Librium 2 at night	Fiorinal 2/day Librium 2 at night	Fiorinal 2/day Librium 1 at night	Librium 4/day and night
2	Librium 2/day Aspirin 4–5/day	Librium 1/day Aspirin 2/day	Aspirin 1/day	Aspirin 1/day
3	Anacin 4–6/day	Same	Same	Same
4	Meprobamate 3/day Elavil 2/day	Same	Same	Same
5	Wigraine Valium	Same	Same	Same
6	Equagesic 3/day Meprobamate 2/day	Equagesic 2/day Meprobamate 1/day	None	None

feedback training, four of the six Group A patients (two had left Colorado) were contacted. Three of the four previously had shown significant declines in headache activity during training. The three reported that their headaches remained at a very low level (roughly one or two mild headaches a month). Because they now felt more relaxed generally, they no longer engaged in a daily period of deep relaxation, using this approach only when feeling particularly tense. The fourth patient (who had *not* shown a significant reduction during training) reported that his headaches continued, although at a reduced rate.

"Real" training for Groups B and C patients. After the 3-mo follow-up, three patients from the pseudofeedback group (B) decided to try "another type" of training. Two of these people showed significant decreases in their headache scores through the training period. The third individual did not improve significantly.

Five of the Group C patients also received training consisting of 16 sessions of EMG feedback. Their training was initiated after their 9-wk "base-line" period was completed. Four of the five showed significant declines in headache activity.

The biofeedback training of the eight former control group patients along with a number of "pilot" headache patients was augmented with cassette tape recordings for home practice. In several instances, portable EMG feedback units were used at home as well.

DISCUSSION

The results of an earlier pilot study with five patients[6] had suggested that training in relaxation of the forehead muscles with EMG feedback might be effective in eliminating muscle contraction or tension headaches. That conclusion was further strengthened by the analysis of the data from this second experiment, which employed two control groups in addition to the experimental group. It now seems apparent that chronic tension headache patients can learn to decrease their resting forehead EMG levels by 50%–70% in three to six 20-min feedback sessions. When they subsequently engage in regular, daily relaxation, the headache activity diminishes considerably. Recently, other laboratories[8,9] have also reported that EMG feedback training is useful in the alleviation of tension headache.

These results are in keeping with a suggestion made independently by Malmo[10] of McGill University Medical School, who has worked extensively with electromyographic recording since the early 1950s. Malmo proposed that systematic muscle relaxation training might well be useful for treating tension headache.

Stages of Progress

As the patients progressed through training, their verbal reports suggested that they first developed a heightened awareness of maladaptive tension levels. This was followed by an increasing ability to remove the tension (and slight-to-moderate headaches) through relaxation. If the patients then applied this new learning to daily stress situations, a change in life style frequently seemed to occur. At this stage, patients typically reported that they no longer overreacted to stress. This "automatic" moderation of arousal level in the face of stress has also been reported by anxiety patients who have received EMG feedback-assisted relaxation training in our laboratory.

Transfer to Real Life

The no-feedback sessions at the end of the 3-mo follow-up revealed that those patients who had received feedback training still retained the ability to produce low forehead EMG levels. The 18-mo follow-up interview indicated that most experimental group patients had also managed to keep themselves relatively free of headaches even though they had been chronic headache sufferers for years prior to the training. Also, in this group, the use of powerful prescription drugs decreased dramatically.

Only one of the pseudofeedback controls produced a significant decline in headache activity over time. This patient was the youngest member of that group. She regularly performed the daily home relaxation practice. Although she was not given specific relaxation instructions, this patient learned to discriminate the internal cues of thorough relaxation such as heaviness and warmth in the arms.

Importance of Daily Practice

This study, as did the pilot study, pointed up the importance of daily home practice. The two experimental group patients who did not show significant declines had found it difficult to carry out the home relaxation assignments. Typically, they reported that the hectic state of affairs at home did not permit quiet periods of relaxation. Other patients stated that they would have preferred more explicit relaxation instructions for home use. A few found the daily home practice to be somewhat boring.

Addition to the Basic Technique

In the present study, only a minimal sort of training was employed—EMG feedback from the frontalis muscle. Probably this training could be strengthened considerably. For example, we have recently begun experimenting with two home practice techniques that should add both structure and novelty to the home training. One technique makes use of a 30-min cassette tape containing relaxation instructions on both sides. The other technique utilizes a battery-powered portable EMG feedback unit (Bio-Feedback Systems, Inc.). The tape and portable unit can be employed singly, sequentially or simultaneously.

Preliminary results indicate that each of these two supplementary methods will be a valuable addition to the minimum procedure used for Groups A, B, and C. By now, tapes and portable equipment have been used in the training of some of the approximately 30 tension headache patients (including those from the B and C groups who later received the "real" feedback) who have been trained in muscle relaxation with EMG biofeedback since the completion of this second study. The overall results indicate that roughly 75% showed significant declines in headache activity.

It is possible that some of those who did not show decreases may have been unwilling to give up their headaches. The headaches may have allowed those patients to avoid certain anxiety-arousing situations, or to manipulate others in their family or at work. In these instances, psychotherapy or behavior therapy is required.[11]

Even though EMG feedback training alone is not effective in all cases, the technique would seem to be of considerable value for a substantial proportion of tension headache cases. The training does not involve drugs or other kinds of therapy and can be accomplished with relatively inexpensive portable equipment. Training can be carried out by a technician (or perhaps by the patient himself) under professional supervision. In most instances, beneficial results can be achieved in 4–8 wk. Since many tension headache patients experience pain in the back of the neck and shoulders, it is possible that faster results could be obtained with some of these patients through feedback from these muscle sites. These locations were not used in this study, since it is more difficult to obtain precise electrode location here than on the forehead.

A variety of evidence suggests that biofeedback techniques may have applications to stress-related disorders other than tension headache. For example, researchers at the Menninger Foundation[12] have explored the use of skin temperature feedback with migraine patients. In our own laboratory, we have for several years regularly employed EMG feedback techniques in the systematic desensitization of phobias.[13] Insomnia may be another potential application. Drowsiness is a frequent accompaniment of profound muscle relaxation; perhaps EMG (and related) feedback techniques would be useful in some instances of sleep-onset insomnia. Observations in support of such a surmise may be found in Jacobson's writings[14] on progressive relaxation and in the autogenic training literature.[15] It may be noted that both these older approaches systematically train patients in the ability to shift readily into a relaxed, low-arousal condition.

ACKNOWLEDGMENT

We are most grateful to Susan Blom and John Nagel, M.D., for their technical assistance.

REFERENCES

1. Sainsbury P, Gibson JF: Symptoms of anxiety and tension and accompanying physiological changes in the muscular system. J Neurol Neurosurg Psychiatry 17:216–224, 1954

2. Ostfeld AM: The Common Headache Syndromes: Biochemistry, Pathophysiology, Therapy. Springfield, Ill, Thomas, 1962, p 19

3. Wolff HG: Headache and Other Pain. New York, Oxford Univ Pr, 1963, pp 582–616

4. Martin MJ: Tension headache, a psychiatric study. Headache 6:47–54, 1966

5. Budzynski TH, Stoyva JM: An instrument for producing deep relaxation by means of analog information feedback. J Appl Behav Anal 2:231–237, 1969

6. Budzynski TH, Stoyva JM, Adler CS: Feedback-induced muscle relaxation: Application to tension headache. Behav Ther Exp Psychiatry 1:205–211, 1970

7. Snedecor GW, Cochran WG: Statistical Methods (ed 6). Ames, Iowa, Iowa State Univ Pr, 1967, pp 152–153

8. Wickramasekera I: Electromyographic feedback training and tension headache: Preliminary observations. Am J Clin Hypn 15:83–85, 1972

9. Raskin M, Johnson G, Rondestvedt JW: Chronic anxiety treated by feedback-induced muscle relaxation. Arch Gen Psychiatry 28:263–267, 1973

10. Malmo RB: Emotions and muscle tension: The story of Anne. Psychology Today 3:64, 1970

11. Dengrove E: Behavior therapy of headache. J Am Soc Psychosom Dent Med 15:41–48, 1968

12. Sargent JD, Green EE, Walters ED: Preliminary report on the use of autogenic feedback techniques in the treatment of migraine and tension headache. Psychosom Med 35:129–135, 1973

13. Budzynski TH, Stoyva JM: Biofeedback techniques in behavior therapy, in Birbaumer N (ed): Beiträge der Neuropsychologie zur Angstforschung. Reihe Fortschritte der Klinischen Psychologie (ed 4). München, Wien, Verlag Urban Schwarzenberg (in press). English version republished in Shapiro D, et al. (eds): Biofeedback and Self-control: 1972. Chicago, Aldine-Atherton, 1973

14. Jacobson E: Progressive Relaxation (ed 2). Chicago, Univ of Chicago Pr, 1938, pp 418–419

15. Schultz JH, Luthe W: Autogenic Training: A Psychophysiological Approach in Psychotherapy. New York, Grune & Stratton, 1959

Chapter 5: Migraine Headache

Introduction

MIGRAINE HEADACHE, in its full-blown form, is an extraordinarily painful malady; it occurs as a part of the much more complex

> migraine syndrome . . . [which] is a pattern of dysfunction integrated within the central nervous system and manifested as wide-spread bodily disturbances, both nonpainful and painful. The outstanding feature is periodic headache, usually unilateral in onset but at times becoming bilateral or generalized. The attacks may vary in duration from a few minutes to several days and, in severity, from trifling symptoms to prolonged disabling illness. The headaches are associated with "irritability," nausea and often photophobia, vomiting, constipation or diarrhea. Although most commonly in the temple, headaches may be experienced anywhere in the head, face and neck.[1]

The pain is

> throbbing and aching, is appreciably reduced by pressure on the common carotid and the affected superficial artery and is characteristically eliminated or reduced by vasoconstrictor agents, particularly ergotamine tartrate. The walls of the dilated cranial arteries and the adjacent tissues become edematous and tender. With sustained vasodilatation for several hours, the easily compressible arteries become rigid and relatively noncompressible, and the pulsatile pain becomes a steady ache. Redness and swelling of the eye with excessive tearing, and redness and swelling of the nasal mucosa, with or without epistaxis [nosebleeds] may occur along with the headache.[1]

The disorder is complex; it runs in families, and it may occur in association with "a generalized accumulation of fluid as part of a nonspecific disturbance in fluid and electrolytes that is found in many persons with and without the migraine syndrome during periods of stress."[1]

In addition,

> there is evidence of a general abnormality of vascular behavior in many migraine subjects, and the extracranial vessels of subjects with migraine show more variability than those of normal subjects in their contractile patterns, even during headache-free periods.[1]

There are also important clues as to pathogenetic biochemical factors:

> Several lines of evidence suggest that serotonin may play a role in the migraine syndrome. Reserpine, which induces a drop in serum serotonin levels, will often induce a migraine attack, and preheadache levels of serotonin have been found to drop spontaneously just before migraine attacks. During migraine attacks, an increased quantity of serotonin metabolites has been found in the urine. Methylsergide, a powerful serotonin antagonist, prevents or reduces the frequency of migraine attacks in most subjects.[1]

Finally, there is a very important emotional factor:

> Patients with migraine headaches are anxious, striving, perfectionistic, order-loving, rigid persons who, during periods of threat or conflict, become progressively more tense, resentful and fatigued. The person with migraine often attempts to gain approval by doing more and better than his fellows and to gain security by holding to a stable environment and a given system of excellent performance, even at a high cost of energy. This pattern brings increasing responsibility and admiration, but little love, so that he feels greater and greater resentment at the pace he feels obligated to maintain. Then tension associated with repeated frustration,

© 1973 by Grune & Stratton, Inc.

> sustained resentment and anxiety, often followed by fatigue and prostration, become the setting in which the migraine attack occurs.[1]

As with tension headache, the common underlying psychologic feature in migraine is the mismanagement and suppression of anger. Migraine patients, as pointed out in the quotation above, are likely to be perfectionistic and hardworkingly dedicated to being so competent and so good that everyone is forced to admire them. This often apparently is part of an attempt to keep their anger from breaking through into consciousness. Pure tension headache patients, on the other hand, seem to be more aware of their anger and engaged in a kind of chronic struggle to hold it back; often, perhaps even typically, tension headache patients are aware of many angry feelings but are proud of their ability to "be rational" and to hold onto their tempers. Thus, in a general way it might be said that migraine patients tend to "repress" anger—i.e., try to keep it out of consciousness—while tension headache patients tend to "supress" anger—i.e., they are aware of it but try not to express it. Many patients, of course, do both, and many patients do have both tension and migraine headache.*

Traditional treatment approaches to migraine headache depend on four major mechanisms: (1) the use of vasoconstrictive drugs like ergotamine tartrate; (2) the use of analgesic drugs like aspirin, propoxyphene hydrochloride (Darvon), or codeine; (3) the daily use of the serotonin-blocking drug, methysergide (Sansert), as a prophylactic drug; and (4) the use of personal counselling and/or psychotherapy

> to allow the patient free and repeated expression of his personal conflicts, resentments and dissatisfactions . . . [to enable him] to recognize the nature of his dilemma and its relationship to the physiologic basis of his pain . . . [and to guide] him toward a more realistic appraisal of his needs . . . .[1]

Unfortunately, however, such a counselling approach generally leaves much to be desired in the way of hard-core results for those whom it does help, "about two of three patients," according to Cecil and Loeb, and is not at all helpful to the remainder. And there are real problems with drug treatment as well. Ergotamine, in many cases, *if given early in the attack,* may be dramatically helpful. But many patients cannot safely take ergotomine at all—it is contraindicated in pregnancy, peripheral vascular (circulatory) disturbance or thrombophebitis; angina pectoris and coronary artery disease; and renal (kidney) disease—and for all patients it is unsafe to take more than 10.0 mg orally† in any one week. In addition, the drug tends to produce unpleasant nausea as a side effect, especially if taken by mouth.

Methysergide is effective in about two-thirds of the cases in preventing attacks, but it also is contraindicated in all the same clinical situations as ergotamine. In addition, it sometimes apparently produces the severe complica-

---

*For them, it is appropriate to use both EMG feedback (as in Chapter 4) and temperature biofeedback (as in Chapter 5). For both tension headache and migraine headache patients, concomitant psychotherapy is also helpful (see Chapter 10); this should include a focus on the effective handling of angry feelings by appropriate self-assertion, and should be supplemented by the behavioral technique, assertive training, if necessary.

†Since up to 8 mg may be required for treating even one attack, this imposes severe limitations.

tion of retroperitoneal fibrosis and, again according to Cecil and Loeb, "any single course of the drug should probably not outlast three months."

The use of analgesic drugs, the last of the four traditional treatment methods, is also beset with problems. Aspirin is not powerful enough as an analgesic to be of help with full-blown migraine attacks, and intermediate drugs like Darvon help only slightly more. And the use of narcotic drugs like codeine or morphine is dangerous because many of the patients have very frequent attacks, and the use of these drugs can lead to addiction.

In the application of biofeedback to the treatment of the migraine syndrome, the painful headache is treated as the target symptom.

The excruciatingly painful headache of migraine syndrome is immediately caused by abnormal vasodilatation of one of the external cranial arteries, most commonly one of the temporal arteries. The vasodilatation, equivalent to a kind of ballooning out, painfully stretches the walls of the artery, and is thus especially painful with the throbbing of each individual heart beat. There are many indications that the vasodilatation is in turn secondary to a central and autonomic nervous system situation characterized by excessive sympathetic outflow (see pages 58–59).

The target physiologic response chosen to combat this situation in the nervous system is warming the hands, since anatomically and empirically it is known that physiologically cool hands can only be warmed by decreasing sympathetic outflow. To this end, the recording instruments used are two thermistors, each measuring body temperature, one in the forehead, and one in the right index finger. The criterion response is hand-warming (usually relative to forehead temperature), because this is correlated with a decrement in the presumptive root problem, excessive sympathetic outflow. The reinforcement is in the form of feedback about success, usually by reading a dial in which the hand sweeps from the midline to the far right as the hands become warmer.

Sargent et al. in this chapter present treatment outcome data (see page 62, and see Table 1) to the effect that of 42 migraine patients treated so far, 34 improved. Of this series, 25 of 42 improved enough to be able to actually abort headaches by using the biofeedback relaxation and hand-warming technique they had learned, and 16 of 42 improved enough to be able to recognize pre-headache symptoms and actually avoid threatened headaches altogether. Putting these outcome data together with what has just been presented in the preceding brief overview of migraine and of traditional treatment approaches to it, the conclusion emerges that this chapter describes a technique of practical value.

To sum up, the most impressive thing about this chapter is the clinical results obtained in a very difficult clinical problem: of the entire treated series 34 of 42 or 81% improved, and 25 of 42 or 60% improved enough to have actually learned to abort headaches.

Lee Birk, M.D.

REFERENCE

1. Beeson PB, McDermott W (eds): Cecil-Loeb Textbook of Medicine (ed 12). Philadelphia, Saunders, 1967, pp 1476–77

Psychosomatic Self-regulation of Migraine Headaches

Joseph D. Sargent, M.D., E. Dale Walters, M.A., and Elmer E. Green, Ph.D.

A historical perspective regarding research and treatment of the migraine syndrome and the studies in animals and humans relating to control of the autonomic nervous system is given. Pilot experience with 75 subjects is presented, and a detailed clinical account of one successful subject with pertinent research records is given. Reference is made to the implications of this clinical research to psychosomatic medicine.

MIGRAINE HEADACHES have been described in the literature for the past 2000 yr, but it has been only in the past three to four decades that this affliction has been subjected to scientific scrutiny, beginning with Wolff and his colleagues. Since then many investigators have intensely studied this disorder; however, its pathophysiology still remains poorly understood.

It is estimated that as much as 5%–10% of the U.S. population suffers from migraine attacks. As yet, no effective treatment has been developed that does not have significant side effects and risks that seriously affect patients' acceptance. The plethora of recommended treatment methods is evidence of the lack of a truly successful treatment for migraine.

For the most part, migraine attacks, although intensely disabling at times, are a benign disorder for which patients are often overly medicated and are frequently given potentially addicting drugs. Because this type of headache poses such a difficult problem, any possible approach that can safely answer this enigma merits study, and such an approach is the use of autogenic feedback training to control blood flow dysfunction in migraine.

BACKGROUND

Possible Mechanisms for Migraine Attacks

Graham and Wolff were the first to show that the pulsation of the temporal artery during the headache phase was increased.[8] Their work was based on observations of ergotamine tartrate effects on extracranial vessels in relief of migraine attacks. Ergotamine tartrate diminished the increased amplitude of the arterial pulsation with corresponding relief of the headache. These results seemed reasonable in view of the previous work with histamine, which had clearly shown that stretched extracranial arteries were capable of producing pain.[3,19]

Schumacher and Wolff, working further with methods to increase intracranial pressure and the administration of amyl nitrite, reached the following conclusions: "The essential migraine phenomena result from dysfunction of cranial arteries and represent contrasts in vascular mechanisms and vascular

---

Reprint requests should be addressed to Dr. Joseph D. Sargent, Department of Neurology, Neurosurgery and Internal Medicine, Menninger Foundation, Topeka, Kans. 66601.

©*1973 by Grune & Stratton, Inc.*

beds. Preheadache disturbances follow occlusive vasoconstriction of cerebral arteries, where the headache results from dilation and distension chiefly of branches of external carotid arteries."[26] Thus, the vascular theory of migraine was born.

A chance cerebral angiogram done on a patient while in a classic migraine attack showed a diminution in the size of the internal carotid system with reflux into the vertebral vessels during the prodromal phase. At the beginning of the headache phase, blood flow returned to normal.[4] O'Brien has shown a profound reduction in blood flow in the cerebral cortex with the changes lasting much longer than the aura. This change may even occur without symptoms and is generalized and bilateral in distribution. From this evidence it can be concluded that each attack of migraine is biphasic with the occurrence of the aura being "an accidental expression of a more generalized process."[14]

Wolff proposed in his neurogenic theory of migraine headache that vasodilation of the cerebral circulation occurred whenever adequate blood supply to the brain is endangered. If cerebrovascular dilation is great enough, the extracranial arteries will dilate and release a number of chemical factors with production of edema and a lowering of pain threshold. What initiates vasoconstriction is not clearly delineated.[30]

In recent years, investigators have postulated that an agent (or agents) causing vasoconstriction may be released to start the headache sequence. Sicuteri has proposed that such liberated chemical substances are amines such as norepinephrine, epinephrine, or serotonin, all powerful vasoconstrictors.[28] Other biochemical agents implicated in the headache sequence are acetylcholine, adenosine, triphosphate, bradykinin, and histamine.[15] Of these, serotonin may be the most important one, since under some circumstances it can also be a vasodilator substance.[16] In the migraine attack, some migrainous subjects have excreted increased amounts of catecholamine end-products, particularly, 5HIAA from serotonin and VMA from norepinephrine and epinephrine.[28] Lance, Anthony, and Hintenberger have shown a corresponding reduction in blood serotonin levels.[12]

According to Friedman and Elkind, "Methysergide maleate (Sansert) has proven to be the most useful prophylactic agent in migraine."[6] Interestingly, this medicine is an anti-serotonin agent and has two actions—inhibition of central vasomotor reflex effects and accentuation of peripheral vasoconstriction produced by catecholamines. Also ergotamine tartrate has significant central effects, in addition to its well-known peripheral vasoconstrictor effect, as demonstrated in man and animals.[8,21,22,30] Thus, Friedman concludes that the "traditional view that migraine consists of phases of vasoconstriction and vasodilation is far too simplified, and it is apparent that migraine is a complex vasomotor disturbance."[7]

Because the migraine syndrome is a multi-faceted clinical disorder, some investigators have postulated a dysfunction in the hypothalamus as the provoking element in the attack. Thus, Graham has suggested that the hypothalamus can profoundly influence the autonomic control of the peripheral vasculature and has postulated a periodic central disturbance of hypothalamic activity or labile threshold accounting for the periodicity of the migraine attack and providing a mechanism whereby emotional disturbances could be mediated by pathways from the limbic system to the hypothalamus.[18] From three groups of clinical observations, Herburg has proposed an etiologic role in migraine headaches for the variation of hypothalamic activity. These groups of clinical observations are as follows: (1) the peripheral vasomotor involvement as seen in the temporal arteries, conjunctiva, and skin; (2) metabolic and vegetative disturbance, such as variations in water balance, food intake, mood, and sleep; and (3) the "accentuated secondary drives" of the migraine personality, which have been related to hypothalamic activity.[11] Rao and Pearce failed to demonstrate in migraine subjects a disturbance in the hypothalamic–pituitary–adrenal axis using metyrapone and insulin hypoglycemia tests. However, a consistently observed pattern of "hypoglycemia unresponsiveness" suggested a possible hypothalamic dysfunction.[20]

Treatment of Migraine

Friedman, commenting on drug therapy in migraine, found "that the results of drug prophylaxis were remarkably similar, irrespective of the drug, and only a few drugs were more effective than a placebo."[7] Ergotamine tartrate is still the drug of choice for the migraine attack and methysergide maleate has proved to be the most useful prophylactic agent in migraine.[7] However, both of these medications have significant adverse side-effects that may decrease patient acceptance. "In general, the surgical therapy of migraine is not effective and should be discouraged."[7] In a small, selected number of cases, psychotherapy and treatment of allergic factors precipitating migraine headaches can be beneficial.

In the U.S., there is a sizable segment of poorly controlled migraine sufferers who might welcome a totally new approach to the treatment of migraine.

Research Experience Leading to Pilot Study

Neal Miller recently performed research that challenges the concept that "learning" in the autonomic nervous system is a reflection of skeletal muscle activity. He has shown that heart rate, gastrointestinal contractions, blood pressure, and the rate of saliva and urine formation in animals can be directly controlled through "operant conditioning techniques" via the autonomic nervous system.[13] In humans, there is scientific evidence for voluntary control of the autonomic nervous system through the training techniques of yoga, biofeedback training,[5,10,23,24,27,29] and the work of Schultz and Luthe on "autogenic training."[25]

Autogenic training, according to Luthe, is a basic therapeutic method of a series of psychophysiologically oriented approaches that are in contrast to other medical or psychologic forms of treatment. It involves the simultaneous regulation of mental and somatic functions. The desired somatic responses are brought about by passive concentration upon phrases of preselected words. The first two specific somatic responses in preliminary training brought under voluntary control are heaviness in the limbs and warmth in the extremities.

In treating migraines, Schultz and Luthe reported that the majority of their patients responded with lessened frequency and intensity of headaches with autogenic training exercises. A number of patients reported a cure after several months of practice and learned to interrupt the onset of an attack by starting autogenic exercises as soon as prodromal symptoms appeared.[25]

Biofeedback training, a recently developed technique, holds promise of accelerating psychosomatic self-regulation. This technique, when combined with autogenic phrases, is called autogenic–feedback training and uses visual and auditory devices to show the subject what is happening to normally unconscious bodily functions as he attempts to influence them by his use of mental, emotional, and somatic visualizations. Work in our laboratory has shown that skin temperature in the hands is directly related to blood flow in the hands,[23] and an increase in skin temperature of the hand is used as an index of voluntary control of the sympathetic section of the autonomic nervous system.

The possibility of using autogenic–feedback training for migraine patients was suggested by the experience of a research subject who, during the spontaneous recovery from a migraine attack, demonstrated considerable flushing in her hands with an accompanying 10° F rise in 2 min. Knowledge of this event quickly spread throughout the laboratory and prompted two individuals with migraine to volunteer for training in hand temperature control. One was wholly successful and learned to eliminate migraine for the most part. The other had a partially beneficial result, and she was able to somewhat alleviate headache intensity and reduce frequency of headache. On the basis of this prepilot experience, it seemed useful to conduct further study with a number of headache patients in a clinical setting.

RATIONALE

Although considerable research must be conducted before we are certain about the neural mechanisms involved in "voluntary controls" training programs, it seems quite clear that the limbic–hypothalamic axis is an essential part. The classic paper of Papez,[17] "A Proposed Mechanism of Emotion," has laid the groundwork for an understanding of bioemotional factors, and additional work has elaborated Papez's position.[1] It seems clear beyond reasonable doubt that the limbic system, the "viseral" or "emotional" brain, is the major responder to psychologic stress and that psychosomatic problems become chronic in somatic processes through numerous interconnections between the limbic system and autonomic control centers in hypothalamic sections of the midbrain. The chain of events might be hypothesized as follows: psychologic response (perception of stimuli)→limbic response→hypothalamic response→autonomic response→somatic response.

In the case of migraine, which seems to be a part of a stress-related syndrome, the somatic response is dysfunction of vascular behavior in the head, related to intense sympathetic dysfunction, if other parts of the syndrome (such as cold hands, due to vasoconstriction) can be used as indicators. Vasoconstriction in the hands is a function only of sympathetic activation and vasodilation is a one-variable indication of decrease of sympathetic outflow. The peripheral vascular structure does not have significant parasympathetic innervation.

With these concepts and facts in mind, it seems reasonable to hypothesize that autogenic–feedback training for hand-warming is effective in amelioration of migraine, because patients are learning to "turn off" excessive sympathetic outflow. Since the sympathetic control centers for vascular behavior are located in subcortical structures, it seems that the attack on vascular dysfunction in the head is linked to a general relaxation of sympathetic outflow, rather than through hydraulic maneuvering of blood in various portions of the body. This hypothesis of sympathetic relaxation rather than blood volume changes per se, as the effective agent in migraine amelioration, is supported by the fact that patients who put their hands in warm water in order to increase the blood volume in the hands usually do not obtain migraine relief. A couple of patients who have obtained a measure of relief in this way have, according to the sympathetic-control hypothesis, merely taught themselves to relax with the conditioned stimulus of warm water.

The limbic system is certainly brought into action by the interaction of patient and machine. Considerable emotion is involved in learning to control the temperature machine, and if this involvement increase the sympathetic activation, then the resultant vasoconstriction causes the hands to cool. In order to "make" the hands get warm, it is literally necessary to learn "passive volition." This includes a condition of relaxed detachment, in which the body is told what to do through autogenic imagery and then is allowed to do it without anxious introspection. Only under this condition, which seems to be opposite to the normal state preceding migraine attack, can the hands be made to become warmer at will. In other words, learning to control hand temperature is a good indicator of learning to control central processes that are associated with vascular dysfunction. It is voluntary control of this functional relationship, in the authors' opinion, that is responsible for migraine relief. It includes normalization of homeostatic balance in hypothalamic control centers.

METHODS

The initial 75 subjects out of a total of approximately 150 in the pilot study have been either self-referred or referred by physicians in the community. Each patient, before participating in the project, had a detailed history, complete physical examination, and laboratory studies (EEG, skull x-rays, echoencephalogram, chest x-ray, serology, CBC, and urinalysis). Subjects with severe psychologic and/or physical disorders were eliminated from the study. There were two with cluster headaches, five with combined headache, 11 with tension headaches, and 57 migraine sufferers.

Each patient received instructions in the use of a "temperature trainer," which indicated the differential temperature between the midforehead and the right index finger. He was also given a typewritten sheet containing autogenic phrases. The first group of phrases helped the subject achieve passive concentration and relaxation of the whole body. The second group of phrases focused on the achievement of warmth in the hands. After learning the phrases, the participant dispensed with the typewritten sheet and visualized the changes while watching the temperature trainer. A positive warmth response, as indicated by the trainer, was accomplished by increasing temperature of the hands in comparison to the forehead and helped the subject to learn to observe the change of feeling that occurred in his hands while practicing. Since absolute temperatures were not measured at either site, it was impossible to know whether a positive response indicated an actual increase in hand warmth or a decrease in forehead temperature. However, results from our laboratory with absolute temperature feedback have indicated that the specific change in temperature occurs in the hands rather than in the forehead. Also, most subjects reported that a positive response with the trainer was associated chiefly with the feeling of change in the hands rather than change in the forehead. The coordination between mind–body or psychosomatic responses is an important aspect of the training exercises, because it allows the subject to overcome his initial doubt with respect to the control of basic physiologic processes. A positive response on the trainer reinforces the patient's confidence in doing his exercises.

One month prior to training, a subject charted daily the type of headache, and if a headache was present, he rated headache severity, presence or absence of associated symptoms, degree of disability from the headache, and duration of headache. Also the type, strength, and total number of units taken in 24 hr for each medication used for headache and its associated symptoms were recorded (see Fig. 1).

After instruction in the use of the temperature trainer and hand temperature control each participant practiced daily at home and recorded presence or absence of relaxation and warmth in the hands, readings from the trainer at the start and end of each practice session, and the interval of time to detect warmth in the hands from the beginning of the session. Later in the training period, the subject tried to control his headache by warming his hands and estimated his success at doing it. The meticulous recording of all data was expected of each participant while in the study.

At first the subject was seen at weekly intervals until he had a consistent, positive response on the meter and an associated change of feeling in the hands. After mastering the hand-warming technique, he practiced on alternate days without the trainer and usually the trainer could be withdrawn within a month after starting. Subsequently, he was expected to continue daily practice sessions and was encouraged to use hand-warming to help control headache. After the trainer was withdrawn, the participant returned to the clinic every 1–3 mo. During the return visits, pertinent data that may have influenced the patient's headache and his response to the exercises were recorded, and he practiced voluntary relaxation on the warmth trainer. The expected follow-up period was a minimum of a year, preferably for 2–3 yr.

As the data were collected, it was scored, and graphs were plotted so that the subject's progress over 1 yr could be viewed at a glance. The variables evaluated to date are (1) headache intensity, (2) the total of individual analgesics used, and (3) total potency of analgesics used. The subjects rated on a 5-point scale the severity of the most intense period of its activity in each 24-hr period. Each analgesic was assigned a number, representing its potency, the extremes of which were aspirin[1] and morphine,[7] and the potency scale represented the sum of strengths of analgesics used in 24 hr.

Each patient's progress was evaluated as to degree of improvement, based on the senior author's global clinical judgement with benefit of the plotted data.

As an outgrowth of this work, it seemed necessary to determine the behavior

MIGRAINE HEADACHE

*a 1—Slight
    2—Moderate
    3—Moderately Severe
    4—Severe

*b 0—No interference with activities
    1—Interference with activities
    2—Had to go to bed
    3—Go to Emergency Room or Doctor's office for treatment
    4—Need to be hospitalized

*c 0—None
    1—Questionable
    2—Present

*d 0—Absent
    1—More than 5 minutes
    2—Between 3 and 5 minutes
    3—Between 1 and 3 minutes
    4—Less than 1 minute

*e 0—None
    1—Questionable
    2—Present

*f 0—None
    1—Partially successful
    2—Successful

1. Date								
2. Type of Headache (check one or more) If headache is present check items 3 thru 6	☐ Migraine ☐ Tension ☐ Sinus ☐ None	☐ Migraine ☐ Tension ☐ Sinus ☐ None	☐ Migraine ☐ Tension ☐ Sinus ☐ None	☐ Migraine ☐ Tension ☐ Sinus ☐ None	☐ Migraine ☐ Tension ☐ Sinus ☐ None	☐ Migraine ☐ Tension ☐ Sinus ☐ None	☐ Migraine ☐ Tension ☐ Sinus ☐ None	☐ Migraine ☐ Tension ☐ Sinus ☐ None
3. Intensity of headache *a (circle one)	1 2 3 4	1 2 3 4	1 2 3 4	1 2 3 4	1 2 3 4	1 2 3 4	1 2 3 4	1 2 3 4
4. Presence of associated symptoms (circle one)	YES NO	YES NO	YES NO	YES NO	YES NO	YES NO	YES NO	YES NO
5. Rate degree of disability from headaches *b (circle one)	0 1 2 3 4	0 1 2 3 4	0 1 2 3 4	0 1 2 3 4	0 1 2 3 4	0 1 2 3 4	0 1 2 3 4	0 1 2 3 4
6. Length of headache (In hours)								
7. Name / Strength of Tab., Cap. or No. in Shot / 24 hrs								
8. Rate presence of warmth in hand *c (circle one)	1 2 3 4 5 0 1 2	1 2 3 4 5 0 1 2	1 2 3 4 5 0 1 2	1 2 3 4 5 0 1 2	1 2 3 4 5 0 1 2	1 2 3 4 5 0 1 2	1 2 3 4 5 0 1 2	1 2 3 4 5 0 1 2
9. Rate ability to bring warmth to hands *d (circle one)	0 1 2 3 4	0 1 2 3 4	0 1 2 3 4	0 1 2 3 4	0 1 2 3 4	0 1 2 3 4	0 1 2 3 4	0 1 2 3 4
10. Rate degree of relaxation *e	0 1 2	0 1 2	0 1 2	0 1 2	0 1 2	0 1 2	0 1 2	0 1 2
11. Change of temperature registered on meter								
12. Rate ability to control headaches with exercise *f (circle one)	0 1 2	0 1 2	0 1 2	0 1 2	0 1 2	0 1 2	0 1 2	0 1 2

Fig. 1. Headache project data collection sheet.

of skin temperature in the forehead and hands as the patient tried to warm his hands. The Biomedical Electronics Laboratory of The Menninger Foundation built a temperature scanner, which measures in rapid sequence skin temperatures from four sites. A number of subjects were evaluated using this temperature scanner.

RESULTS

Work in the headache project, begun almost 4 yr ago, was initially reported after accumulating data on 28 subjects, of whom 19 were afflicted with migraine.[23] A later report was based on the data from 33 migrainous individuals. Of the 33, 32 had migraine attacks and 68%-90% of the patients were considered to be improved in the judgment of three raters.[24]

Of the initial 75 subjects in the headache project, approximately 81% of the migraine patients followed for over 150 days were helped to a significant extent. The degree of improvement ranged from slight to very good (see Table 1).

Since the initial study with 75 patients, we have worked with approximately 75 additional patients using absolute temperature feedback. Those data have not been completely scored to date. To understand fully what we have done in this study, we feel that it will be particularly helpful to follow one participant from entrance into until voluntary withdrawal from the project.

Illustrative Case

Mrs. L.O. was first seen by me in consultation in January, 1971, in a community hospital for a long, complex illness. As a result of this encounter, the patient was started on Tofranil at 10 mg t.i.d. for endogenous depression. Interestingly, the symptom of headache assumed little importance of its own at that time in the midst of other complaints. Eventually her personal physician increased the Tofranil to 100 mg daily with considerable improvement of her depression, but the headache problem continued unabated to the time of my next consultation in October, 1971.

At the time of the second consultation the patient was 58 yr old and now complained principally of headaches that seemed typical of migraine and were located always on the right side of the head. A complete physical examination with emphasis on the nervous system and laboratory workup including an EEG, echoencephalogram, and skull x-rays revealed no other causes for headache except for an "abnormal EEG with photic sensitivity and a spike focus in the left temporal region." A repeat EEG in August, 1972, was normal.

She was accepted for participation in the headache project in October, 1971, and concluded her participation in January, 1973. Data were collected on this patient for just over 1 hr. Figure 2 shows the patient's progress as indicated by (1) ratings of headache severity, (2) number of analgesic drugs used, and (3) sum of the potency of analgesic drugs used. Base-line data for 1 mo prior to training is also shown. On visual inspection, it can be seen that steady improvement occurred in the control of headache. By the 20th week, mean severity of headache was reported as slight to none and remained at that level except for several slight episodes.

Figure 3 shows the skin temperature behavior of Mrs. L. O. from four body

Table 1. Classification of Degree and Type of Improvement and Evaluation of Treatment for the Initial 75 Headache Patients*

Degree of Improvement	Type of Improvement	Number of Migraine Patients	
None	Headache activity continued at the same level with little or no reduction in medication	8	19% Not Improved
Slight	Shortened headache duration, for instance, from 24 hr to 12 hr, reduced severity of headache, for instance, from severe to moderate, and reduced frequency of headache, for instance, from 20 headache days/mo to 15/mo	9	81% Improved
Moderate	All in the slight category and, in addition, aborting headache after its onset by voluntarily relaxing, and some reduction of drug use	9	
Good	All in the slight and moderate categories and, in addition, detection of *preheadache* symptoms and voluntarily relaxing to avoid headache, and considerable reduction of drug use	10	
Very good	All in the slight, moderate and good categories and, in addition, almost complete elimination of drug use for headache relief except for a few brief, isolated episodes	6	
	Total	42	

*The data of the following groups of patients are not included in this table: (1) 15 migraine patients, eight with tension headache and one with cluster headache who did not participate in the project for a criterion of 150 days and (2) five patients with mixed headache (vascular and tension components), one with cluster and three with tension headache who participated for over 150 days, but represented too few cases for evaluation.

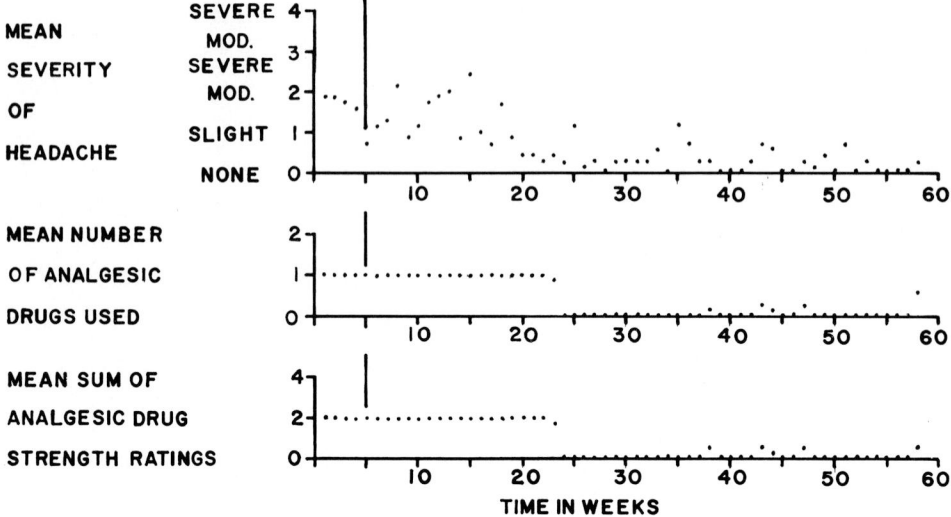

Fig. 2. Clinical progress for 1 yr of Mrs. L.O. in the reduction of severity of headache and analgesic drug use during base line, training, and follow-up.

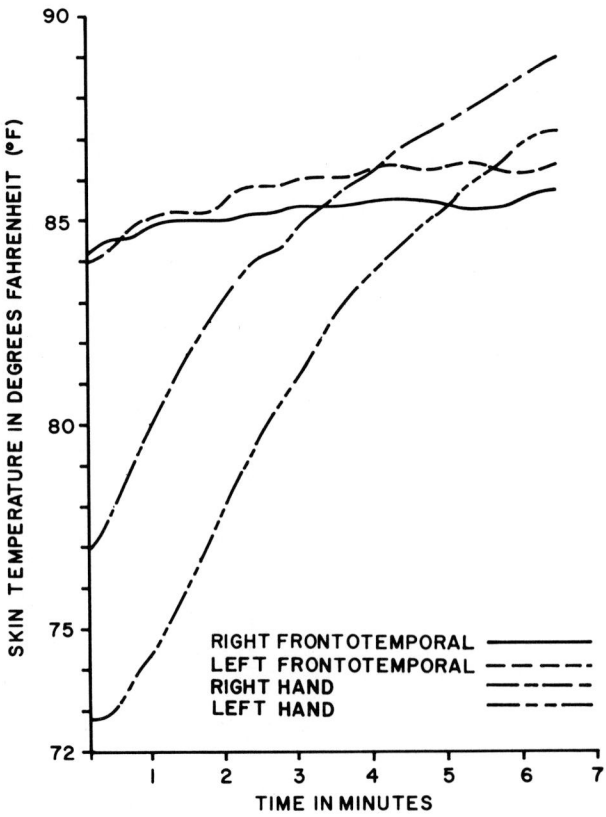

Fig. 3. Skin temperature behavior of Mrs. L.O. from four body locations over time in a practice session "without headache" during a follow-up office visit.

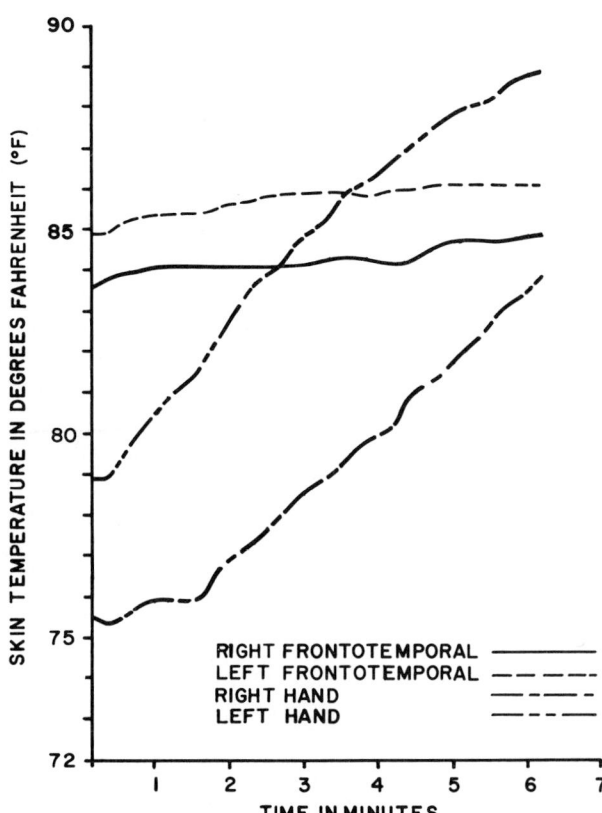

Fig. 4. Skin temperature behavior of Mrs. L.O. from four body locations over time in a practice session with right frontotemporal migraine during a follow-up office visit.

locations over time in a practice session "without headache" during a follow-up office visit. A similar record is shown in Fig. 4 of Mrs. L. O. during another follow-up session with a moderately severe frontotemporal migraine, which was partially relieved by hand-warming. Comparison of the headache and nonheadache sessions of Mrs. L. O. indicates some differences in skin temperature behavior: (1) During nonheadache, right-hand skin temperature is warmer throughout the session than left-hand skin temperature, but during headache, right-hand skin temperature is cooler through the session than left-hand skin temperature; (2) zero-time or starting right-hand skin temperature for the headache and nonheadache sessions are approximately the same, i.e., within $1\frac{1}{2}°$ F and (3) zero-time or starting left-hand skin temperature is warmer by 6° F during headache than during nonheadache. What these observations may mean in terms of vascular behavior in migraine headache is, at present, not certain; however, they will be the subject of continuing research.

DISCUSSION

The results of the initial 75 patients, some of whom were discussed in a previous paper, were reevaluated according to degree of improvement defined by behavioral criteria. It is of interest that a significant degree of improvement was seen in 81% of the 42 migraine patients who were followed for more than 150 days. Furthermore, some individuals do not seem to be helped by using hand-warming to control migraine headache. Nineteen per cent of the migraine patients received little or no reduction of headache activity and drug use in relief of headache.

Many patients who develop voluntary control of migraine headache progress through a hierarchial series of behaviors. Patients who exemplify headache control at the "good" level, for instance, demonstrate relatively consistent behaviors of detection of preheadache symptoms and voluntary relaxation to avoid migraine attacks; however, this does not exclude, at certain times, headaches that may become temporarily beyond an individual's immediate control, such as awakening from a sound sleep with a moderately severe headache.

From our clinical experience, it seems all normal individuals have the physiologic capability to produce warmth in their hands. Psychologic factors seem to be important in determining success or failure in learning to increase blood flow into hands. Persons who were comfortable with the hypothesis that thoughts and feelings have an influence over bodily processes seemed to learn much faster. Also it seems as though psychologic-mindedness is helpful in learning psychosomatic self-regulation of migraine headache. Younger persons seem to respond quicker to the training than older individuals. A possible explanation for this finding may be that a person's life values increase in rigidity with increasing age, a person may then adjust less readily to new situations. The issue of being in command of situations seems important in patients who could not give up their headache; symptom substitution was found in only one person out of approximately 150 that we have seen. Although the above psychologic factors may be important in learning hand blood flow control in management of migraine attacks, we have no systematic data to support these claims. This is an area in which we plan to do further research.

In our opinion, most of the clinical studies in headache research are carried out for too brief a period of time. In our project, we have a number of subjects who have been followed for 1–3 yr. These extensive follow-ups will help provide hypotheses concerning whether successful subjects can sustain their improvement over a long period of time and whether initially unsuccessful subjects can improve if followed long enough.

The absolute skin temperature scanner has given us flexibility by monitoring four different skin sites at a time and recording these on a paper strip. These permanent tracings are now obtained on all new patients accepted into the project, and therefore, data are available on skin temperature behavior in subjects while voluntarily relaxing.

Since many migraine patients also have tension headache at times, the work of Budzynski, Stoyva, and Adler should be cited here. They report that "in general the results seemed to indicate that chronic tension headache sufferers can be trained to voluntarily lower their striate muscle tension in the face of daily life stresses and to reduce the incidence of tension headaches."[2] In their program, tension headache patients are given a thorough medical examination to confirm the diagnosis of tension headache. Then, patients received feedback for muscle action potentials or electromyographic activity (EMG) generated in the forehead area. Patients generally received two or three 30-min feedback training sessions per week from 4–8 wk and worked at a reducing frontalis EMG to low levels. Patients were encouraged to practice relaxation training at home at least once a day. It was found that (1) both headache activity and EMG levels declined as training progressed and (2) patients reported changes in their day-to-day lives outside the laboratory such as a heightened awareness of maladaptive rising tension, an increasing ability to reduce such tension, and a decreasing tendency to overreact to stress.

Because headache poses such a difficult problem, any possible approach that can safely answer the headache problem merits study. Such an approach is the use of autogenic feedback training to increase hand blood flow for treatment of migraine and the use of frontalis EMG feedback training for tension headaches.

Biofeedback and voluntary control may have usefulness in the treatment of a a great number of psychosomatic disorders and may provide new tools to explore the mind–body interface.

The authors think that an important trend is beginning to take place in the areas of psychosomatic disorders and medicine. This is the increasing involvement of the patient in his own treatment. The traditional doctor–patient relationship is giving way slowly to a shared responsibility in which the patient is helped to become aware of his problems, both physical and emotional, and can therefore become a responsible partner in going toward psychosomatic and physical health.

In summary, (1) most migraine patients, aided by Autogenic Feedback Training, learn to voluntarily regulate their headaches; (2) patients develop psychosomatic self-regulation of migraine headache by voluntarily relaxing the sympathetic section of the autonomic nervous system in the hand, thereby increasing the blood flow to that area; (3) the degree of improvement varies across migraine patients, as some patients' improvement is better than others; (4) there seems to be a hierarchy of behaviors through which the migraine patients progress toward regulating their headaches; and (5) during training sessions in the clinic, it has been observed that significant increases occur in hand skin temperatures, while only small changes occur in frontotemporal skin temperatures.

REFERENCES

1. Brady JV: The paleocortex and behavioral motivation, in Harlow HF, Woolsey CN (eds): Biological and Biochemical Bases of Behavior. Madison, Univ of Wisconsin Pr, 1958

2. Budzynski T, Stoyva J, Adler C: Feedback-induced muscle relaxation: Application to tension headache, in Barber TX, et al (eds): Biofeedback and Self-Control. Chicago, Aldine-Atherton, 1971

3. Clark D, Hough M, Wolff HG: Experimental studies on headache observations on histamine headaches. Arch Neurol Psychiatry 140:23, 1932

4. Dukes HT, Vieth RG: Cerebral arteriography during migraine prodrome and headache. Neurology 14:636, 1964

5. Engel BT, Melmon KR: Operant conditioning of heart rate in patients with cardiac arrhythmias. Cond Reflex 8:130, 1968

6. Friedman AP, Elkind AH: Appraisal of methysergide in the treatment of vascular headaches of the migraine type. JAMA 184:125–128, 1963

7. Friedman AP: Migraine headaches. 223: 1399–1402, 1972

8. Graham JR, Wolff HG: The mechanism of the migraine headache and the action of ergotamine tartrate. Arch Neurol Psychiatry 39: 737, 1938

9. Green EE, Ferguson DW, Green AM, et al: Preliminary report on Voluntary Controls Project: Swami Rama. Research Department, The Menninger Foundation, June, 1970

10. Green EE, Green AM, Walters ED:

Voluntary control of internal states: Psychological and physiological, in Barber TX, et al (eds): Biofeedback and Self-Control. Chicago, Aldine-Atherton, 1971

11. Herburg LJ: The hypothalamus and the aetiology of migraine, in Smith R, (ed): Background to Migraine. London, Heinemann, 1967

12. Lance JW, Anthony M, Hintenberger H: The control of cranial arteries by humoral mechanism and its relation to the migraine syndrome. Headache 7:93–102, 1967

13. Miller NE: Learning of visceral and glandular responses. Science 163:434–445, 1969

14. O'Brien MD: The relationship between aura symptoms and cerebral blood flow changes in the prodrome of migraine, in Dalessio DJ, Dalsgaard-Nielsen T, Diamond S (eds): Proceedings of the International Headache Symposium, May 16–18, 1971, Elsinore, Denmark. Basle, Switzerland, Sandoz, Ltd, 1971

15. Ostfield AM: Migraine headache, its physiology and biochemistry. JAMA 174:110–112, 1960

16. Page IH: Serotonin (5 hydroxy tryptamine). Physiol Rev 34:536–588, 1954

17. Papez JW: A proposed mechanism of emotion. Arch Neurol Psychiatry 38:725–743, 1937

18. Pearce J: Migraine: Clinical Features, Mechanisms and Management. Springfield, Ill, Thomas, 1969

19. Pickering GW, Hess W: Observations on the mechanism of headache produced by histamine. Clin Sci 51:77, 1933

20. Rao LW, Pearce J: Hypothalamic-pituitary-adrenal axis studies in migraine with special reference to insulin sensitivity. Brain 94:289–298, 1971

21. Rothlin E: Recherches experimentales sur l'ergotamine, alcaloi de specifique de l'ergot de seigle. Arch Int Pharmacodyn Ther 27:459, 1923

22. Rothlin E, Cerlitti A: Untersucmumgere uber die kreislauf wirkumg des ergotamine. Helv Physiol Pharmacol Acta 7:333, 1941

23. Sargent JD, Green EE, Walters ED: The use of autogenic feedback training in a pilot study of migraine and tension headaches. Headache 12:120–124, 1972

24. Sargent JD, Green EE, Walters ED: Preliminary report on the use of autogenic feedback training in the treatment of migraine and tension headaches. Psychosom Med 35:129–135, 1973

25. Schultz JH, Luthe W: Autogenic Therapy, vol 1. New York, Grune & Stratton, 1969

26. Schumacher GA, Wolff HG: Experimental studies of headache. Arch Neurol Psychiatry 45:199, 1941

27. Schwartz GE, Shapiro D, Trusky B: Learned control of cardiovascular integration in man through operant conditioning. Psychosom Med 33:57–62, 1971

28. Sicuteri F: Vasoneuroreactive substances and their implications in vascular pain, in Friedman AP (ed): Research and Clinical Studies of Headache. Baltimore, Williams & Wilkins, 1967

29. Weiss T, Engel BT: Operant conditioning of heart rate in patients with premature ventricular contractions. Psychosom Med 38:301–321, 1971

30. Wolff GH: Headache and Other Head Pain (ed 2). New York, Oxford Univ Pr, 1963

Chapter 6: Cardiac Arrhythmias

Introduction

INEVITABLY, this is a difficult chapter for the non-physician, or even the non-cardiologist. This is especially true of Parts II, III, and IV, which are highly technical. This material is included in spite of this, however, because of its appreciable clinical promise, and even current clinical usefulness, in the case of Part 2; and because of its admirable methodological sophistication. Despite initial appearances to the contrary, this material is not too difficult for medically trained psychiatrists, who should be able to summon back from memory enough of their understanding of cardiac function to be well rewarded by understanding the exciting pioneering work being described in these papers.

Parts 1, 2, 3, and the first section of Part 4, "Training in Heart-Rate Control," all share a common paradigm: In all, ventricular heart rate (VR) is the target response, and the aim is to teach patients with various kinds of cardiac disease and various kinds of aberrant heart rhythms to be able to alter these aberrant rhythms at will, through learning how to increase, to decrease, and to alternately increase and decrease VR. A green light, the top light shown in the picture of the feedback display system (see Fig. 1), is used as a discriminative stimulus for increased VR; i.e., when the green light is on, this signals that increases in rate will be reinforced by feedback, delivered by means of the yellow light, the middle one of the three lights. When the yellow light is on, this is a direct feedback signal to the patient that he is performing successfully at that time. In addition, cumulative feedback is provided, via a meter calibrated from 0–100; this runs "whenever the patient is performing successfully, and at the end of the time (therefore) provides the patient with a measure of the percentage of time he was successful" during the whole of a given timed trial. The red light, at the bottom of the three lights, is in a parallel way used as discriminative stimulus for decreased rate.

Thus, in Parts I, II, and III, and in the first section of Part IV, the measuring physiologic instrument used was an electrocardiogram or EKG, and the criterion response was an increase or a decrease in VR. The reinforcing stimulus was visual feedback, in the form of the yellow light being on, plus the readings on the percentage meter that indicate how successful the patient was over the whole timed trial. The green and red lights are used as discriminative stimuli, the green light to indicate that increased VR will be reinforced, and the red light to indicate that decreased VR will be reinforced.

In Part I Dr. Engel summarizes the rationale, methodology, and clinical achievements to date of using biofeedback to modify cardiac arrhythmias. In addition, in his Discussion (see page 76), he calls attention to the fact that his data leads to the conclusion that there are six factors that are necessary for successful cardiac learning. Four of these replicate the anatomy of the relevant feedback loop: functioning physical receptors "which are stimulated by the cardiac response of interest;"* intact efferent nerves, to convey the impulses to

---

*That is, for example, there must be intact sensory receptors that enable the patient to learn to sense his heart beat and/or heart rhythm.

© 1973 by Grune & Stratton, Inc.

the central nervous system (CNS); adequate motivation, to insure that the CNS processes effectively the impulses conveyed there by the afferent nerves; and intact efferent nerves, to convey "command" type impulses from the CNS to the heart. The remaining two factors relate to the functional capacity of the heart itself, and to the heart as it functions within a homeostatic system. That is, if the heart is too severely diseased and/or too electrically unstable it will not be possible for the patient to learn control of its function; and if because of disease elsewhere in the body, the body as a whole cannot tolerate more normal heart function, the body's homeostatic or natural balance-seeking forces will stand in the way of any learned normalization of heart function. In biofeedback, as in the rest of life, there are built-in physiologic limitations; even the most astute practitioners of operant conditioning and behavioral shaping have yet to succeed in teaching cats to bark or dogs to purr.*

Part 2 describes the application of Dr. Engel's basic biofeedback method (described in abbreviated form previously in the italicized paragraph of this Introduction) to the clinical treatment of eight patients suffering from frequent premature ventricular contractions, or PVC's. This arrhythmia occurs in association with sudden death, and can lead to dangerous diminutions in coronory blood flow or cerebral blood flow.† Also by serial EKG evidence this rhythm, very frequent PVC's, is known to be the precursor of the dangerous heart rhythm paroxysmal ventricular tachycardia, which in turn often develops into the highly unstable and severely disabling rhythm of ventricular flutter, which in turn frequently is superseded by the rhythm of ventricular fibrillation, an event that is uniformly fatal unless quickly reversed.

In view of this, and in view of the fact that drug treatment (with quinidine or procaine amide) is not uniformly successful, Dr. Engel's reported results in using biofeedback techniques for the treatment of frequent PVC's are therefore to be recognized as having current clinical value.

Of the eight patients, all learned some degree of heart rate control; five showed a marked decrease in PVC's in association with learning heart rate control, and four have shown persistence of low PVC frequency in follow-up study, one for as long as 21 mo. Even those without medical training will be struck by the transformation in the EKG record produced by 39 sessions of biofeedback training (see Fig. 6, page 89).

Part 3 is included for the cardiologists among us. It has important theoretical implications for the physiology of the atrioventricular node (see pages 101, 111, and 113). Basically, however, it amounts to a report on the use of Dr. Engel's basic biofeedback technique (again, see the italicized paragraph in this Introduction) in six patients with chronic atrial fibrillation stable on digitalis regimens. All six of these subjects achieved some degree of heart rate control: two could reliably slow VR, two could reliably speed it, and two could slow or speed it.

---

*For this behavioral truism I am indebted to Dr. Lynch, the author of Chapter 12 of this volume.

†It is notable, for example, that two-thirds of the patients who did *not* learn to control their PVC's in this study are now dead!

INTRODUCTION

Part 4 amounts to a case report of a single case of Wolff–Parkinson–White syndrome.

Wolff–Parkinson–White syndrome, as some readers will remember, is recurrent paroxysmal tachycardia associated with a congenital defect in AV (atrioventricular) conduction; it is thought to result from an abnormal dual pathway for the transmission of impulses from the atrium to the ventricle. In addition to the normal pathway via the AV node and bundle, an abnormal accessory pathway exists, not subject to the normal physiologic delay of the AV node. Episodes of tachycardia are thought to result when the impulse descends via the normal pathway to the ventricles and re-enters the atrium via the accessory pathway, establishing a self-perpetuating circus. Traditional treatment measures "relate entirely to the paroxysmal tachycardia, and are managed in the same way as the ordinary variety, except that quinidine is somewhat more likely to help, and digitalis less ..."[1]

The EKG characteristics of the two conduction pathways are quite distinguishable: The pattern of the accessory pathway is one marked by a very short P-R interval (0.10 sec or less) and a prolonged QRS duration. In the case reported, with the accessory Wolff–Parkinson–White conduction, the P-R interval was 0.10 sec, and the QRS duration 0.12 sec, while for the normal pathway the P-R interval was 0.18 sec, and the QRS duration 0.07 sec.

This paper is of special interest, because by biofeedback the patient learned not only to control her heart rate, (i.e., to increase it or decrease it on signal) but she also learned some control over which of the two alternate AV conduction pathways were to be used, the normal pathway, or the Wolff–Parkinson–White pathway. During periods when normal conduction was rare (< 10% of total beats), she learned to increase normal conduction tenfold, from an average of 1.8% normal beats to 18.2% normal beats, and during periods when normal conduction was moderate (10%–90% of total beats), she was able to increase normal conduction from an average of 38.1% to an average of 55.9%.

To sum up, then, it seems safe to say that Chapter 6 describes biofeedback techniques of surprising powerfulness and range, techniques capable of producing significant clinical improvement in cardiac function (as in Part 2) and also capable of providing data leading toward important theoretical advances and refinements (as in Parts 3 and 4) in our knowledge of cardiac physiology.

Lee Birk, M.D.

REFERENCE

1. Beeson PB, McDermott W (eds): Cecil-Loeb Textbook of Medicine (ed 12). Philadelphia, Saunders, 1967, p 685

---

*This was accomplished by auditory feedback, by arranging that normally conducted QRS complexes only would trigger a clicker. The patients' instructed aim was to increase the frequency of these clicking sounds.

Part I

Clinical Applications of Operant Conditioning Techniques in the Control of the Cardiac Arrhythmias

Bernard T. Engel, Ph.D.

THE PURPOSE of this article is to review the experiments that my colleagues and I have performed to evaluate the clinical application of biofeedback technology in the control of the cardiac arrhythmias. Although this report will focus on our clinical experiences, the interested reader may also want to read some of our other reports, where we have discussed control mechanisms[4] or psychosomatic aspects of our findings,[5] or where we have presented an animal model in which it is possible to study control mechanisms in greater detail.[8]

Cardiac arrhythmias are complex in that they include abnormalities in the site of impulse formation, in the spread of impulses through the conduction system, in the rate at which the heart beats or in the rhythm with which the heart beats. Furthermore, many patients will manifest more than one kind of arrhythmia, and these arrhythmias may interact or they may be independent. This degree of complexity precludes any simple classification scheme. Therefore, in the ensuing paragraphs our findings will be presented in terms of a predominant arrhythmia, rather than in any special order.

Before turning to our results, however, I would like to mention the rationale for initiating this research. By the time we began our experiments, we already had carried out three cardiac conditioning studies with normal subjects,[7,9,10] and Miller and his colleagues had shown that it was possible to operantly condition heart rate in the rat.[12] Furthermore, there was extensive literature that showed that the nervous system could play a major role in modulating the prevalence of cardiac arrhythmias,[13] and that showed that tempermental variables affected the prevalence of many arrhythmias.[14] These data indicated that the nervous system exercised a significant role in cardiac function, and that at least some aspects of this nervous control were associated with volitional behavior.

TRAINING PROCEDURES

Although there are important variations in our procedures depending upon such factors as the specific arrhythmia we are trying to bring under voluntary control, the patient's current stage of training, or his tolerance for long training sessions, there also are certain important consistencies. Figure 1 shows our laboratory as it would appear to a patient. Arrayed in front of him are a vertical

---

Reprint requests should be addressed to Dr. Bernard T. Engel, Gerontology Research Center, Baltimore City Hospitals, Baltimore, Md. 21224.

© *1973 by Grune & Stratton, Inc.*

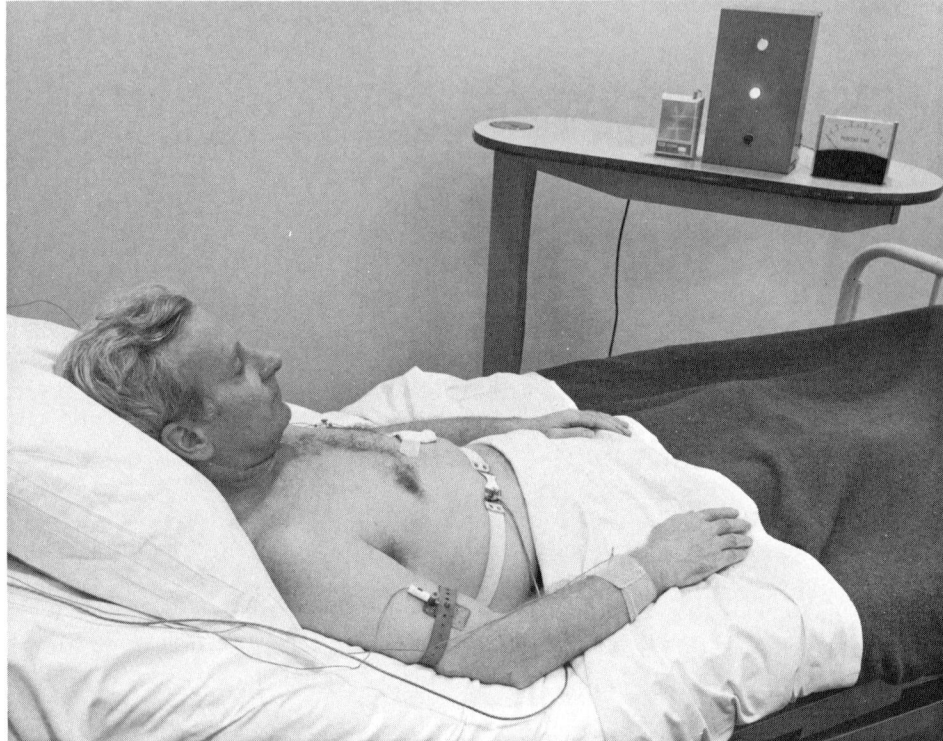

Fig. 1. A subject during a typical training session. The devices attached to the subject record his ECG and his breathing. See text for a discussion of the devices on the table.

display of three lights, a meter, and an intercom. The lights, from top to bottom, are green, yellow, and red. The green light is a cue to the patient to speed his heart, the red light is a cue to slow his heart, and the yellow light is a feedback signal to the patient that he is performing successfully. The meter is calibrated from zero to 100: it runs whenever the patient is performing correctly, and at the end of each training session it provides the patient with a measure of the percentage of time he was successful. The intercom permits the patient and the experimenter, who is in an adjacent room, to communicate.

Most patients were trained in a series of sessions, during which they were required to learn to decrease the prevalence of their arrhythmias, to increase the prevalence of their arrhythmias, to alternately decrease and increase the prevalence of their arrhythmias—e.g., to cyclically alternate every 4 min—and finally to decrease the prevalence of their arrhythmias without feedback. In addition to the training sessions in the laboratory, most patients were hospitalized and had their ECGs monitored while they were on the ward, and all patients were seen subsequent to training in the clinic or by their private physicians.

Each patient had ready access to all of his data: i.e., he could see his cardiograms or the rhythm strips taken in the laboratory or on the ward. We tried to explain the nature of his arrhythmia to each patient so he could interpret his rhythm strip. While there were considerable individual variations among patients in their desire to see the data, most patients tended to accept the feedback information and to spend relatively little time inspecting rhythm strips.

EXPERIMENTAL RESULTS

Patients With Premature Ventricular Beats (PVCs)

We have studied patients with PVCs extensively because of the association of this arrhythmia with sudden death[3,11] and because drug therapy often does not suppress these ectopic beats satisfactorily. We have reported the results of one study with a group of eight patients who had PVCs, usually in conjunction with other cardiac disease,[15] and we have reported our results with one patient who had PVCs in association with Marfan's syndrome.[6] Six of these nine patients learned to control the prevalence of their ectopic beats while in the laboratory, and five of these six patients showed evidence of being able to maintain this control outside of the laboratory. The two patients whom we have followed systematically—one for 5 yr and the other for about 1 yr—continue to show evidence of good control: Each has only rare instances of PVCs as measured by ECGs taken during clinic visits or by continuous, 10-hr tape recordings taken while the patient performed his normal daily activities.

We have discussed some of the clinical implications of our findings as well as some of the behavioral aspects of our findings elsewhere.[4-6,15] There is one observation worth repeating here, however. We carried out studies with autonomic drugs in order to enable us to identify the mechanisms mediating each patient's control of his ectopic beats. The drug studies indicated that in one patient PVC control was associated with increased vagal tone and that in another patient PVC control was associated with reduced sympathetic activity. This finding shows the flexibility of the operant conditioning technique, since it was effective in PVC control despite the diverse mechanisms by which PVCs are mediated. We believe that the reason this is so is that the operant technique requires the subject to evolve his own controls rather than having these controls imposed upon him by the therapist. It seems likely that there is a similarity between the learning of cardiac control and the learning of other motor skills. If this is so, then the importance of the patient evolving his own controls lies in the fact that once he has learned such a motor skill he can easily retain it and improve it without further formal training; and it also lies in the fact that the patient—like an athlete—develops a high degree of self-confidence in his ability to perform his skill whenever he desires to do so. The self-confidence undoubtedly also helps to maintain and strengthen the patient's motivation to maintain his skill.

Patients With Tachyarrhythmias

We have seen several patients with tachyarrhythmias including sinus tachycardia, paroxysmal atrial tachycardia, supraventricular tachycardia, and atrial fibrillation.[1,6] In all of these studies, our goal was to see if the patient could learn to control his ventricular rate, and in all cases our results were positive: All of these patients learned to control their rates.

Since the results of these studies have been published, it will not be necessary to review them here. There was one noteworthy behavioral finding, however, that was consistent among all of these patients. As each patient learned to control his rate, he showed evidence of diminished anxiety about his heart. The expression of this decline in anxiety took a number of forms; however, two kinds of comments tended to predominate. Several of the patients said that they "knew" that they could control their hearts, and as a result the tachycardia seemed to them to be less threatening; some patients said they had a renewed sense of mastery over themselves, and they said that they did not feel as dependent upon their physicians as they once did. These expressions of attitude are quite revealing, since they indicate the degree of concern with which these patients view their arrhythmias, and since they suggest that such patients will be highly motivated to learn cardiac control, and that once they receive evidence that such learning is possible, they also will be highly motivated to practice the skills that they have learned.*

Patients With Conduction Defects

We have seen three patients with third-degree block and one patient with type A, Wolff–Parkinson–White syndrome (WPW).[2] The patients with third-degree block were studied to determine whether learned rate control is possible in a functionally isolated ventricle. The results were negative: Patients with complete heart block cannot voluntarily increase their ventricular rates. Interestingly, however, one patient was able to generate PVCs, which suggests that it may be possible to bring ventricular functions other than rate under voluntary control.

The patient with WPW was trained to control her ventricular rate and also was trained to control her patterns of intracardiac conduction. The patient learned to increase and decrease her heart rate reliably, and she learned to increase and decrease the prevalence of normally conducted beats and abnormally conducted beats reliably. She also was able to control her cardiac conduction patterns away from the laboratory and after a hiatus of 10 wk.

DISCUSSION

Our clinical studies have dealt with the questions of whether patients can learn to control their cardiac arrhythmias, and whether such learning may be therapeutic. The answer to the first question is yes, and the answer to the second question also seems to be yes. However, there are a number of important issues that must be resolved before such a conclusion can be drawn. We have discussed these issues as well as possible applications to other kinds of cardiovascular disease at some length already.[6] Therefore, I will devote the remainder of this article to a consideration of some of the patient-related factors that seem to us to be important determinants of learning.

One factor that is probably necessary if learning is to occur is that the pa-

---

*Our studies tell us nothing about why these patients learn. Furthermore, there are no studies of which I am aware that deal with the question of why most medical patients are so strongly motivated to get better. It is my belief that we will never understand the nature of psychosomatic illnesses until we understand the mechanisms of actions of motivation. It is my hope that those among us who argue so strongly for the importance of motivation in behavior will begin to *do* the experiments that will show us how it works.

tient have a set of peripheral receptors that are stimulated by the cardiac response of interest. In the initial stage of training, our feedback lights permit the visual system to subserve this function, however, the clinical efficacy of our procedures ultimately depends upon the fact that the subject will be able to utilize internal receptors that do not require any gadgetry. Our experience indicates that most patients are able to appreciate their heart beats or heart rhythms. The subjective reports suggest that some patients can sense their hearts directly while other patients report that they refer their cardiac changes to other sensations—e.g., diaphoresis.

A second factor mediating learning is the presence of afferent nerves, which transmit information from the peripheral receptors to the central nervous system (CNS). In our study with the patient with WPW, we trained her to control her ventricular rate using visual feedback, and we trained her to control her cardiac conduction using auditory feedback. Ultimately, she reported that she was able to sense her heart beat directly, and that she was able to recognize the presence of a tachyarrhythmia and the presence of aberrantly conducted beats. Although we did not test her impressions systematically, our informal observations suggested that her reports were true, and that she could recognize the differences between a normal sinus rhythm and an arrhythmia.

The third factor that we believe to be an important determinant of learning is a set of CNS properties, which enables the patient to recognize the information transmitted about his heart, and which provides the patient with behavioral characteristics—e.g., motivation*—necessary to mediate learning and to maintain performance. Obviously, this is a very complex factor that subsumes much of psychology. Nevertheless, from our point of view, the CNS comprises only one factor in the feedback loop.

The fourth factor that is important in learning to control cardiac function is the presence of efferent nerves to the heart, which are capable of producing the desired changes in cardiac function. The results from the study with patients with third-degree block document the importance of this factor. The extrinsic autonomic nerves to the ventricles do not mediate chronotropic function, and these patients were unable to modify their ventricular rates voluntarily.

The fifth factor that we believe to be important in learning is the functional capacity of the heart itself. Among the three patients with PVCs who failed to learn to control their heart rhythms, two had hearts that were probably too diseased to permit normal function: One patient had severe cardiomegaly, and the other patient had an extremely, electrically unstable heart that produced multi-focal PVCs of at least four different electrical configurations.

---

*Based upon conversations I have had with a number of psychiatrists—especially those psychiatrists who are psychodynamically oriented—it is my impression that their understanding of the distinction between learning and motivation is confused. Learning is the process whereby new information or new relationships among known events or things are acquired. Motivation is a set of internal phenomena that initiates, maintains, or directs behavior. Obviously, motives can be learned, and learning is highly unlikely in the absence of motivation. However, learning and motivation are conceptually independent phenomena and the distinction between them should be clear: Learning deals with the *how* and *what* of behavior, and motivation deals with the *why* of behavior.

The sixth factor that seems to be important in learning is the homeostatic systems, which include the heart. If these systems will not tolerate a more normal cardiac function, then it will be impossible for the patients to maintain such a response. In the case of the cardiac arrhythmias, this should not be a significant limitation; however, in other diseases this factor may become very important. For example, it may not be possible for patients with essential hypertension to maintain normal blood pressures because hypertrophic changes in their arterioles may have raised their total peripheral resistance to the point where some organs cannot be perfused adequately under normotensive conditions.

ACKNOWLEDGMENT

I wish to express my appreciation to Dr. George W. Ainslie, Jr., for his helpful comments on an early draft of this manuscript.

REFERENCES

1. Bleecker ER, Engel BT: Learned control of ventricular rate in patients with atrial fibrillation. Psychosom Med 35:161-175, 1973
2. Bleecker ER, Engel BT: Learned control of cardiac rate and cardiac conduction in a patient with Wolff-Parkinson-White syndrome. N Engl J Med 288:560-562, 1973
3. Chiang BN, Perlman LV, Ostander LD, Jr, et al: Relationship of premature systoles to coronary heart disease and sudden death in the Tecumseh epidemiologic study. Ann Intern Med 70:1159-1166, 1969
4. Engel BT: Operant conditioning of cardiac function: A status report. Psychophysiology 9:161-177, 1972
5. Engel BT: Operant conditioning of cardiac function: Some implications for psychosomatic medicine. Behav Ther (in press)
6. Engel BT, Bleecker ER: Application of operant conditioning techniques to the control of the cardiac arrhythmias, in Obrist PA, et al (eds): Contemporary Trends in Cardiovascular Psychophysiology. Chicago, Aldine-Atherton, (in press)
7. Engel BT, Chism RA: Operant conditioning of heart rate speeding. Psychophysiology 3:418-426, 1967
8. Engel BT, Gottlieb SH: Differential operant conditioning of heart rate in the restrained monkey. J Comp Physiol Psychol. 73:217-225, 1970
9. Engel BT, Hansen SP: Operant conditioning of heart rate slowing. Psychophysiology 3:176-187, 1966
10. Levene HT, Engel BT, Pearson JA: Differential operant conditioning of heart rate. Psychosom Med 30:837-845, 1968
11. Lown B, Wolf M: Approaches to sudden death. Circulation 46:130-142, 1971
12. Miller NE: Learning of visceral and glandular responses. Science 163:434-445, 1969
13. Scherf D, Schott A: Extrasystoles and allied arrhythmias. New York, Grune & Stratton, 1953
14. Stevenson IP, Duncan CH, Wolf S, et al: Life situations, emotions, and extrasystoles. Psychosom Med 11:257-272, 1949
15. Weiss T, Engel BT: Operant conditioning of heart rate in patients with premature ventricular contractions. Psychosom Med 33:301-321, 1971

Part II

Operant Conditioning of Heart Rate in Patients With Premature Ventricular Contractions

Theodore Weiss, M.D.* and Bernard T. Engel, Ph.D.

Operant conditioning of heart rate (HR) was carried out in 8 patients with premature ventricular contractions (PVCs). All of the patients showed some degree of HR control. Five of these patients showed a decrease in PVCs in association with the learning of HR control. Four patients have shown persistence of a low PVC frequency after study, the longest followup being 21 months. Pharmacologic studies suggested that decreased PVC frequency was mediated by diminished sympathetic tone in 1 patient and increased vagal tone in another. These findings suggest that some aspects of cardiac ventricular function can be brought under voluntary control. Once such control has been acquired, it can mediate clinically significant changes in cardiac function.

FOR MANY YEARS, and in a multiplicity of experimental situations, the technics of operant conditioning have been employed to modify and control somatic behavior—ie, actions involving the use of skeletal muscle.[1] In the last decade, a large volume of additional research has accumulated, indicating that visceral and other involuntary responses also are amenable to operant control.[2,3] Response systems studied have included heart rate,[4-7] blood pressure,[8,9] rate of urine formation,[10] regional blood flow,[11] vasoconstriction,[12] and galvanic skin potential.[13-15]

In addition to reports of operant conditioning of visceral responses in normal man and in animals, there are three studies in which patients with pathologic visceral responses showed improvement after operant training. Engel and Melmon[16] conditioned more regular cardiac rhythms in patients with several kinds of cardiac arrhythmias, and White and Taylor[17] and Lang[18] each conditioned patients to stop or decrease ruminative vomiting.

Several studies have shown the effects of neural impulses on premature ventricular contractions (PVCs).[19] Hypothalamic lesions and stimulation,[20-22] afferent vagal stimulation,[20,23] efferent cardiac sympathetic nerve impulses,[20,24] and cardiac sympathectomy[25] all have been shown to produce dramatic changes

---

*Dr. Weiss is now at the Department of Psychiatry, University of Pennsylvania.

Republished by permission of Psychosomatic Medicine (Vol. 3, No. 4, July–August 1971).

From the Section of Physiological Psychology, Laboratory of Behavioral Sciences, Gerontology Research Center, National Institute of Child Health and Human Development and Baltimore City Hospitals.

The authors would like to thank Drs. Gustav C. Voigt and Kenneth M. Lewis for permitting them to draw patients from the Clinic, and for regular consultation on the patients; Drs. Lewis A. Kolodny and Jay J. Platt for referring Patients 6 and 7, respectively; Mr. Reginald E. Quilter for assisting in the development and maintenance of various instruments used in this study; and Mr. Richard H. Mathias for assisting in the analysis of the ward telemetry data.

Received for publication Aug 6, 1970; revision received Nov 23, 1970.

Address for reprint requests: Bernard T. Engel, PhD, Baltimore City Hospitals, Baltimore, Md. 21224.

in PVC frequency. Also, both increases and decreases in PVC frequency have been reported using classic conditioning technics.[26,27]

Because of these considerations, we undertook a study of patients with PVCs to see if operant conditioning could produce clinically significant control of this arrhythmia.

MATERIALS AND METHODS

Patients

Selection. Eight patients with PVCs were obtained from Baltimore City Hospitals, and from referrals by private physicians.

Hospitalization procedure. Patients were hospitalized for the duration of the study and given passes each weekend. After admission, they were given a complete physical examination and a standard battery of laboratory tests including a 12 lead EKG and PA and lateral chest X-rays.

Experimental Design

Laboratory. All formal cardiac training took place in the laboratory although each patient was encouraged to practice his technics outside the laboratory as well.

While in the laboratory, the patient lay in a hospital bed in a sound-deadened room. At the foot of the bed was a vertical display of three differently colored light bulbs, an intercom and a meter.

The three lights provided the patient with feedback information about his cardiac function. The top light (green) and the bottom light (red) were cue lights. The middle light (yellow) was the reinforcer; it was on when the patient was producing the correct heart rate (HR) response. Our system enabled us to feed back this information to the patient on a beat-to-beat basis.

When the fast (green) cue light was on, a relative increase in HR would turn on the reinforcer light. When the slow (red) cue light was on, a relative decrease in HR would turn on the reinforcer light.

The meter accumulated time. Whenever the patient was performing correctly, the meter arm moved, and when he performed incorrectly, it stopped.

One to three 80-minute conditioning sessions were carried out daily. A typical session began with about 10 minutes for the attaching of EKG leads, and of a strain gauge around the lower chest to monitor breathing. Then, the patient lay quietly for 20 minutes more. During the last 10 minutes of this period, a baseline HR was obtained. The feedback lights were off throughout the baseline period. Two to three minutes were allowed for setting the trigger level for heart rate (HR) conditioning. The trigger level was the HR (eg, in a speeding session) at or above which the reinforcer light would go on. Then the patient had either one 34-minute period during which the feedback lights were on, or two such periods of 17 minutes each, separated by a 10-minute rest period.

Because this was primarily a clinical study, the patient's responses at any stage of the study always dictated the procedure. In general, however, we followed a standard sequence for conditioning. During the initial or control session, the patient simply lay in bed in the laboratory for the prescribed time period. The feedback lights were never turned on. Next, HR speeding was taught for about 10 sessions, followed by HR slowing for about 10 sessions. For about 10 further sessions, a differential contingency was taught, in which the patient alternately had to increase and decrease his HR during periods of 1–4 minutes throughout the session. During these sessions, the green and red cue lights would come on alternately so that the patient would know whether to speed or to slow.

The last training contingency usually was a range situation in which the patient had to maintain his HR between preset upper and lower limits. Only the yellow light would be on when the HR was within this range. When the rate was too fast, the yellow light would go off and the red light would go on, cueing the patient to slow down. When the rate was too slow, the green light would come on, cueing the patient to speed up. Because a premature beat caused the HR to go above range, and the compensatory pause caused the HR to go below range, this contingency also gave the patient prompt feedback every time he had a PVC.

In the range contingency, feedback was phased out gradually. Initially, the feedback was available for 1 minute and unavailable for the next. In later sessions, it was available for 1 minute and unavailable for 3; in the final sessions, it was on for 1 minute and off for 7. By this procedure, the patient was weaned from the light feedback and made to become aware of his PVCs through his own sensations.

Each patient was told in detail about the nature of the experiment, and he was allowed to inspect all his data throughout the study.

Ward. The patient's EKG was monitored three nights per week for 10 minutes out of every hour, using a telemetry apparatus.

Pharmacologic studies. In 3 patients, studies were carried out with the use of some or all of the following autonomically active drugs—isoproterenol, propranolol, atropine, edrophonium, phenylephrine and phentolamine—administered intravenously. This was done in the laboratory after conditioning had been completed in order to elucidate the mechanism underlying HR and rhythm changes.

Followup. Clinical follow-up was done in the Baltimore City Hospitals Cardiac Clinic by Dr. Weiss, and by the referring physicians. The visits usually included an EKG with a 1–2 minute rhythm strip.

Apparatus

Laboratory. Variations in interbeat interval were detected by a Beckman-Offner cardiotachometer and converted into electrical signals whose magnitudes were proportional to HR. The cardiotachometer output was also fed into a BRS Electronics Schmitt trigger, which was used to control the patient's feedback. The input to the Schmitt trigger was regulated by a zero suppression circuit on the amplifier to permit adjustment of the trigger point. In order to reduce the hysteresis in the Schmitt triggers, we grounded the emitters. an EKG from a precordial lead was recorded on a Beckman-Offner dynograph, and on magnetic tape using an Ampex SP 300 tape recorder.

Ward. The EKG signal from two chest electrodes was transmitted to a Parks model 220-1 converter and a telemetry receiver in an adjacent room, where the EKG was recorded on a tape recorder for subsequent analysis.

Analytic Procedures

Laboratory. All heart beats were counted automatically, and mean HRs were calculated from these data. PVCs were counted manually, all being counted when they were less frequent (under 10/min); and two to four 1-minute samples per 10 minutes being counted when they were more frequent.

Ward. Mean HR was determined by counting five to six 10-beat samples or five 30-second samples distributed across each 10-minute epoch. All PVCs were counted.

Pharmacologic studies. Heart rate was counted either automatically or manually from a continuous EKG record. All PVCs were counted manually from the same record.

Clinical history and followup. Heart rate and PVC frequency generally were determined from EKGs. Some data were derived from physical examinations.

RESULTS

The results will be presented on a patient-by-patient basis. However, since the findings do suggest some general principles, these will be presented as well. Each of the tables summarizes some of the major findings for each patient; however, specific references to these data will be made in the individual patient presentations.

Patient 1

LR, a 52-year-old Caucasian female, had a history of five myocardial infarctions (MI) in the 13 years prior to study. In association with the last two, 8 months and 5 months prior to study, she had PVCs. Maintenance quinidine therapy was required to suppress them after the last MI. She had been on digoxin for 1 year. Because of persistent diarrhea, the quinidine was discontinued 2 weeks prior to study, and PVCs increased in frequency from about one to two per minute to ten per minute.

Laboratory. Table 1 reports the proportion of sessions during which this patient performed successfully as measured by changes in heart rate or (during

Table 1. Ratios of Sessions During Which Each Patient Performed Successfully To Total Number of Sessions for Each Contingency

Patient	Speed	Slow	Differential	CRF	Range					
					1:1		1:3		1:7	
					On	Off	On	Off	On	Off
1 (Study 1)	4/9	4/6	7/9	5/6	—	—	—	—	—	—
1 (Study 2)	—	—	—	8/10	3/5	4/5	2/4	3/4	2/4	2/4
2	11/14	5/7	9/9	10/10	2/2	2/2	2/2	2/2	3/3	3/3
3	5/11	9/10	8/10	2/3*	4/4*	4/4*	3/4*	3/4*	5/5*	5/5*
4	6/10	5/10	10/10	5/5	11/11	11/11	7/7	7/7	—	—
5	1/10	9/9	12/14	15/15	—	—	—	—	—	—
6	1/6	5/11	—	13/16	—	—	—	—	—	—
7	2/8	7/10	—	2/4	—	—	—	—	—	—
8	—	16/18	—	15/15	—	—	—	—	—	—

During the range sessions, successful performance was defined as maintenance of HR within the correct range for more than 50% of the time.
*Slow.

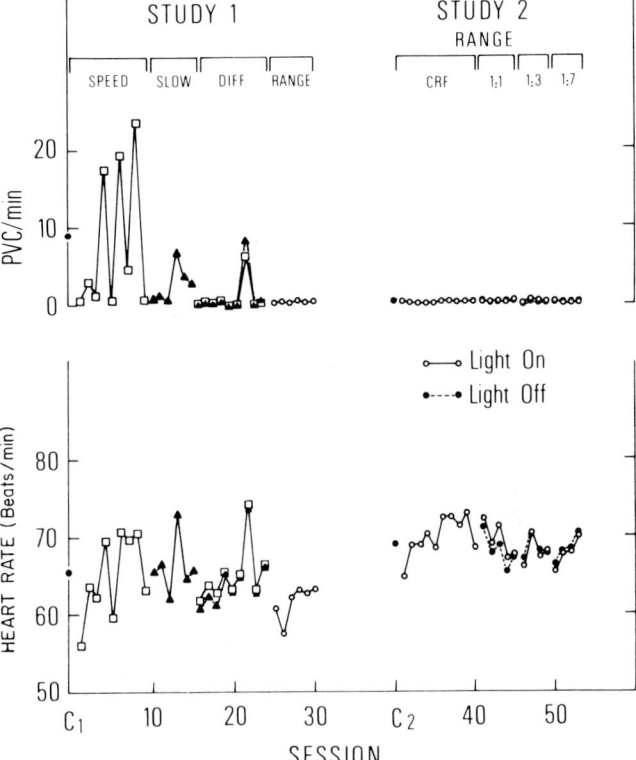

Fig. 1. Patient 1. PVC and HR levels during training; C1 and C2 are initial sessions during Studies 1 and 2, respectively, when no feedback was provided. Diff, differential conditioning; CRF, continuous feedback; 1:1 feedback on 1 minute, off 1 minute; 1:3 feedback on 1 minute, off 3 minutes, etc; boxes, speeding; triangles, slowing; circles, range.

the range sessions) by percentage of time heart rate was within the correct range. Figure 1 shows the absolute heart rates and the frequencies of occurrence of PVCs during the training periods of each session.

During speeding training, the patient was able consistently to increase her HR from baseline in the afternoons but not in the mornings (when she also had few PVCs). In association with these successful performances, her PVCs increased to over 23/min (Fig. 2). The patient said that she thought about relaxing to speed her heart. During the slowing sessions, the patient was able consistently to decrease her HR from baseline, and PVCs were consistently less frequent—1-4/min (Fig. 2). She said that she concentrated on breathing maneuvers.

The patient differentiated consistently although she did not increase her HR with respect to her baseline rate during the speeding phases of the sessions. PVC incidence was quite low, under 1/min. At this time, the patient reported that her heart was functioning in a dysrhythmic fashion, when actually it was beating quite regularly. Her cardiograms were shown to her, and the differences between her rhythm strips during the speeding sessions and the present sessions were explained to her in detail. After her misconceptions had been clarified, she subsequently learned to recognize correctly the presence of PVCs.

During the range sessions, the patient consistently maintained her HR within the predetermined, 10-beat range (usually 60-70 beats/min) and PVCs were very infrequent, generally about 0.2/min.

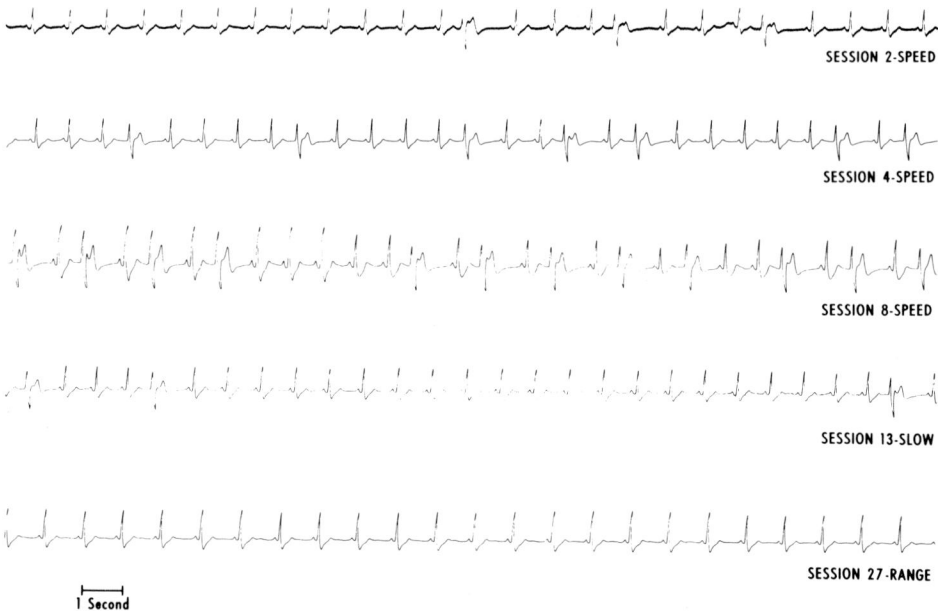

Fig. 2. Patient 1. EKG rhythm strips during conditioning. These tracings show increase in PVCs during speeding conditioning, and decrease in PVCs during slowing and range conditioning.

After a 3-week recess, the patient's digoxin was stopped. The only discernible effect was an increase in baseline HR of about 5 beats/min to about 68. Twenty-three further range sessions were carried out. Gradually, the patient's feedback was decreased until it was present only 1 minute out of 8 by the last four sessions. PVCs remained very rare, about 0.1/min. She was discharged off all medications.

Ward. Cardiac activity on the ward (Tables 2 and 3) paralleled events in the laboratory—ie, her PVC incidence was highest during the period when she was speeding, and lower during the period when she was slowing.

Pharmacologic studies. After the study, we tested the patient with pharmacologic agents. Atropine (1.0 mg) speeded her HR to 98 but did not produce

Table 2. Premature Ventricular Contraction Frequencies (PVCs/min) on Ward During Different Phases of Study

Patient	Speeding	Slowing	Differential	Range or PVC Avoidance
1	10.7	7.6	2.0	0.8
2	1.4	2.3	1.1	0.5
3	34.4	30.0	12.4	—
4	6.6	5.7	5.0	2.1
5	10.2	6.6	4.9	3.8
6	3.1	7.1	—	6.5
7	16.6	4.7	—	9.4
8	—	15.2	—	10.2

Table 3. Heart Rates (beats/min) on Ward During Different Phases of Study

Patient	Speed	Slow	Differential	Range or PVC Avoidance
1	66.9	67.5	66.8	67.0
2	51.7	50.9	50.7	50.4
3	82.9	83.4	69.7	—
4	61.0	57.1	56.0	53.2
5	77.3	75.0	71.5	74.0
6	62.5	79.2	—	66.8
7	74.4	76.1	—	72.7
8	—	83.4	—	88.7

PVCs. Isoproterenol (0.5–1.5 μg/min) speeded her heart rate and produced PVCs when the HR was above 90. The PVC configuration was the same as those she had spontaneously and during conditioning to speed her heart rate. This suggests that decreased sympathetic tone accounts for her diminished PVC incidence.

Followup. Twenty-one months of follow-up data have been obtained. PVCs remained quite low for 4 months, none being seen on five EKGs. Subsequently, they became more variable—commonly about 1/min, but as high as 6/min. The patient continues to be able accurately to identify PVCs. She says she rarely has significant numbers of them at home. When she does, she sits down and rests, and they stop within 20 minutes and do not return.

Patient 2

IW was a 62-year-old Caucasian male with a history of one MI 7 years prior to study. Thereafter, he had intermittent angina on exertion. PVCs were noted first in 1965; they were present on four of six EKGs taken thereafter, at times in a bigeminal rhythm. The average frequency was 14/min on EKG, and 3–5/min clinically. Two months prior to study, his angina worsened. An exercise tolerance test, performed to clarify the relationship between his angina and his PVCs produced bigeminy and multifocal PVCs in association with a heart rate of 95–100 beats/min. Modest exercise, raising HR from the usual level of about 55–80 beats/min, was associated with a temporary cessation of PVCs. When the HR slowed below 60, the PVCs returned. A subsequent therapeutic trial on diphenylhydantoin produced no significant change in the PVC frequency or in the patient's angina.

Laboratory. The patient performed successfully in all phases of the study as measured by changes in heart rate (Table 1). Figure 3 reports his absolute heart rates and PVC incidences during each training session.

In order to speed his heart, the patient said that he thought about "pushing or forcing" his heart to the left, and about its beating rapidly. In several of the speeding sessions, he had long periods of bigeminal rhythm, the PVCs having two configurations. One configuration was like that of the patient's usual PVCs, with the major vector in the same direction as that of the regular QRS. It will be referred to as the *usual type PVC*. The other configuration was seen in the laboratory only in association with HR speeding. Its major vector was in the opposite direction from that of the normal QRS. It will be referred to as the *speeding type PVC*. Apart from the bigeminy, the patient's PVCs were infrequent during speeding, usually less than 1/min. The patient also had several prolonged episodes of bigeminy on the ward recordings of the night after speeding session 11, and on the following night. Both times, these occurred during waking hours when he said he would practice HR control. Many of the bigeminal PVCs on telemetry were of the speeding type. This type of PVC had not been seen on telemetry prior to then.

PVCs were more frequent during slowing, usually 1.5–5/min. They were of the usual type. No bigeminy was seen. He said that he concentrated on the "heart slowing down and stopping."

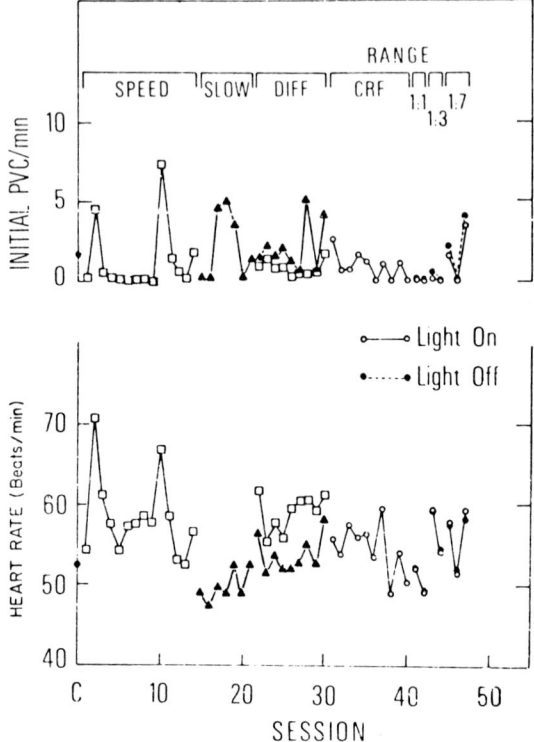

Fig. 3. Patient 2. PVC and HR levels during training.

During the differentiation sessions, PVCs occurred more and more frequently in the slowing periods and less frequently in the speeding periods (Fig 4). The PVCs were of the usual type. The patient said that he used the same technics for HR speeding and slowing described above. At comparable heart rates, PVCs were most frequent during HR slowing, least frequent during HR speeding and of intermediate frequency during the baseline periods. These findings suggest that the active processes involved in slowing and speeding the heart were more important in modulating PVC frequency than was the heart rate per se.

During range conditioning sessions, PVCs generally were infrequent, usually less than 1/min.

Ward. Telemetry data showed little variation in HR (Table 3). Apart from periods of bigeminy during the waking hours, PVCs were infrequent (Table 2). As in the laboratory, they were most frequent during the slowing contingency.

Pharmacologic studies. Studies with autonomically active drugs were done in this patient. Isoproterenol (0.5–1.0 µg/min) led to a HR increase from the resting level of 52 beats/min to 93 beats/min, and to bigeminy and ventricular tachycardia. The PVCs were of the speeding type. The ventricular tachycardia stopped after the isoproterenol infusion was stopped. No antiarrhythmic agents were required. Atropine (1.0 mg) also speeded the HR to 86 beats/min and increased PVC frequency from zero to 8/min. These PVCs were of the usual type. Both edrophonium (1–10 mg) and propranolol (0.5 mg every 3 minutes for six times) separately slowed the heart to about 48 beats/min, but neither

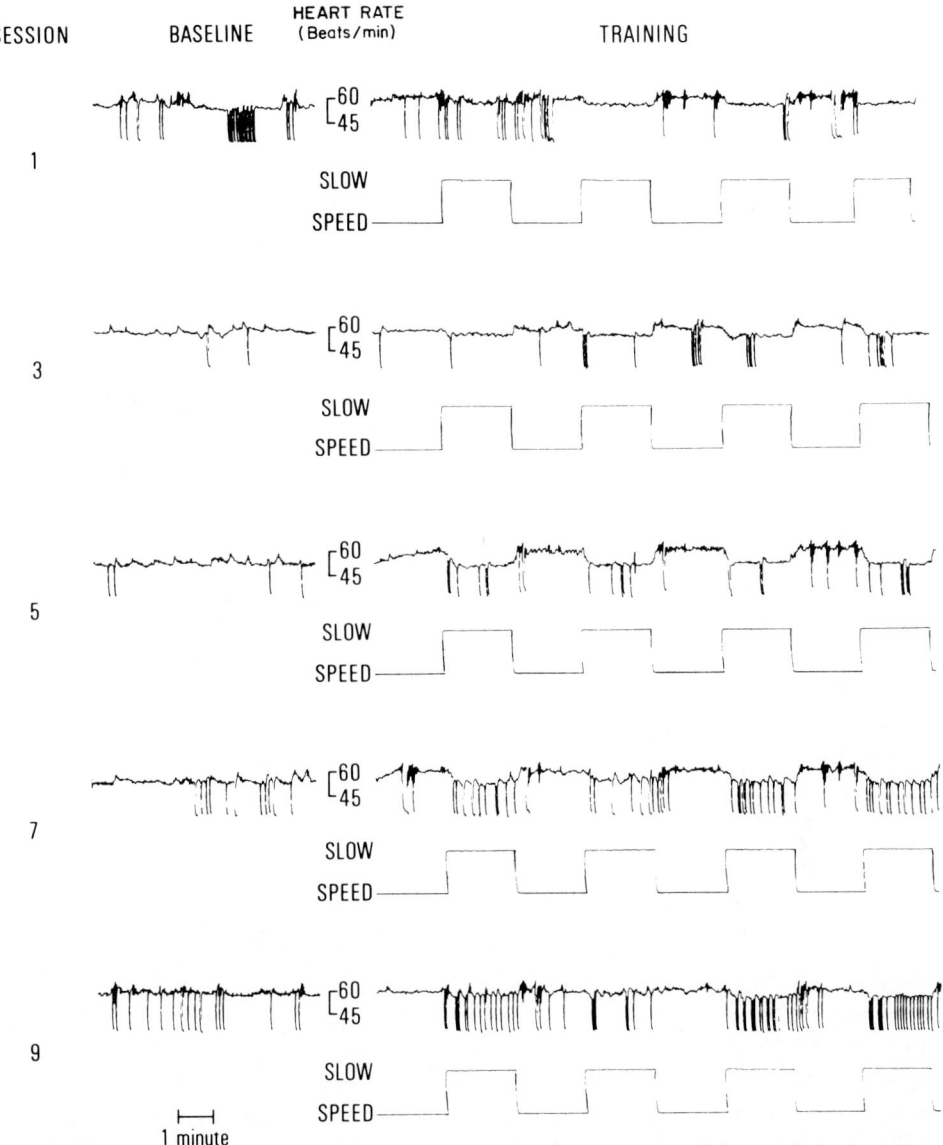

Fig. 4. Patient 2. Differential HR conditioning. Tracings are cardiotachometer records. PVCs are shown by long vertical lines. As differentiation proceeds, patient speeds and slows appropriately, and PVCs are progressively more concentrated in slowing periods.

affected the frequency of PVCs. They generally remained below the baseline frequency of 2.5/min. When isoproterenol was readministered (same dosages) after propranolol administration, PVCs increased in frequency to about 10/min although HR did not increase. Their configuration was of the usual type. These results suggest that PVCs of the speeding type were related to increased sympathetic tone. They do not clarify the mechanism underlying the usual type of PVCs.

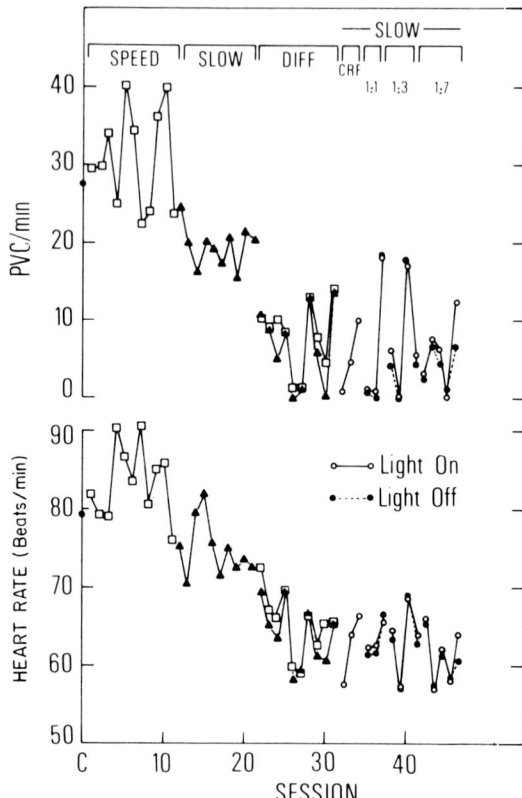

Fig. 5. Patient 3. PVC and HR levels during training. Slow₁ refers to first block of slowing sessions; Slow₂ to second block.

Followup. The patient has been followed for 10 months since the study. Initially, he continued to have very rare PVCs, averaging 0.4/min on three EKGs. When they were more frequent at home, he said he could decrease them by concentrating on a steady heart beat. His angina continued to worsen, and 4 months after discharge, he had another MI. After recovery from this, the patient's PVCs were somewhat more frequent, averaging 2.2/min in the clinic and, according to him, more at home. He said that it took 15–20 minutes to stop them with HR speeding at home. We therefore readmitted him 9 months after the first study. At that time, PVCs were rare, less than 1/min in the laboratory and on the ward. Because they originated consistently from two foci, quinidine was added to the patient's regimen. This reduced them even further, to one every 4–5 minutes.

Patient 3

MK was an obese 36-year-old Caucasian female with an 8-year history of documented PVCs. They were present on four of six EKGs taken during the 8 years prior to study. The average frequency was 12.8/min. During the last several months before the study, she had had three to four syncopal episodes. An EKG taken by her private physician shortly after one of these revealed unifocal PVCs at a frequency of 21/min. The syncopal episodes had occurred

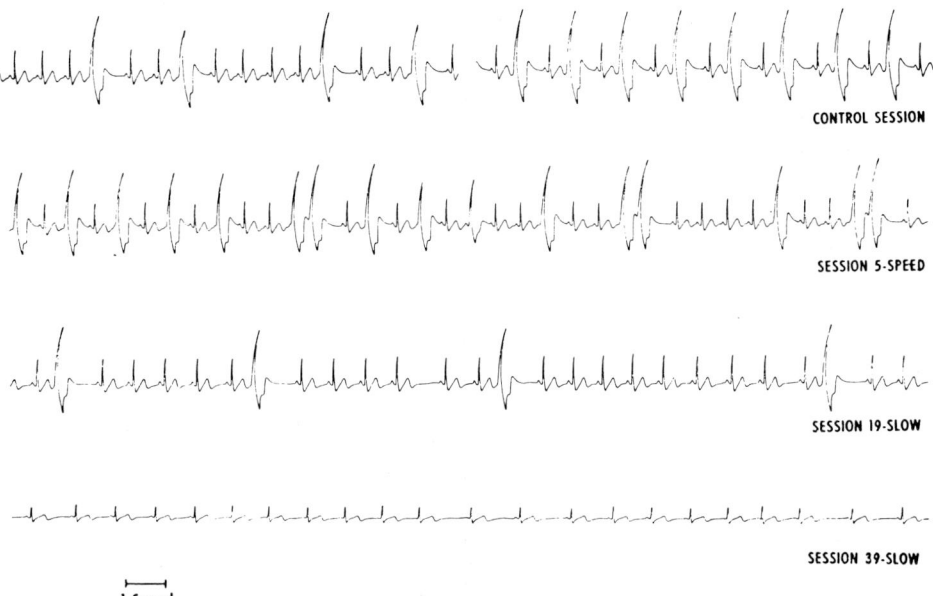

Fig. 6. Patient 3. EKG rhythm strips during conditioning.

when she was angry or excited. She also reported "a big thumping feeling" in her chest in association with strong emotions and moderate physical exertion such as walking half a mile. To stop this, she said that she sat down and relaxed for half an hour or more.

Laboratory. The patient did not speed consistently from baseline (Table 1); however, she did perform successfully in all other phases of the study. During the speeding sessions, PVC frequency was high—up to 40/min (Fig 5)—and at times, coupling of PVCs occurred (Fig 6). The patient said that she thought about arguments with her children and about running through a dark street during the speeding sessions.

During the slowing sessions, PVC frequency fell to about 20/min (Fig 5). The patient said she thought about swinging back and forth in a swing during these sessions.

The patient differentiated well although she speeded from baseline during the speeding blocks in only one session. She slowed during the slowing blocks in all ten sessions. PVCs became much less frequent, usually under 10/min, and at times there were none for periods ranging up to 8 minutes. She said that she concentrated on the same things described above during the conditioning periods.

Because PVC's were least frequent at the lower HRs, slowing of the HR under 65 beats/min rather than range control was taught next. The patient's HR was under 65 beats/min during twelve of the sixteen sessions. She said that she thought about swinging on a see-saw and about relaxing during these sessions. PVC frequency was usually under 10/min; it was at zero for periods as long as 17 minutes (Fig 6).

The patient frequently decreased her PVCs when the training portion of the

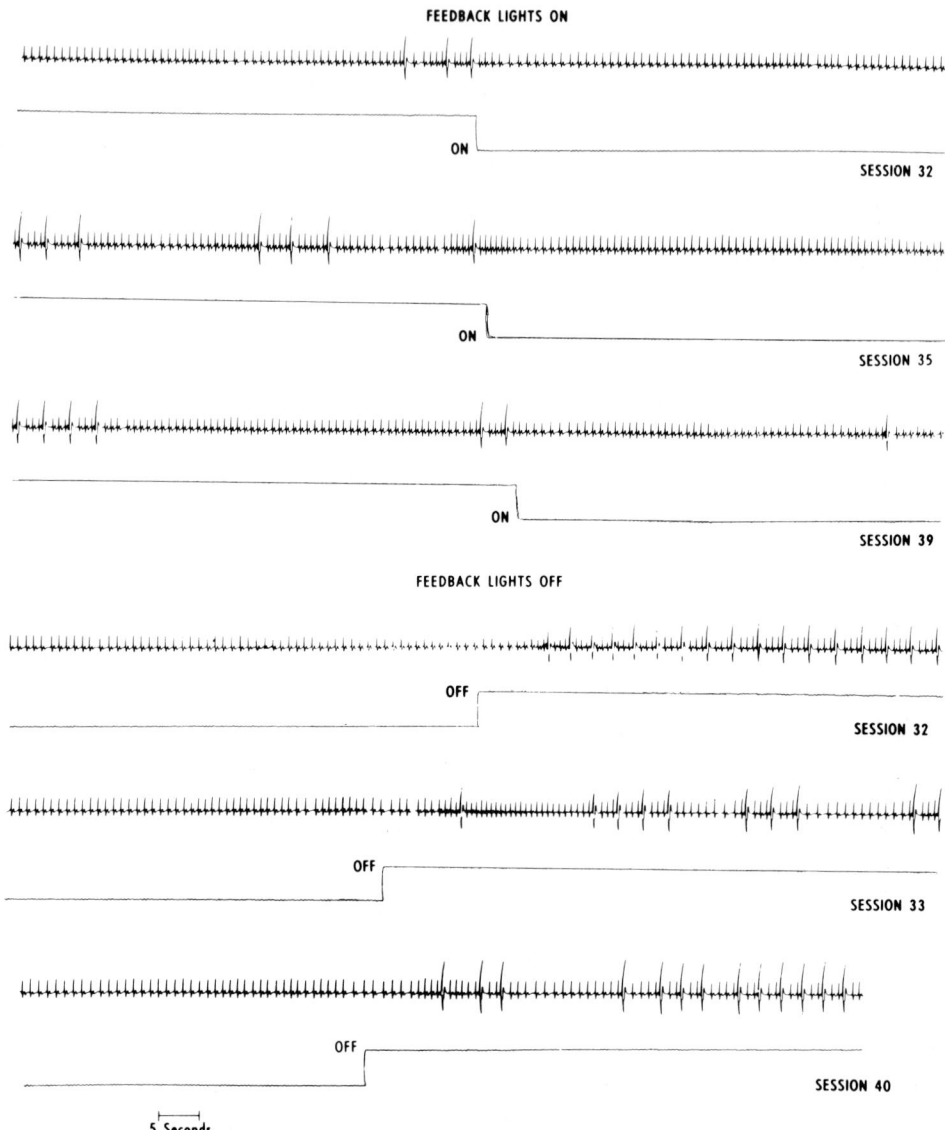

Fig. 7. Patient 3. EKG rhythm strips at onset and offset of feedback during HR slowing. These tracings show that patient was able to stop having PVCs when feedback began, and PVCs returned at end of sessions.

session began and the feedback lights were turned on (Fig 7). Also, the PVCs often returned promptly when the training portion of the session ended and the lights were turned off (Fig 7). During the training sessions in which the light was off part of the time, PVC frequency was as low or lower when the light was off as when it was on (Fig 5).

Ward. Cardiac activity on the ward generally paralleled events in the laboratory. Heart rate (Table 3) was highest during speeding and slowing, intermediate during the second slowing block (not shown in Tables 2 or 3), and lowest during the differential conditioning sessions. The PVC pattern was the same as that for HR (Table 2). Their lowest average frequency was about 12/min during the differential contingency. At the end of the study, they averaged about 19/min.

Pharmacologic studies. Both edrophonium (1–10 mg) and propranolol (0.5 mg every 3 minutes for eight times) separately slowed the heart from about 80 to about 73 beats/min. Neither had any effect on PVC frequency which remained at about 20/min. When administered together (edrophonium, 10 mg at the end of the above administration of propranolol), they slowed the heart from 75 to 60 beats/min and abolished PVCs from a prior level of 20/min. Phenylephrine (7–28 µg/min) increased the blood pressure from 104/70 to 138/76, slowed the HR from 77 to 54 beats/min, and abolished PVCs from a prior level of 12/min. Isoproterenol (0.5–1.0 µg/min) speeded the HR from 78 to 95 beats/min and stopped PVCs, the prior level being 25/min. Atropine (1.5 mg) speeded the HR from 75 to 97 beats/min and PVCs increased from 19/min to a bigeminal rhythm with 48/min. Phentolamine (5 mg), given at a time when PVC frequency was low (1/min), had no obvious effect on PVCs. It decreased the blood pressure from 108/68 to 90/62, and increased the HR from 75 to 82 beats/min.

These findings suggest that in this patient strong vagal tone inhibits PVCs, regardless of sympathetic input. Weaker vagal tone associated with β-sympathetic inhibition also inhibits PVCs. Vagal blockade leads to frequent PVCs.

Followup. The patient has been followed for 3 months since the study. PVCs have continued to be frequent on EKG during clinic visits, averaging 17.1/min on three EKGs. However, the patient says that she is able to stop them at home using the HR slowing technic learned in the laboratory. She has not been able to do so in the clinic. She has had no dizziness or syncope since the study.

Patient 4

RL was a 68-year-old Caucasian male with a history of an MI 4 months prior to study. Three months prior to study and after discharge from the hospital, the patient began to have PVCs. These were typically bigeminal or trigeminal, with a frequency of over 20/min, and were unifocal. The PVC occurred well after the preceding T wave, and after exercise, it occurred even later. Also, the PVCs did not increase with exercise; and the patient was unaware of their occurrence. For these reasons, no medications were given to control them.

Laboratory. The patient did not perform reliably during the slowing and speeding training sessions (Fig 8 and Table 1), and his PVC frequency was highly variable throughout these sessions. He did differentiate consistently, however. Furthermore, he speeded from baseline during the speeding blocks in six of the sessions, and slowed from baseline in seven of them. He said that he moved his shoulders to increase his HR, and lay still and stared at the light to slow his HR. PVC frequency was variable, but was under 10/min in seven of the ten sessions. The PVCs were more frequent in the speeding blocks in seven of the ten sessions.

During the range sessions, the patient said that he generally just watched the

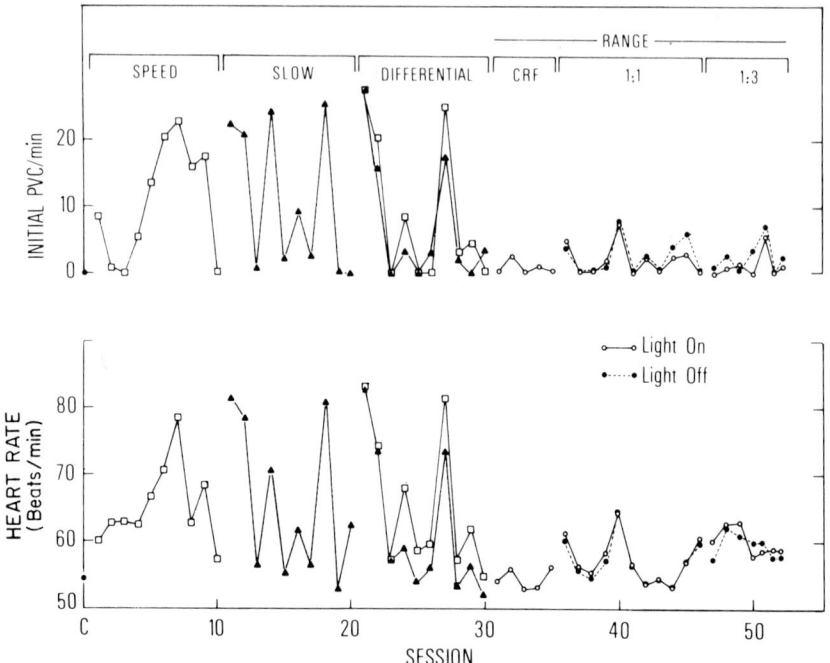

Fig. 8. Patient 4. PVC and HR levels during training.

light to keep PVCs infrequent. He said that sometimes he also moved his shoulders. PVC frequency was low, under 8/min throughout. During the first five sessions of the range contingency, when the feedback was on during the entire training period, the patient had 2.1 PVCs/min or less (Fig 8). As the feedback was phased out, PVCs became somewhat more frequent. It is of note that the patient could not tell when he was having PVCs except when the feedback lights were on or when he took his pulse.

Ward. Ward data paralleled the laboratory data. Heart rates (Table 3) were highest during speeding and slowing and lowest during the range training. Similarly, PVCs (Table 2) were most frequent during speeding and slowing and least frequent during the range contingency.

Pharmacologic studies. No drug studies were performed on this patient.

Followup. Because PVCs were noted to come from two foci (Fig 9), the patient was started on quinidine at the time of discharge. PVC frequency has been low on followup visits, averaging 3.2/min on 5 EKGs. Because the patient was unable to detect PVCs except by taking his pulse, he was given twenty-four further training sessions to learn PVC detection. This was done 1 month after the first study. Whereas the patient initially was unable to detect any of his PVCs except by taking his pulse, by the end of the second study, he was able to detect them accurately 35–40% of the time without the light feedback. He said that he felt a sensation of warmth across the precordium when PVCs were occurring. When PVCs were frequent—eg, 15/min—he also noted diaphoresis.

In one additional followup visit after the second study, there were no PVCs on EKG. During the clinic visit, the patient was able to sense that he was

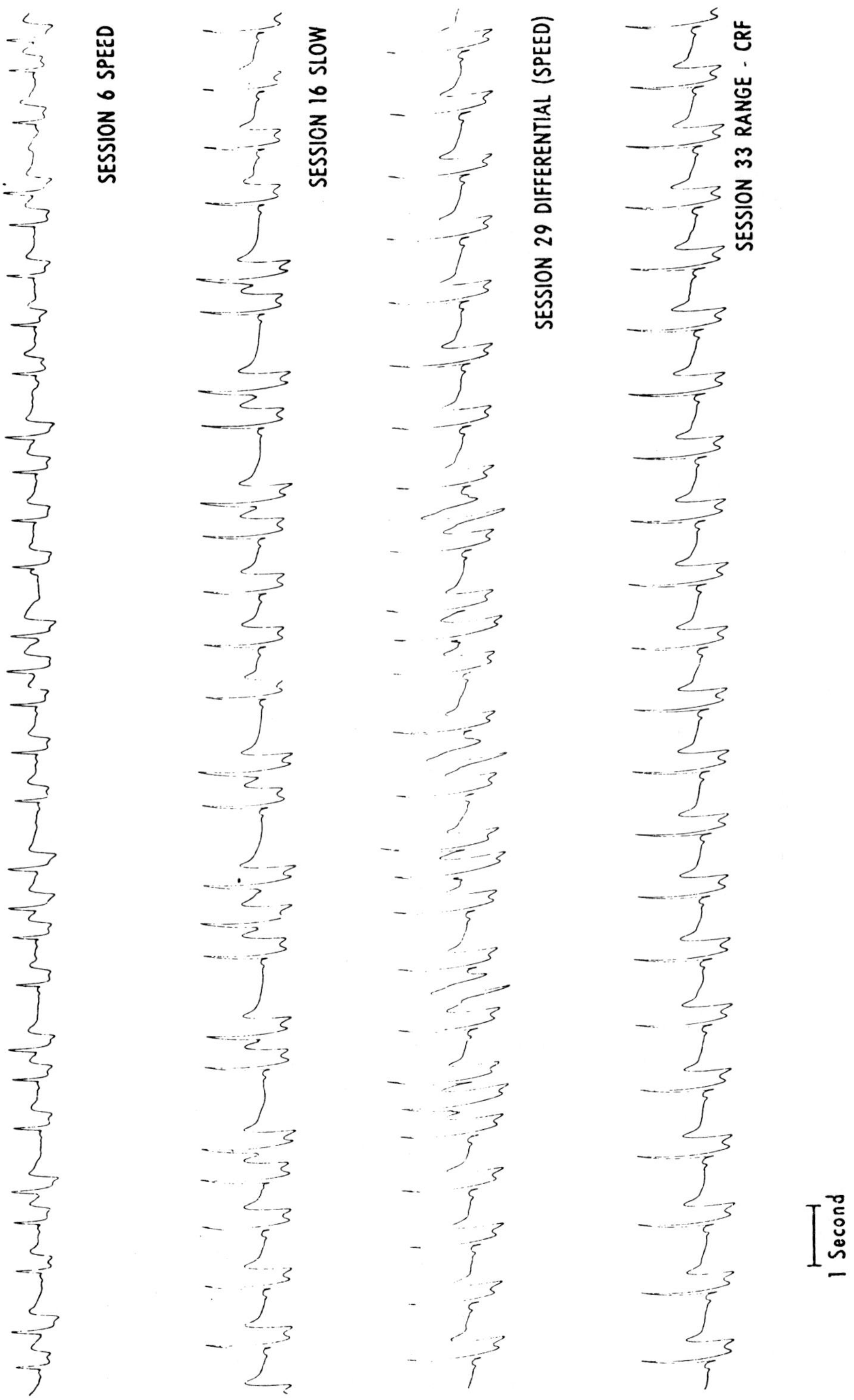

CARDIAC ARRHYTHMIAS

SESSION 6 SPEED

SESSION 16 SLOW

SESSION 29 DIFFERENTIAL (SPEED)

SESSION 33 RANGE - CRF

1 Second

Fig. 9. Patient 4. EKG rhythm strips during conditioning.

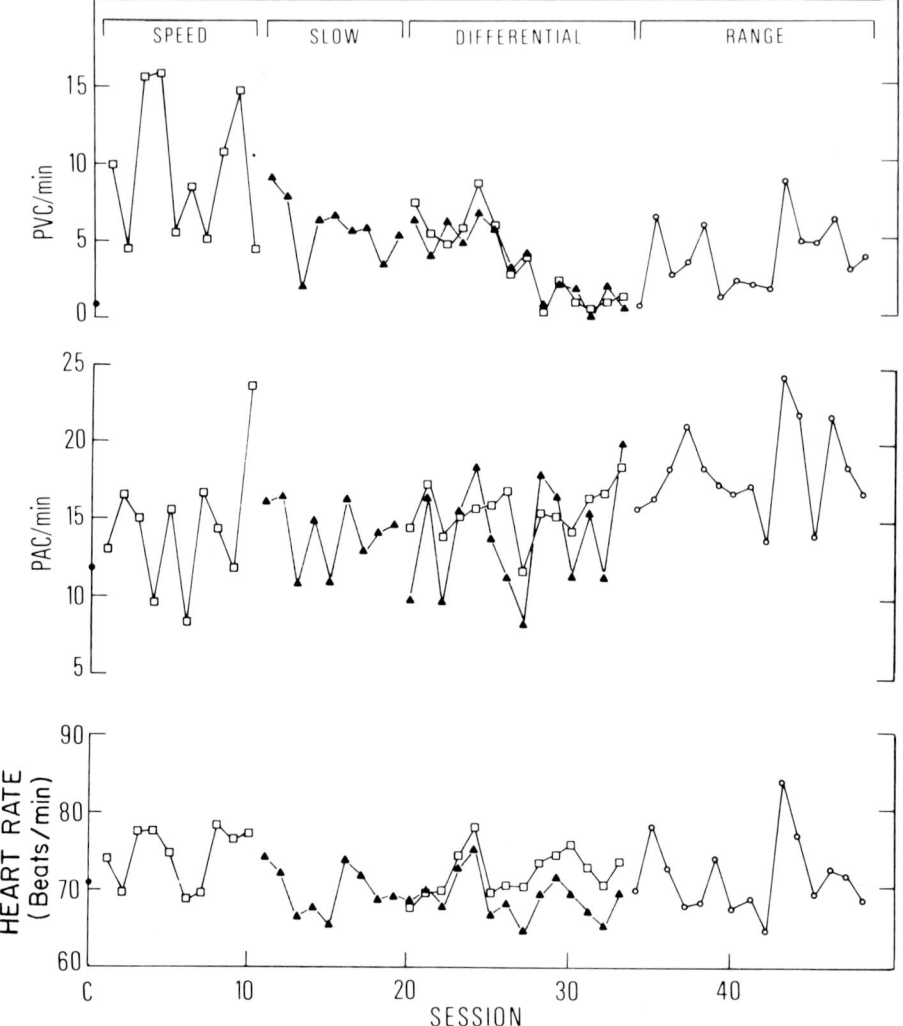

Fig. 10. Patient 5. PVC and HR levels during training.

having infrequent PVCs (6/min). He reported that at home he also could sense his PVCs by the precordial warmth—verified by taking his pulse—and by sitting quietly, he could abolish them in half an hour. They stayed away for variable periods of time thereafter, usually for about an hour.

Patient 5

CA was a 73-year-old Caucasian male with a 19-month history of documented PVCs.

On thirteen visits to his private physician during the 19 months prior to our study, the patient was described as having no ectopic beats on five occasions, few to moderate ectopic beats ("few," "occasional," "slight irregularity of pulse," "irregularity of heart rate") on six occasions, and many ectopic beats on two occasions. The patient said that he could not sense the PVCs.

Laboratory. The patient was unable to speed his heart during the speeding sessions; however, he was consistently successful at slowing his heart (Table 1). The patient differentiated well (Fig 10). He slowed from baseline during all sessions, and he speeded from baseline in five of the sessions, including four of the last seven. In order to speed his heart, the patient said that he thought about bouncing a rubber ball. To slow his heart, the patient said that he counted the amount of time the reinforcement light was on.

PVC frequency was highly variable during the speeding sessions (Fig 10). During slowing, PVC frequency declined to about 5/min, and during the differentiation sessions, they fell still further so that there were fewer than three PVCs/min during the last six of these sessions. During the range sessions, PVC frequency remained low, averaging 4/min.

PACs increased slightly during the study, from about 14/min during speeding to about 18/min during the range condition (Fig 10). The patient said that he still could not tell when the PVCs occurred.

Ward. There was little fluctuation in HR on the ward (Table 3). As in the laboratory, PVCs (Table 2) were most frequent during speeding and were fewest during the later range and differential contingencies. PACs on telemetry also paralleled their behavior in the laboratory, being least frequent early (9.5/min during speeding) and more frequent later (17.1/min during the range contingency).

Pharmacologic studies. Drug studies were not done on this patient.

Followup. During 5 months of followup, the patient has been seen three times by his private physician. He was described as having no ectopic beats on two occasions, few to moderate ectopic beats on one occasion, and many ectopic beats on no occasions. An EKG taken 5 months after the study revealed 0.3 PVC/min and 22 PACs/min.

Patients 6, 7 and 8 all failed to learn to control their PVCs. Brief summaries of their cases are included in this report because they highlight important aspects about the limitations of operant training in the control of PVCs.

Patient 6

LS was a 60-year-old Negro male with a 5-year history of cardiac disease, including five hospitalizations for congestive heart failure.

His activities were severely limited by exertional dyspnea and palpitations, and less frequently by angina. He has paroxysmal nocturnal dyspnea about two nights per week. Chest X-ray revealed massive cardiomegaly, with a cardiac/thoracic ratio of 20/27.5. For almost 4 years prior to study, he had had premature atrial and ventricular contractions. Either or both of these were present on eight of nine EKGs during the 4 years prior to study. PVCs averaged 3.7/min and PAC, 1.6/min.

Laboratory. This patient was unable consistently to slow or speed his heart rate; however, he was quite successful at maintaining his rate within a ten-beat range (Table 1). His absolute heart rate declined from about 90 beats/min in the early sessions to about 65 beats/min by the end of speeding (slow training was given first in his case). The most likely explanations for this decline in HR are that during his period of hospitalization, he took his medications more regularly, and he reduced his alcohol consumption substantially.

During all training conditions, the frequency of his premature beats was highly variable, ranging from 1/min to 15/min. EKG tracings in the laboratory and on the ward were such that PVCs could not be differentiated from PACs; thus, all are listed together as premature beats.

It should also be noted that the patient drank heavily while on weekend passes so that he was too inebriated to return on Sunday evening as requested, and had to be fetched the next morning.

Followup. In 4 months of clinic followup, the patient continued to have many premature beats. On two EKGs, PVCs averaged 5.9/min and PACs, 9.7/min. His clinical status was unchanged. Thereafter, he was lost to followup. It was learned later that he died at home 10 months after the study.

Patient 7

EC was a 48-year-old Negro male with a history of hypertension for 27 years and cardiomegaly for 5 years, with hospitalization for congestive heart failure 4 years prior to study. After discharge from the hospital, the patient returned to work (manual labor) but he was so limited by dyspnea on exertion, that he was forced to quit. He proved to be little motivated to take a less strenuous job, and despite several professional attempts at rehabilitation, he has not worked since. At the time of study, he was functional Class II-B. The patient had had PVCs for 18 months prior to study, these being consistently present on physical examinations and on EKGs during that time. Their average frequency on three EKGs during that period was 9.0/min. The patient was an active Baptist, attending services twice a week.

Laboratory. The patient did not consistently speed his heart from baseline (Table 1); however, he did raise his absolute heart rate throughout the speeding sessions from 61 beats/min at the beginning to 78 beats/min by the end. He said he prayed to speed his heart. Although the patient did consistently slow his heart from baseline during the slowing sessions, his absolute heart rate did not change, remaining at 75 beats/min throughout these sessions. He said he tried to manipulate his breathing, and he prayed to slow his heart.

During the speeding sessions, PVC frequency increased from 6/min to 24/min. During the slowing sessions, PVC frequency was variable, ranging from 10/min to 20/min.

In an effort to enable this patient to gain control over his PVCs, he was given four sessions of training in the range contingency, and nine sessions of training in a PVC avoidance contingency in which a soft tone sounded whenever he had a PVC; his task was to silence the tone. However, PVCs persisted generally between 7 and 20/min, with an average of 12.4/min. HR averaged 76.2. The patient said that he tried mild exercise in bed, as well as praying and changing his breathing to decrease his PVCs.

Ward. Telemetry data (Tables 2 and 3) indicated that HR did not change throughout the study. However, the incidence of PVCs decreased during the slowing conditioning and then returned to prestudy levels during the range and PVC avoidance training.

Pharmacologic studies. No drug studies were done on this patient.

Followup. During 17 months of follow-up, he has continued consistently to have PVCs, averaging 6.1/min. His clinical status is unchanged. The patient subsequently revealed that he was afraid that if his PVCs improved, he might lose his disability benefits and have to return to work. It is possible that this concern affected his performance during the study.

Patient 8

JF was a 77-year-old Caucasian male with a history of two probable MIs, the second one being 3 years prior to admission. He was not hospitalized on either occasion, and subsequent EKGs did not reveal definite evidence of an old MI. He also had had diabetes mellitus for 7 years. Shortly after the second probable MI, the patient developed CHF, and was hospitalized. PVCs were noted then for the first time. They did not respond to amelioration of the CHF (digoxin, chlorothiasize and potassium chloride), procaine amide, dilantin, or discontinuing digoxin for several months. They were consistently present thereafter, being seen on all of the nine EKGs taken from that time until the study. They were multifocal in origin, and their average frequency was 12.4/min. The patient said that he could not tell when they occurred.

Laboratory. Although there was evidence of heart rate control (Table 1) and a fall in absolute HR from an initial 90 beats/min to 76/min during slowing training, PVC frequency did not decrease. It should be noted that this patient had PVCs of at least four different configurations. Sometimes certain ones were more frequent; sometimes others were. This posed severe difficulties for our HR and PVC detection system. It also made it quite difficult to provide accurate feedback to the patient.

Ward. Telemetry data paralleled events in the laboratory in that HR was lower during the slowing periods (Table 3), and PVCs remained frequent (Table 2).

Pharmacologic studies. No drug studies were performed on this patient.

Followup. Followup for 8 months revealed no significant changes in the patient's cardiovascular status. PVCs were present on all of four EKGs taken during these visits, with an average frequency of 10.0/min. The patient died suddenly at home 2 weeks after his last clinic visit.

DISCUSSION

This study shows that patients can be taught to control the prevalence of their PVCs. Patients 1–4 showed clear evidence of PVC control in the laboratory, and evidence of transfer of the learned effect to the ward. Patient 1 has sustained her low PVC rate for 21 months, and each of these other 3 patients who have been followed for shorter periods of time reports that he is able to detect and modify his PVCs while at home. Also, Patient 5 has maintained a low PVC frequency for 5 months after the study.

The presence of PVCs is associated with an increased probability of sudden death.[28] Corday et al have demonstrated experimentally that PVCs can diminish coronary artery blood flow[29] and cerebral blood flow.[30] The fact that Patient 1 has had no further myocardial infarctions in the 21 months of followup, as contrasted with three in the 11 months preceding the study, may be related to her decreased PVC frequency.

In the patients in this study, at least two different mechanisms of PVC control appear to have been involved. The drug studies in Patient 1 suggested that reduced sympathetic tone to the heart was responsible for the decreased incidence of PVCs. As the cardiac sympathetic nerves are known to influence the ventricle strongly,[31,32] this effect probably occurred directly at the ventricular level. In Patient 3, the drug studies suggested that increased vagal tone decreased her PVC frequency. This may have represented a direct vagal effect on the ventricle, as there is anatomic evidence for vagal innervation of the ventricle in mammals,[33,34] and physiologic evidence for vagal effects on the mammalian ventricle.[35,36]

The flexibility of operant conditioning is demonstrated by the fact that PVCs were reduced whether they were mediated primarily by the sympathetic or by the parasympathetic nervous system. This underscores the fact that operant conditioning can be used to alter pathologic conditions mediated by different mechanisms.

Heart rate per se does not determine the presence or absence of PVCs. Similar HRs in Patient 2 were associated with different PVC frequencies depending on the experimental contingency under which they occurred. Also, in Patient 1, HRs between 90 and 100 beats/min induced by isoproterenol were associated with PVCs, whereas similar HRs induced by atropine were not. In Patient 3, the opposite occurred. Atropine-induced HRs above 90 beats/min were associated with PVCs, while similar HRs induced by isoproterenol were not. This also suggests that extensive, short-term, experimental drug studies—of the type carried out in Patient 3—might be useful in clarifying the mechanisms of PVCs in different patients.

The imagery which patients reported while controlling their heart rates has been presented. However, the reports are highly idiosyncratic, and no consistent pattern is apparent.

There seem to be six elements that are important for successful learning of PVC control. These are: (a) peripheral receptors which are stimulated by the PVC; (b) afferents which carry the information to the CNS; (c) CNS processing to enable to the patient to recognize the PVC and to provide the motivation and flexibility necessary to enable learning to occur; (d) efferents to an effector organ which can bring about the desired change in the pathologically functioning heart; (e) a heart which is not too diseased to beat more regularly; (f) a homeostatic system in the patient which will tolerate the more normal functioning of the heart.

Patient 4 illustrates the role of the afferent system. He did well at controlling his PVCs when he had continuous feedback in the range portion of Study 1, but did more poorly as the feedback was phased out. After Study 2, he was able to detect his PVCs, and then to reduce their frequency.

Patient 1 illustrates the importance of CNS processing. She had to learn to be comfortable with infrequent PVCs, whereas early in the study, she had been interpreting frequent PVCs as comfortable. This underscores the fact that physicians cannot always rely on the naive patient's interpretation of his physiologic state. The concern which Patient 7 expressed regarding his disability benefits suggests that motivation is also an important, CNS-mediated factor.

The grossly enlarged heart of Patient 6 and the electrically very unstable one of Patient 8 illustrate the importance of the heart itself. These hearts may have been too diseased to beat regularly for prolonged periods of time.

Early intervention may facilitate the learning of PVC control—eg, during convalescence from an infarction as in Patient 4. (The severity of the arrhythmias which the patients were able to generate in the course of conditioning was striking. Therefore, it would seem advisable not to attempt to condition patients during the acute, postinfarction period.)

This study was not concerned with optimization of technics. It should be possible to accomplish comparable results in much shorter periods of time, as more nearly optimal conditioning technics are employed. For example, studies should be feasible on an outpatient basis; and pretesting with autonomically active drugs such as those used in this study should suggest whether the patient will benefit more from being taught to slow or to speed.

REFERENCES

1. Skinner BF: The Behavior of Organisms. New York, Appleton-Century-Crofts, 1938
2. Kimmel HD: Instrumental conditioning of autonomically mediated behavior. Psychol Bull 67:337–345, 1967
3. Miller NE: Learning of visceral and glandular responses. Science 163:434–445, 1969
4. Shearn DW: Operant conditioning of heart rate. Science 137:530–531, 1962
5. Hnatiow M, Lang PJ: Learned stabilization of heart rate. Psychophysiol 1:330–336, 1965
6. Engel BT, Hansen SP: Operant conditioning of heart rate slowing. Psychophysiol 3:176–187, 1966
7. Levene HI, Engel BT, Pearson JA: Differential operant conditioning of heart rate. Psychosom Med 30:837–845, 1968
8. DiCara LV, Miller NE: Instrumental learning of systolic blood pressure responses by curarized rats: dissociation of cardiac and vascular changes. Psychosom Med 30:489–494, 1968
9. Shapiro D, Turksy B, Gershon E, et al: Effects of feedback and reinforcement on the control of human systolic blood pressure. Science 163:588–590, 1969
10. Miller NE, DiCara LV: Instrumental learning of urine formation by rats: Changes in renal blood flow. Amer J Physiol 215:677–683, 1968
11. DiCara LV, Miller NE: Instrumental learning of vasomotor responses by rats: learning to respond differentially in the two ears. Science 159:1485–1486, 1968
12. Snyder C, Noble M: Operant conditioning of vasoconstriction. J Exp Psychol 77:263–268, 1968
13. Fowler RL, Kimmel HD: Operant conditioning of the GSR. Psychol Rep 7:555–562, 1960
14. Kimmel HD, Baxter R: Avoidance conditioning of the GSR. J Exp Psychol 65:212–213, 1964
15. Shapiro D, Crider A: Operant electrodermal conditioning under multiple schedules of reinforcement. Psychophysiol 4:168–175, 1967
16. Engel BT, Melmon KL: Operant conditioning of heart rate in patients with cardiac arrhythmias. Conditional Reflex 3:130, 1968
17. White JD, Taylor D: Noxious conditioning as a treatment for rumination. Ment Retard 5:30–33, 1967
18. Lang PJ, Melamed BG: Case report: avoidance conditioning therapy of an infant with chronic ruminative vomiting. J Abn Psychol 74:1–8, 1969
19. Scherf D, Schott A: Extrasystoles and allied arrhythmias. New York, Grune and Stratton, Inc, 1953, pp 253–274
20. Korth C: The production of extrasystoles by means of the central nervous system. Ann Intern Med 11:492–498, 1937
21. Weinberg SJ, Fuster JM: Electrocardiographic changes produced by localized hypothalamic stimulations. Ann Intern Med 53:332–341, 1960
22. Attar HJ, Gutierrex MT, Bellet S, et al: Effect of stimulation of hypothalamus and reticular activating system on production of cardiac arrhythmia. Circ Res 12:14–21. 1963
23. Scherf D, Blumenfeld S, Yildiz M: Experimental study on ventricular extrasystoles provoked by vagal stimulation. Amer Heart J 62:670–675, 1961
24. Gillis RA: Cardiac sympathetic nerve activity: changes induced by ouabain and propranolol. Science 166:508–510, 1969
25. Estes EH Jr, Izlar HL Jr: Recurrent ventricular tachycardia: a case successfully treated by bilateral sympathectomy. Amer J Med 31:493–497, 1961

26. Peimer IA: Conditioned reflex extrasystole in man. Fiziol Zh SSSR Sechenov 39:286-292, 1953

27. Perez-Cruet J: Conditioning of extrasystoles in humans with respiratory maneuvers as unconditional stimulus. Science 137:1060-1061, 1962

28. Chiang BN, Perlman LV, Ostander LD Jr, et al: Relationship of premature systoles to coronary heart disease and sudden death in the Tecumseh epidemiologic study. Ann Intern Med 70:1159-1166, 1969

29. Corday E, Gold H. DeVera LB, et al: Effect of the cardiac arrhythmias on the coronary circulation. Ann Intern Med 50:535-553, 1959

30. Corday E, Irving DW: Effect of cardiac arrhythmias on the cerebral circulation. Amer J Cardiol 6:803-807, 1960

31. Rushmer RF: Autonomic balance in cardiac control. Amer J Physiol 192:631-634, 1958

32. Sarnoff SJ, Brockman SK, Gilmore JP, et al: Regulation of ventricular contraction: influence of cardiac sympathetic and vagal nerve stimulation on atrial and ventricular dynamics. Circ Res 8:1108-1122, 1960

33. Mitchell GAG: Cardiovascular Innervation. Edinburgh and London, Livingstone, Ltd, 1956

34. Hirsch EF, Kaiser GC, Cooper T: Experimental heart block in the dog. III. Distribution of the vagus and sympathetic nerves in the septum. Arch Path 79:441-451, 1965

35. Wildenthal K, Mierzwiak DS, Wyatt HL, et al: Influence of efferent vagal stimulation on left ventricular function in dogs. Amer J Physiol 215:577-581, 1969

36. Daggett WM, Nugent GC, Carr PW, et al: Influence of vagal stimulation on ventricular contractibility, O_2 consumption and coronary flow. Amer J Physiol 212:8-18, 1967

Part III

Learned Control of Ventricular Rate in Patients With Atrial Fibrillation

Eugene R. Bleecker, M.D., and Bernard T. Engel, Ph.D.

Six patients with chronic atrial fibrillation (AF) and rheumatic heart disease on stable digitalis regimens were trained to slow and to speed ventricular rate (VR). Two subjects were more consistent in their ability to slow VR; two subjects were more consistent in their ability to speed VR; and the remaining two subjects were able to slow and to speed VR reliably. All subjects were able to control VR differentially during sequential slowing and speeding phases of experimental training sessions. Analyses of R-R interval histograms revealed that all subjects significantly changed the statistical frequency distributions of their R-R intervals. During VR slowing one subject generated a junctional escape rhythm. Another subject produced frequent premature ventricular contractions during speeding of VR under effective β-adrenergic blockade with propranolol. This control of VR in AF is neurally mediated at the level of the atrioventricular node. Studies with autonomic drugs indicate that this central nervous system control of VR in this arrhythmia usually occurs through activation of efferent cholinergic pathways.

NORMAL MEN[7-11] and monkeys[12] can be trained to slow, speed, or cyclically slow and speed their heart rates. Normal men can also decrease beat-to-beat heart rate variability.[13] Fields[14] demonstrated that rats can be trained to control their P-R intervals.

There is unresolved debate concerning the control of atrioventricular (A-V) transmission and the periodicity and rhythmicity of atrial and ventricular rate patterns in patients with atrial fibrillation (AF). Bootsma et al.[1] state that ventricular rhythm in AF is random and is not related to alterations in the electrophysiologic properties of the A-V node. These investigators contend that the role of the A-V node is limited to adjusting ventricular rate (VR) by modifying the rate of atrial impulses penetrating the A-V conduction system. Other investigators[2-6] assert that there is demonstrable periodicity and regularity of VR in AF. They further conclude that VR patterns are influenced by the state of A-V nodal tissue, by concealed conduction of atrial beats, and by changes in A-V nodal effective refractory period.

The purposes of the present study are to determine whether patients with chronic AF can be trained to slow and speed VR and to identify some of the autonomic nervous system mechanisms which mediate the voluntary control of VR in AF. The results of this study should help to clarify the intracardiac

---

Republished by permission of Psychosomatic Medicine (Vol. 35, 1973, p 161).

From the Section of Physiological Psychology, Laboratory of Behavioral Sciences, Gerontology Research Center, National Institute of Child Health and Human Development, Baltimore City Hospitals, Baltimore, Md.

Address for reprint requests: Bernard T. Engel, PhD, Gerontology Research Center, Baltimore City Hospitals, Baltimore, Md. 21224.

Received for publication May 2, 1972; revision received August 7, 1972.

mechanisms of voluntary cardiac control; and they should resolve some of the questions about the control of VR in patients with AF.[18]

METHOD

Six patients with AF were recruited from the Baltimore City Hospitals and Johns Hopkins Hospital cardiac clinics. The only criteria for patient selection were a history of rheumatic valvular heart disease, freedom from serious neurologic disorders, and that each patient was maintained on a stable dosage of a digitalis preparation for at least three months prior to study. Pertinent clinical data for each patient are contained in Table 1. During the three-week period of study each patient was hospitalized on a research ward.

Each patient was trained in the laboratory to speed and to slow his VR. Three first were trained to slow VR while the other three were trained initially to speed VR.

Table 1. Clinical Data on Patients *

Patient	Age	Sex	Diagnosis	Duration CHF	Medications—Cardiac (Daily Dosage)	ECG	Classification†
FP	56	F	RHD MS MI Postoperative mitral commissurotomy History cerebral embolus	2 years	0.25 mg digoxin 5 mg warfarin 25 mg hydrochlorothiazide KCL	AF VR = 60–70 RAD	II B
JB	28	M	RHD Aortic and mitral Starr Edwards protheses History subacute bacterial endocarditis	3 years	0.25 mg digoxin on even dates 0.125 mg digoxin on odd dates 7.5 mg warfarin	AF VR = 80–90 PVC LVH	II B
WF	62	M	RHD AS AI MI	5 years	0.75 mg digoxin 50 mg hydrochlorothiazide KCL	AF LVH VR = 50–60	III C
EW	31	F	RHD MS MI History duodenal ulcer disease	12 years	0.1 mg digitoxin 100 mg hydrochlorothiazide	AF VR = 70–80 LVH	II B
MW	56	F	RHD MS AI Gout	6 years	0.25 mg digoxin 40 mg furosemide KCL	AF VR = 70–80 VPC	II B
WL	57	M	RHD MS MI AI Postoperative mitral commissurotomy (twice)	20 years	0.75 mg digoxin 50 mg hydrochlorothiazide KCL	AF VR = 70–80 LVH	II–III C

*Abbreviations: RHD, rheumatic heart disease; AS, aortic stenosis; AI, aortic insufficiency; MI, mitral insufficiency; MS, mitral stenosis; CHF, congestive heart failure; AF, atrial fibrillation; VR, ventricular rate; LVH, left ventricular hypertrophy; RAD, right axis deviation; PVC, premature ventricular contractions; ECG, electrocardiogram.

† New York Heart Association Functional and Therapeutic Classifications.

While in the experimental laboratory the subject lay semireclined in a hospital bed in a quiet room. Arrayed in front of the patient was a vertical display of three differently colored lights which provided feedback information about VR. The top light (green) and the bottom light (red) were cue lights which informed the patient about the experimental conditions. The middle light (yellow) was lit whenever the patient produced the correct change in VR, and therefore provided him with beat-to-beat information about his VR.

A typical experimental session began with a 30-min period during which electrocardiographic leads were attached, and the patient adapted to the experimental situation and stabilized his VR. During the last 512 sec of this period (the baseline period), automatic data processing equipment monitored and recorded the frequency of the subject's ventricular contractions. The last phase of the experimental sessions was a 1,024-sec training period during which the patient actively tried to control his VR. The specific durations of the baseline period (512 sec) and the training period (1,024 sec) were chosen because the data processing equipment used in these experiments employed a binary counting system to measure time. When the patient was being trained to speed his VR, the green light was lit throughout the entire training period. When the patient speeded his VR above his baseline VR, the yellow light would go on and remain on as long as VR was above baseline VR. As soon as his VR fell below baseline rate, the yellow light would go off. Each subject was instructed to keep the yellow light on as long as possible and he knew that speeding his VR was the correct way to do this. During training to slow VR the procedure was identical to that outlined for speeding except that the red light rather than the green light remained lit, and that relatively slow VR now controlled the yellow light. Of course, no lights were lit during the resting and baseline periods.

After a series of training sessions in slowing VR and a series of training sessions in speeding VR, each patient was tested further under alternating conditions. During the training phase of these sessions the patient was required alternately to speed and slow his VR over four consecutive 256-sec intervals which were signaled by the red and green cue lights. The patient knew that these lights meant he should try to slow and speed VR respectively.

In five patients (WL refused participation) pharmacologic studies were carried out using some or all of the following autonomic drugs—isoproterenol (0.5–2.0 ug/min IV infusion), propranolol (0.075 mg/kg IV in divided 1-mg dosages), atropine (0.05 mg/kg IV in divided 1-mg dosages), and edrophonium (10 mg initially IV followed after 10 min by 1 mg/min IV). The dosage of isoproterenol was adjusted so that resting VR would be increased approximately 25 beats/min. The beta adrenergic blockade achieved with propranolol was sufficient to prevent any change in VR during isoproterenol infusion. The dosage of atropine sulfate used was considered adequate to block transmission of efferent cholinergic pathways but far less than the pharmacologic dosage (0.5 mg/kg) required in animals to prevent the effects of electrical stimulation of the peripheral ends of the cut vagus nerve.[15] All drug studies were performed after training in VR control was completed in order to investigate the mechanisms of VR and rhythm changes.

The laboratory apparatus employed in these experiments has been previously described by Weiss and Engel.[16]

Data were analyzed statistically in two ways. During the baseline and training periods of each session, electrocardiograms were recorded continuously on an analog tape recorder. These tapes subsequently were played back through a computer which generated R-R interval histograms, both on a visual monitor and on punched paper tape. The R-R interval data were transformed to rates subsequently. Differences between baseline VR and training level VR and between the slow and fast training levels during the alternating sessions were compared by means of T-tests. Rate histograms were generated by standardizing the data within each condition (baseline, slow, fast) and the differences between the distributions of the rate histograms were compared by means of the chi-square statistic. The standardization procedure made the chi-square test independent of differences in central tendency (mean VR) and variability (standard deviation of VR). For the purposes of this analysis eight intervals were generated: > 1.75S + VR; 1.75S + VR to 1.25S + VR; 1.25S + VR to 0.75S + VR; 0.75S + VR to 0.25S + VR; 0.25S + VR to −0.25S + VR; −0.25S + VR to −0.75S + VR; −0.75S + VR to −1.25S + VR; < −1.25S + VR, where S is the standard deviation of ventricular rate and the VR is the average ventricular rate for that condition. It should be clear that these tests of distribution are independent of any differences in the mean or standard deviations of VR.

In addition to the statistical procedures described above, individual interval histograms and individual rhythm strips were visually inspected. The frequency of occurrence of premature ventricular contractions was determined by direct count from individual rhythm strips.

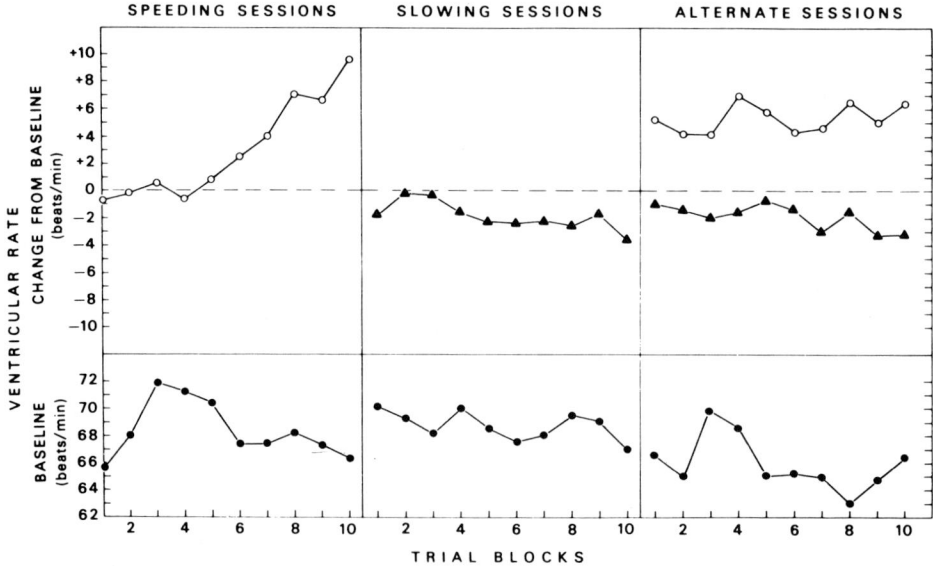

Fig. 1. Mean baseline VRs for all patients during training (bottom graph); mean changes from baseline VR during training (top graph). VR during slowing is represented by triangles and during speeding by circles. Training has been divided into ten trial blocks by averaging temporally related training sessions.

RESULTS

Figure 1 graphs mean VR for the entire experimental group during baseline recordings and mean changes in VR during training. Training has been divided into ten trial blocks by averaging temporally related sessions when the number of individual sessions for each phase of training exceeded ten. Mean baseline VR remained relatively stable throughout speeding and slowing sessions but decreased slightly (2.5 beats/min) during differential training. During training to speed VR there is an increase in the magnitude of mean VR changes (−0.5 beats/min to +9.5 beats/min) recorded during successive trial blocks. A similar but less marked trend (−0.8 beats/min to −3.5 beats/min) is noted during VR slowing. In the alternate sessions the performances of the six patients demonstrate consistent differences between the fast and slow phases of each trial block (average difference in VR is 7.2 beats/min). Table 2 lists the trial-block data for each patient during the differential training sessions.

Table 3 lists the ratio of individual training sessions in which a subject either slowed or speeded VR correctly to the total number of training sessions for that contingency. The results in this table and the trial-block data of Table 2 indicate that FP and JB were more consistent in their ability to slow VR; WF and EW consistently speeded VR; and WL and MW were able to speed and to slow their ventricular rates reliably. Although the initial sessions in VR speeding do not reflect EW's ability to speed VR, once this patient learned this response she performed consistently as illustrated during speeding of VR in alternate sessions. WF and EW were able to speed as much as 30% and 60% respectively above baseline VR during each of several sessions.

The most critical demonstration of a subject's ability to control VR is his

Table 2. Mean VR (Beats/Min) for Baseline and Cyclical Fast and Slow Training Trial Blocks*

Subject		1	2	3	4	5	6	7	8	9	10	$\bar{x}$
FP	base	51.5	53.0	58.8	51.2	54.0	58.0	53.8	44.5	51.7	55.2	53.2
	fast	48.4	51.1	56.5	49.0	54.5	54.5	54.4	45.6	50.0	59.5	52.4
	slow	46.3	48.7	54.0	46.6	51.0	51.3	50.0	44.5	48.0	55.8	49.6
JB	base	93.5	79.6	88.6	93.4	83.3	79.8	85.8	73.7	79.1	75.6	83.2
	fast	89.7	81.2	84.6	91.1	82.5	80.0	79.0	75.1	76.1	76.3	81.6
	slow	90.0	80.6	84.0	89.6	80.1	78.2	76.8	72.2	72.3	69.6	79.3
WF	base	50.2	52.3	52.8	52.2	55.7	53.3	51.4	52.3	55.6	68.5	54.4
	fast	54.2	56.7	60.3	58.2	61.3	62.0	63.5	65.2	66.8	80.2	62.8
	slow	53.7	52.6	54.2	52.7	57.1	54.6	53.8	56.6	55.3	64.1	55.4
EW	base	75.6	74.5	75.6	71.3	70.5	68.8	73.0	74.2	71.6	68.2	72.3
	fast	106.7	95.6	97.4	94.1	93.8	94.0	90.7	91.5	89.2	86.3	93.9
	slow	82.0	75.4	77.7	73.5	74.0	72.0	73.2	71.9	69.3	68.3	73.7
MW	base	75.0	71.0	85.2	88.1	73.0	72.8	68.6	71.0	72.7	72.0	74.9
	fast	72.0	69.8	88.6	90.8	74.8	75.5	70.8	70.8	73.8	73.5	76.0
	slow	71.0	67.3	85.6	89.5	72.4	72.7	67.7	68.4	69.4	69.1	73.3
WL	base	54.7	59.8	58.2	55.2	54.0	58.4	57.7	62.8	57.7	58.8	57.7
	fast	60.3	62.5	56.0	60.6	58.6	60.3	59.4	69.7	62.1	61.8	61.1
	slow	51.2	55.5	52.0	50.5	52.1	54.5	50.8	56.1	54.6	53.4	53.0

*See legend to Fig. 1 for definition of a trial block.

Table 3. Ratio of Sessions in Which Each Subject "Correctly" Modified VR to Total Training Sessions for All Patients

Subject	Slow Training Sessions	Fast Training Sessions	Alternate Training Sessions*		
			Alt.	Slow	Fast
FP	17/19	5/17	21/23	19/23	7/23
JB	14/19	10/19	24/31	24/31	9/31
WF	7/17	11/13	20/24	4/24	24/24
EW	7/24	4/10	15/15	3/15	15/15
MW	19/20	11/21	22/25	18/25	17/25
WL	12/12	13/16	12/12	12/12	11/12

*Alt. column refers to subject's ability to correctly cyclically control VR during slowing and speeding phases, while the slow and fast columns reflect speeding and slowing of VR with respect to baseline VR.

ability to speed and slow VR during alternate sessions. All subjects differentiated between fast and slow cues in this phase of training. Differential control of cardiac rate when comparing the slow and fast phases of each alternate session is statistically significant ($p < 0.05$) in 30% of JB's, 50% of FP's, 70% of MW's, 95% of WF's, and 100% of WL's and EW's alternate sessions.

Figure 2 presents a representative R-R interval histogram for each patient during alternate training sessions. Each histogram is based on all of the ventricular beats which occurred during 512-sec recordings of baseline (middle), speeding (top), and slowing (bottom). These histograms illustrate statistically significant shifts from baseline VR *distribution* achieved by these subjects during voluntary control of VR. Statistically significant shifts in distribution of VR

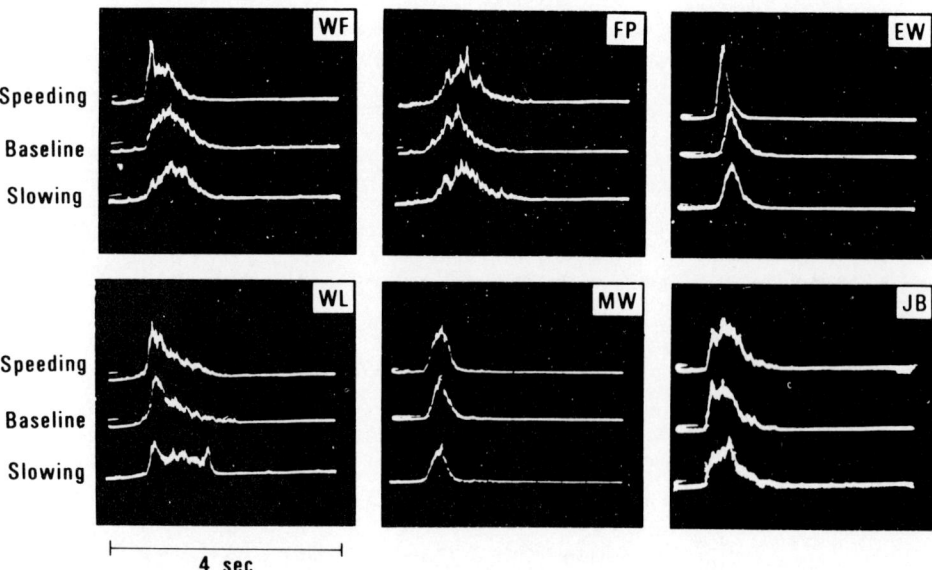

Fig. 2. Representative R-R interval histograms for each patient during alternate training in VR control. Each histogram represents the R-R intervals for all ventricular beats during the 512-sec period of baseline recordings (middle histogram), speeding of VR (top histogram), and slowing of VR (bottom histogram). Time scale for the abscissa of each histogram is 4 sec.

Table 4. Probability Levels of Statistical Differences in VR Distribution During Training*

Patient	Slowing B-S	Speeding B-F	Alternate B-S	B-F	F-S
FP	<0.01	NS	<0.05	<0.01	NS
JB	<0.01	<0.01	<0.01	NS	NS
WF	NS	<0.01	<0.05	<0.01	<0.01
EW	<0.01	<0.01	<0.01	<0.01	<0.01
MW	<0.01	NA†	<0.01	<0.01	<0.05
WL	<0.01	NS	<0.01	<0.01	<0.01

* Abbreviations: B, baseline; S, slow; F, fast; NS, not significant.
† Distribution data were not available.

(Table 4) during speeding were noted in WF, JB, and EW; during slowing in FP, MW, JB, EW, and WL. In alternate sessions WF, MW, EW, and WL generated significant differences in distribution of VR between the fast and slow phases of each session. The probabilities in this table were obtained by combining the chi-square values from all of the sessions during each of the conditions. It should be clear that these changes in VR distribution are independent of any changes in the mean or standard deviation of rate.

Studies with autonomic drugs were performed in FP, WF, MW, EW, and JB. Neither isoproterenol, propranalol, nor edrophonium abolished the ability of these subjects to voluntarily modify VR (Figure 3). Atropine abolished differential modification of cardiac rate in FP, WF, MW, and JB (Table 5). However, EW could still alter VR although less well than previously. EW's performance under autonomic drugs will be presented in detail later. Figure 3 illustrates that similar increases in mean baseline VR were achieved with atropine and isoproterenol infusion, and similar decreases in mean baseline VR were achieved with propranolol and edrophonium infusion.

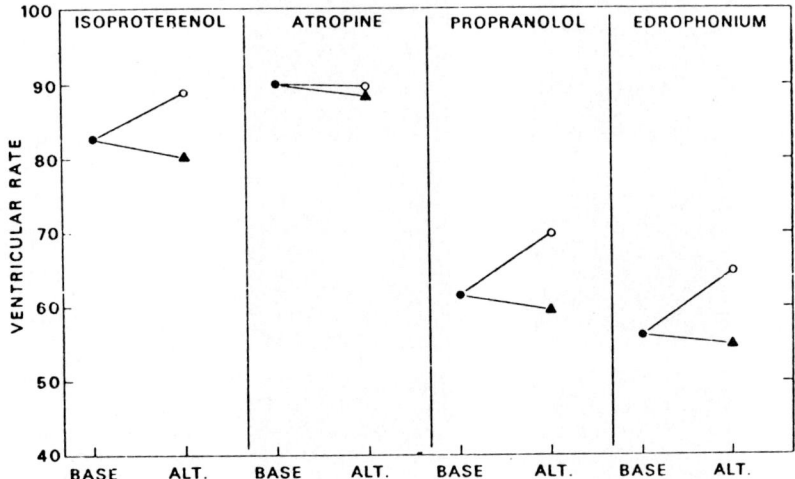

Fig. 3. Effect of autonomic drugs on voluntary control of VR in AF. During alternate training sessions the VRs graphed are mean values for all patients. (Solid circles = VR during baseline recordings, open circles = VR during the speeding phase of the alternate sessions, triangles = VR during the slowing phase of the alternate sessions.)

Table 5. Ratio of Sessions in Which Each Subject "Correctly" Modified VR to Total Sessions for Each Drug During Alternate Sessions *

Patient	Isoproterenol	Atropine	Propranolol	Edrophonium
FP	3/3	0/2		
JB	2/2	0/2	2/2	1/1
WF		0/2		
EW	2/2	2/2	4/4	1/1
MW	2/2	0/2	2/2	1/1

*Correct performance refers to greater than one heartbeat difference during cyclical slowing and speeding of VR.

Patients WF and WL were given extensive training to try to teach them to decrease the variabilities of their ventricular rates. During training to control VR variability, the yellow light would be on as long as the patient maintained his VR within the predefined limits. As soon as the patient speeded his heart above the upper limit (approximately 7.5 beats above baseline VR), the red light would go on and the yellow light would go off. Similarly, if the patient slowed below the lower limit (approximately 7.5 beats below baseline VR), the yellow light would go off and the green light would go on. WF was able to reduce VR variability from baseline (as measured by the standard deviations of VR) in 14 of 21 sessions, which is statistically significant ($p < 0.05$), and WF reduced VR

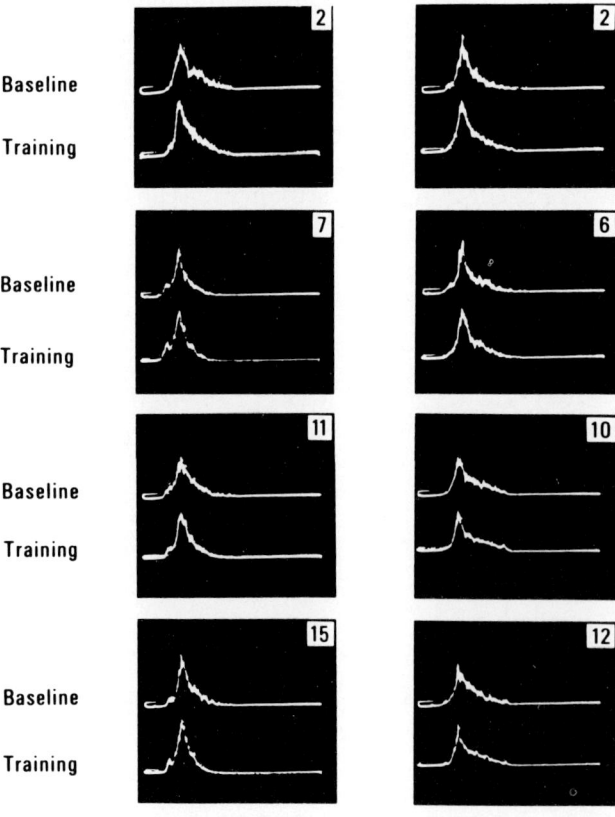

Fig. 4. R-R interval histograms during progressive stages of slowing and speeding training in patient WL. (Number on histogram refers to training session number.)

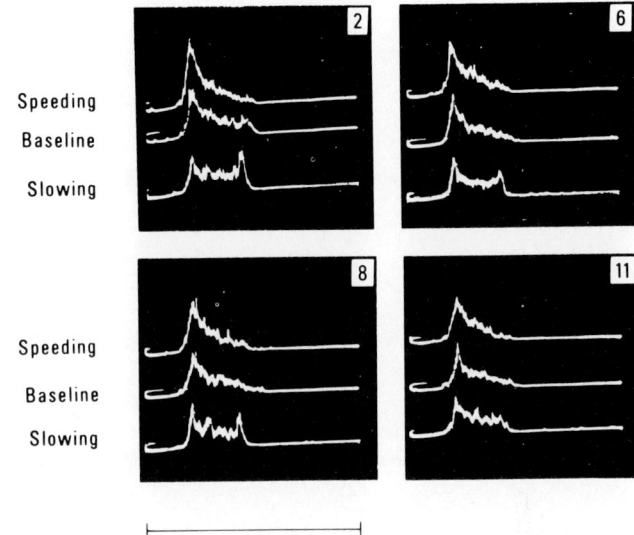

Fig. 5. R-R interval histograms during progressive stages of alternate training sessions in patient WL. The second modal peak during slowing occurs at a VR of approximately 40 beats/min.

variability in 24 of 30 sessions, which is statistically significant ($p < 0.05$). However, neither patient showed any evidence of day-to-day reduction in VR variability.

Results in the performance of two subjects require detailed presentation. R-R interval histograms during various stages of slowing and speeding training in WL (Figure 4) indicate that during speeding there is a shift in the histograms toward faster VR. During slowing training WL generated an increasing number of slow heartbeats including what appears to be a second mode at the tail of the distribution. This is further illustrated by the histograms from alternate training sessions (Figure 5). During slowing WL generated a bimodal distribution of

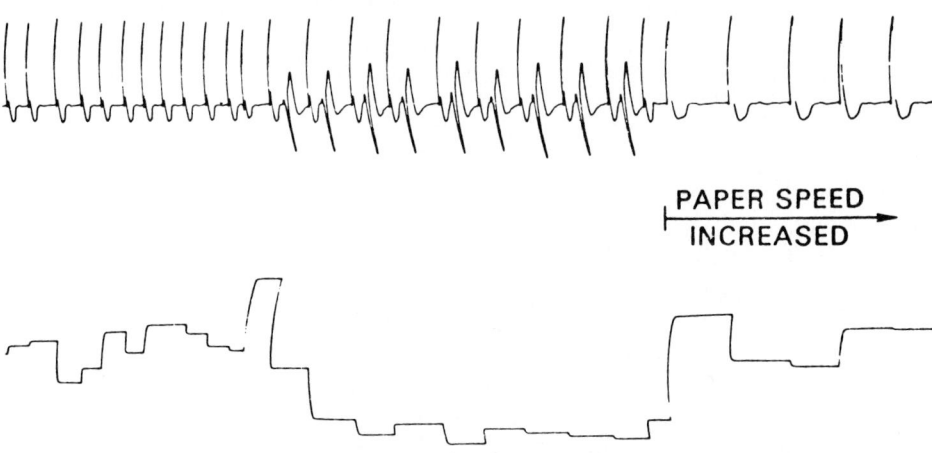

Fig. 6. Cardiotachometer (bottom) and electrocardiographic tracings illustrating the effects of premature ventricular contractions on feedback to patient EW during slow training sessions. The cardiotachometer is triggered by the normally directed R wave. A PVC with reversed electric polarity does not trigger the detection system and is perceived as a slow VR (decrease in magnitude of cardiotachometer tracing).

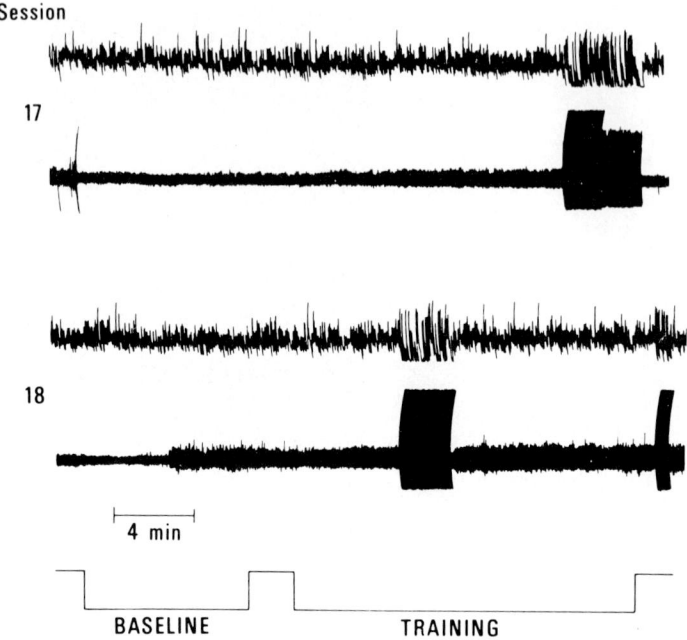

Fig. 7. Cardiotachometer (top) and electrocardiographic (bottom) tracings showing periods of reinforcement of PVCs during slow training sessions 17 and 18 in patient EW. PVCs appear as extra-wide excursions on the electrocardiographic tracings. Note the very slow paper speed.

R-R intervals. One mode occurs at a rate similar to the baseline modal rate while the second peak corresponds to a VR of approximately 40 beats/min. This second grouping of ventricular beats may represent an A-V junctional escape pacemaker which is activated during voluntary VR slowing. Inspection of WL's rhythm strips reveals evidence of numerous fixed R-R intervals of approximately 1.5-sec duration during voluntary slowing of VR. The QRS complexes are the same configuration and magnitude as WL's usual QRS complex.

Patient EW not only increased VR but also changed cardiac rhythm such that she would have frequent bursts of premature ventricular contractions (PVCs) often in a bigeminal rhythm. EW experienced difficulty slowing VR and during this training she generated runs of PVCs which we reinforced because the yellow light was triggered by the normally directed R wave and a PVC with reversed polarity was perceived by our detection system as a very slow rate (Figure 6). Figure 7 shows two slowing sessions in which EW generated long runs of PVCs that were reinforced as if they represented VR slowing. We then stopped reinforcement and PVCs only occurred sporadically.

During drug studies EW demonstrated frequent PVCs throughout the period of isoproterenol administration (Figure 8). However, after adequate beta adrenergic blockade with propranolol, EW selectively generated PVCs during VR speeding. This response was so intriguing that two days later the patient was retested with propranolol (sessions 2A and 2B) and again produced PVCs only during periods of speeding of VR (Figure 9). During the two 256-sec speeding phases of propranolol in session 1A, EW emitted 104 and 102 PVCs, respectively; during session 1B she emitted 158 and 175 PVCs; during session 2A she

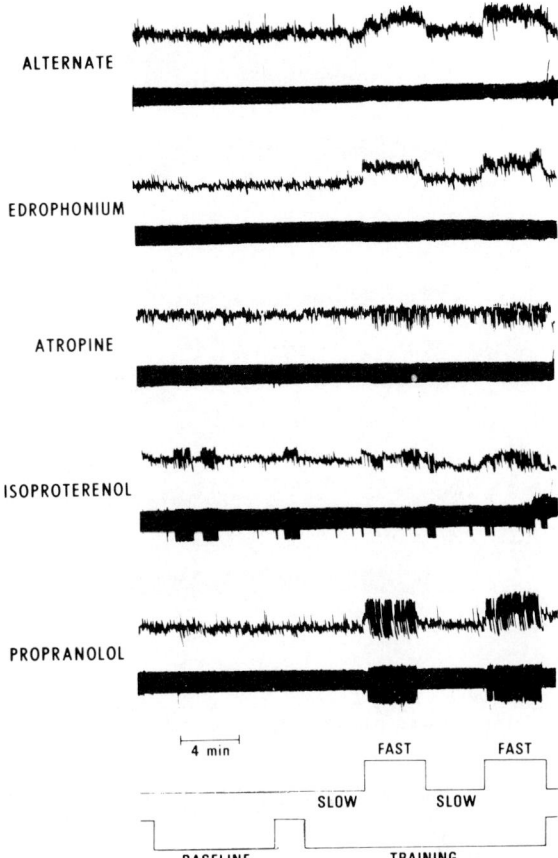

Fig. 8. Effects of autonomic drugs on ventricular rate and rhythm during alternate training sessions in patient EW. PVCs appear as wide excursions on the electrocardiographic tracing (bottom). During isoproterenol administration PVCs occurred throughout the baseline, slow, and fast phases of training. During propranolol administration PVCs are noted only during the speeding phases of the alternate training sessions. Note very slow paper speed. (In the cardiotachometer tracing [upper] higher deflections indicate faster VR while lower deflections indicate slower VR.)

generated 3 and 22 PVCs; and finally during session 2B she emitted 25 and 69 PVCs, respectively. During the baseline periods and the slowing phases of the alternate sessions there were no PVCs.

DISCUSSION

The results of this study indicate that digitalized patients with AF can be operantly conditioned to modify VR differentially. This control of VR probably is mediated neurally at the level of the A-V node. Studies with autonomic drugs suggest that blockage of efferent cholinergic pathways by the administration of atropine sulfate abolishes voluntary control of VR in patients with established AF.

Cyclical control of VR as well as alteration of beat-to-beat VR variability in subjects with normal sinus rhythm would be effected by direct changes in the sino-atrial node pacemaker.[17] Unpublished data from this laboratory from patients with third-degree heart block suggest that these patients cannot modify their VR voluntarily. These findings indicate that pacemakers below the A-V node are not under direct central nervous system control, while the present study suggests that voluntary central nervous control of VR can be achieved by direct neural alterations of the A-V node.

During training in control of VR, significant changes in the statistical dis-

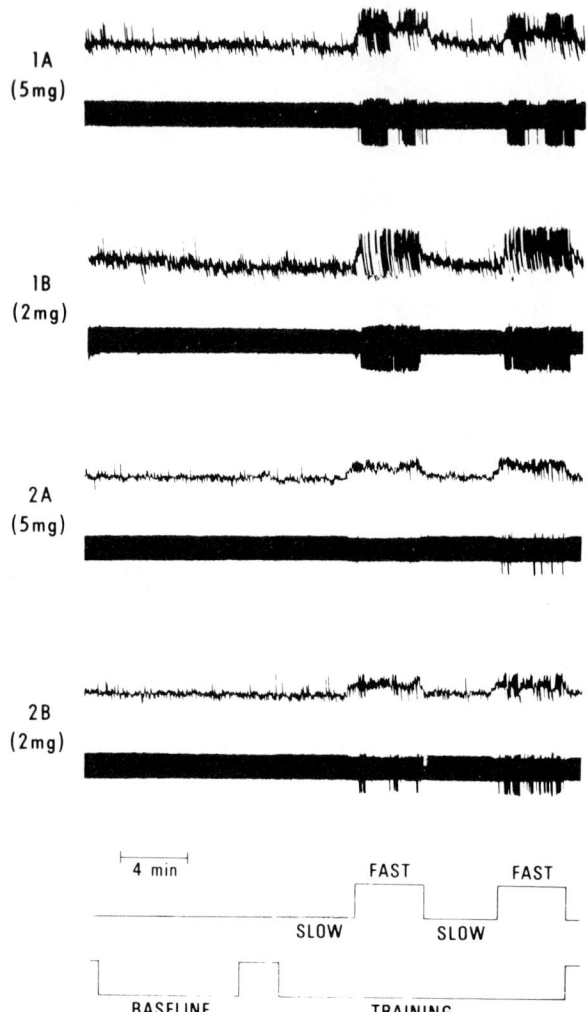

Fig. 9. Electrocardiographic (bottom) and cardiotachometer (top) tracings from the alternate training session in patient EW during which propranolol was administered. These tracings show that PVCs (wide ECG excursions) were generated only during the speeding phases of each alternate training session but none were generated during slow or baseline phases. The intravenous dosage of propranolol is listed under the session number. Propranolol sessions 1A and 1B were run sequentially on one day and propranolol sessions 2A and 2B were run sequentially on a subsequent day.

tribution of VR patterns were noted. Patient WL during slowing of VR generated bimodal distributions of R-R intervals, suggesting that he not only lengthened his R-R intervals, but that he also initiated an A-V junctional escape pacemaker. Analyses of his histograms revealed the second peak to correspond to a VR of about 40 beats/min. Inspection of electrocardiogram rhythm strips revealed R-R intervals of 1.5 sec during training periods of VR slowing. There is evidence that an A-V junctional escape pacemaker in AF is caused by pathologic A-V block which is usually the result of digitalis toxicity.[5,19] WL exhibited this escape rhythm during slowing when he may have modified A-V conduction tissue by increasing refractory period and/or increasing conduction time. This patient was chronically maintained on a stable dosage of digoxin. There was no evidence of digitalis toxicity during the immediately preceding baseline recording periods or during temporally contiguous periods of speeding of VR. Increase in vagal tone to the heart by carotid sinus stimulation[20] and by administration of edrophonium chloride[21] have been reported to be useful in the early detection of digitalis excess. One may conclude that this A-V junctional escape rhythm was caused either by direct modification of the A-V node during voluntary VR slowing or that learned modification of VR was additive to that of digitalis, thereby unmasking latent digitalis toxicity.

An explanation is lacking for patient EW's selective ability to generate PVCs during speeding of VR under the influence of adequate beta adrenergic blockade with propranolol. This subject consistently generated PVCs during each 256-sec speeding interval during the four different alternate sessions performed with propranolol. EW was the only subject who remained able to modify VR and especially perform VR speeding during efferent vagal blockade after a total of 4 mg of intravenously administered atropine. We speculate that this patient was able to speed her VR by way of vagal inhibition (in the presence of propranolol) and by increased sympathetic outflow (in the presence of atropine). We believe this mechanism is atypical since no other patient speeded with efferent vagal blockade with atropine.

Bootsma et al.[1] minimize the function of the A-V node to "scaling of atrial impulses." The present study indicates that the central nervous system, acting on the A-V node, can modify not only VR but can also shift the statistical distribution of ventricular beats. Furthermore, we have noted the generation of an A-V nodal escape rhythm during VR slowing.

Attempts to train two patients to chronically reduce VR variability were unsuccessful. Although changes in vagal tone to the A-V node can modulate VR, these alterations of nervous input to the node apparently are unable to decrease R-R variability sufficiently to produce clinically significant, long-term changes in variability of VR.

It seems worthwhile to investigate further the interaction of training to alter VR in AF with the effects of medications such as digitalis and quinidine. It also seems worthwhile to explore the mechanisms of this technique in relation to electrophysiologic diagnostic procedures such as direct recordings of His bundle electrocardiograms.

ACKNOWLEDGMENT

We wish to thank Dr. Gustav C. Voigt, chief of the Cardiac Division, Baltimore City Hospitals, for his advice and consultations on the patients. We wish to thank Dr. J. O'Neal Humphries for referring patients WL, EW, and JB from The Johns Hopkins Hospital Cardiac Clinic. We wish to acknowledge our appreciation to Mr. Reginald E. Quilter, who assisted in the development and maintenance of various instruments used in this study, to Miss Diana Dumps for technical assistance in data analysis, and to Mrs. Estelle Carter for secretarial help in the preparation of this manuscript.

REFERENCES

1. Bootsma BK, Hoelen AJ, Strackee J, Meyler FL: Analysis of R-R intervals in patients with atrial fibrillation at rest and during exercise. Circulation 41:783–794, 1970

2. Moe GK, Abildskov JA: Observations on the ventricular dysrhythmia associated with atrial fibrillation in the dog heart. Circ Res 14:447–460, 1964

3. Braunstein JR, Franke EK: Autocorrelation of ventricular response in atrial fibrillation. Circ Res 9:300–304, 1961

4. Horan LG, Kistler JC: Study of ventricu-

lar response in atrial fibrillation. Circ Res 9:305–311, 1961

5. Urbach JR, Grauman JJ, Straus SH: Quantitative methods for the recognition of atrioventricular junctional rhythms in atrial fibrillation. Circulation 39:803–817, 1969

6. Battersby EJ: Pacemaker periodicity in atrial fibrillation. Circulation 17:296–302, 1965

7. Shearn DW: Operant conditioning heart rate. Science 137:530–531, 1962

8. Engel BT, Hansen SP: Operant conditioning of heart rate slowing. Psychophysiology 3:176–187, 1966

9. Engel BT, Chism RA: Operant conditioning of heart rate speeding. Psychophysiology 3:418–426, 1967

10. Levine HI, Engel BT, Pearson JA: Differential operant conditioning of heart rate. Psychosom Med 30:837–845, 1968

11. Frazier TW: Avoidance conditioning of heart rate in humans. Psychophysiology 3:188–202, 1966

12. Engel BT, Gottlieb SH: Differential operant conditioning of heart rate in the restrained monkey. J Comp Physiol Psychol 73:217–225, 1970

13. Hnatiow M, Lang PJ: Learned stabilization of cardiac rate. Psychophysiology 1:330–336, 1965

14. Fields C: Instrumental conditioning of the rat cardiac control systems. Proc Natl Acad Sci USA 65:293–299, 1970

15. Goodman LS, Gilman A: The Pharmacologic Basis of Therapeutics, 4th ed. New York, Macmillan, 1970

16. Weiss T, Engel BT: Operant conditioning of heart rate in patients with premature ventricular contractions. Psychosom Med 33:301–321, 1971

17. Miller NE, DiCara L: Instrumental learning of heart rate changes in curarized rats. J Comp Physiol Psychol 63:12–19, 1967

18. Brody DA: Ventricular rate patterns in atrial fibrillation. Circulation 41:733–735, 1970

19. Kastor JA, Yurchak PM: Recognition of digitalis intoxication in the presence of atrial fibrillation. Ann Intern Med 67:1045–1054, 1967

20. Lown B, Levine SA: The carotid sinus: Clinical value of its stimulation. Circulation 33:766–790, 1961

21. Pitt B, Kurland GS: Use of edrophonium chloride (Tensilon) to detect early digitalis toxicity. Amer J Cardiol 18:557–565, 1966

Part IV

Learned Control of Cardiac Rate and Cardiac Conduction in the Wolff–Parkinson–White Syndrome

Eugene R. Bleecker, M.D., and Bernard T. Engel, Ph.D.

A patient with Type A Wolff-Parkinson-White syndrome (WPW) was trained to control heart rate. The patient was then trained to increase and decrease both normal conduction and WPW conduction. Pharmacologic studies performed to delineate the mechanism used by this patient to modify conduction revealed that vagal blockade with atropine produced normal conduction while increased vagal tone favored WPW conduction. This study describes the ability of a patient to learn to modify heart rate and cardiac conduction independently.

IT HAS BEEN SHOWN that normal men can be trained to slow, speed and cyclically slow and speed heart rate.[1-4] Patients with premature ventricular contractions can be trained to decrease and to control them.[5] Patients with chronic atrial fibrillation can be trained to change ventricular rate by the modification of vagal tone to the atrioventricular node.[6] Our purpose in this study was to determine whether a patient with intermittent Wolff–Parkinson–White syndrome can learn to control heart rate and also to modify the pathway of cardiac conduction.

CASE REPORT

A 29-year-old woman was admitted to the Gerontology Research Center in 1972. Since the age of 19 she had had episodes of rapid tachycardia associated with dyspnea, syncope and chest pain and treated with combinations of various medications: propranolol, quinidine, procainamide, diphenylhydantoin, digoxin and sedatives. Ten-hour Holter continuous monitoring and exercise treadmill stress tests performed during the last 3 years documented the presence of intermittent conduction typical of the Wolff–Parkinson–White syndrome, sinus tachycardia and supraventricular tachycardias (200 to 240 beats per minute) with a conduction pattern typical of the syndrome. She received only sedatives and analgesics during the month before this study.

Admission physical examination revealed a normally developed, asthenic woman with a blood pressure of 110/80 and regular pulse rate of 110. An electrocardiogram revealed intermittent Type A conduction typical of the Wolff–Parkinson–White syndrome. The heart was vertical, with a +70° axis. During normal conduction the PR interval was 0.18 second, and the QRS dura-

---

Republished by permission of New England Journal of Medicine (Vol. 288, No. 11, March 15, 1973, pp. 560–62).

From the Section of Physiological Psychology, Laboratory of Behavioral Sciences, Gerontology Research Center, National Institute of Child Health and Human Development, Baltimore City Hospitals, Baltimore, Md. 21224, where reprint requests should be addressed to Dr. Engel.

tion 0.07 second. During Wolff–Parkinson–White conduction the PR interval was 0.10 second, and the QRS duration 0.12 second.

METHODS

Training in Heart-Rate Control

The patient was first trained to slow and then to speed and finally sequentially to slow and speed her heart rate. While in the laboratory she lay in a hospital bed. Each session began with a rest period during which electrocardiographic leads were attached, and she stabilized her heart rate. During the last 512 seconds of this base-line period her heart rate was recorded. The last phase of the experimental session was a training period of 1024 seconds when she was trained to control her heart rate. During speeding training, a green light was put on that she could see throughout the entire training period. When the patient speeded her heart rate above the base-line rate, a yellow light went on and remained on as long as the rate was above base line. As soon as the heart rate fell below the base-line rate, the yellow light went off. The patient was instructed to keep the yellow light on, and she knew that speeding her heart rate was the correct way to accomplish this purpose. During slowing training the procedure was identical to that outlined for speeding except that a red light rather than the green light remained on, and that a relatively slow heart rate now controlled the yellow light. After a series of sessions to slow and a series of sessions to speed the rate, she was required alternately to speed and to slow the rate during 4 consecutive 256-second intervals that were signaled by the red and green cue lights. The laboratory apparatus employed has previously been described.[5] Differences between base-line and training heart rates and between the slow and fast training phases were compared by means of t-tests.

Training to Control Cardiac Conduction

After rate training was completed, she was trained to control the prevalance of normal and Wolff–Parkinson–White beats. This control was made possible by selection of a right precordial electrocardiographic lead in which the major QRS deflection of Wolff–Parkinson–White-conducted beats and normally conducted beats were opposite, and then by selectively triggering a clicker from normally conducted QRS complexes only. During training sessions designed to teach her to increase normal conduction she was told to increase the frequency of these sounds. During training to increase Wolff–Parkinson–White conduction she was instructed to decrease the frequency of these sounds. She was then required alternately to increase and decrease the frequency of clicks over consecutive 128-second intervals that were signaled by cue lights. Finally, she was trained to increase normally conducted beats without feedback.

At the conclusion of training, pharmacologic studies were carried out to investigate the mechanisms of rhythm change. The following autonomic drugs were administered: isoproterenol (1.0 to 1.5 μg per minute, intravenous infusion); phenylephrine (0.02 to 0.05 mg per minute intravenously); propranolol (5.0 mg intravenously); and atropine (1.5 mg intravenously). The beta-adrenergic blockade achieved with propranolol was sufficient to prevent any change in heart rate during an isoproterenol infusion. During administration of these drugs the patient tried to increase and decrease normal conduction.

Differences in the frequencies of normally conducted and Wolff-Parkinson-White beats were compared statistically by means of the chi-square test.

RESULTS

Training in Rate Control

The patient decreased her heart rate by an average of 3.4 beats per minute during 26 slowing training sessions: she slowed her rate from base line in 19 of the 26 sessions. She increased it an average of 2.5 beats per minute during 15 speeding training sessions, and she speeded from base line in 11 of the 15 sessions. The most critical demonstration of her ability to control her heart rate occurred during the sequential, alternating phase, when she performed successfully in 20 of 21 sessions, and when the average heart-rate difference between the speeding and slowing segments was 5.5 beats per minute.

Training in Rhythm Control

When she received reinforcement to increase normal conduction, she did so significantly ($p \leq 0.05$) in four of eight training sessions. She also was able to increase Wolff-Parkinson-White conduction significantly in two of three sessions when she was trained to do so.

Her performance during the alternating training sessions was divided into three categories depending on her base-line rhythm. When normal conduction was rare (base-line rhythm less than 10 per cent normal conduction), she was able to increase normal conduction significantly during all five sessions from an average of 1.8 to an average of 18.2 per cent. When normal conduction was moderate (base-line rhythm between 10 and 90 per cent normal conduction) she was able to increase normal conduction significantly in five of seven sessions from an average of 38.1 to an average of 55.9 per cent, and to decrease normal conduction significantly in four of seven sessions to an average of 31.4 per cent. In six of these seven sessions she significantly differentiated between the increase and decrease of normal conduction phases. During sessions when normal conduction was predominant (base-line rhythm greater than 90 per cent), she was able to decrease normal conduction significantly in five of ten sessions, from an average of 99.7 to an average of 90.4 per cent. Figure 1 shows representative electrocardiographic tracings from an alternating session in which she increased and decreased normal conduction.

During the last stage of training the patient was taught to increase normal conduction without feedback. In these training sessions, 128-second periods of feedback were alternated with 128-second periods of no feedback, and she was instructed to increase normal conduction during the entire training session. She increased normal conduction significantly in all eight sessions during both the feedback and the no-feedback phases. The mean proportional increase of normal conduction from base line was 13 per cent during both feedback and no-feedback phases of training.

When heart rate and rhythm were compared, normal conduction tended to be associated with a fast rate although on numerous occasions, the rate was low and she had predominant normal conduction. Drug studies were done to clarify the relation between heart rate and conduction and to identify autonomic mechanisms mediating the patient's performance. Administration of phenyl-

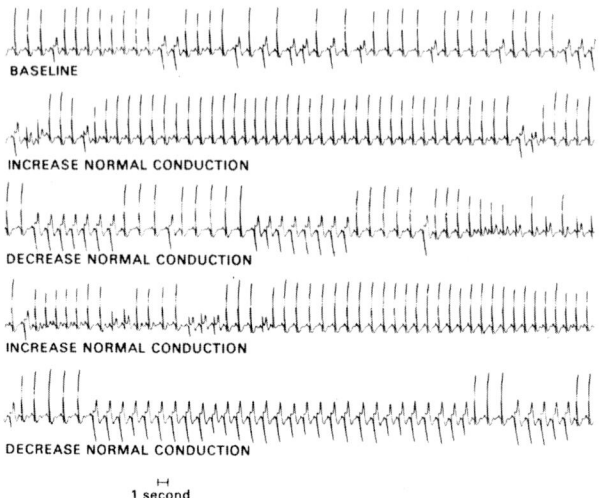

Fig. 1. Representative rhythm strips from an alternate training session during which the patient was sequentially increasing and decreasing normal conduction. QRS complexes with upright R waves and normal PR intervals were normally conducted.

ephrine increased Wolff–Parkinson–White conduction and decreased heart rate during the base-line period. During the training session she was able to increase normal conduction from 5 to 12 per cent and also increased heart rate from 82 to 91 beats per minute. During beta-adrenergic blockade with propranolol the heart rate was 81 beats per minute, with 4 per cent normally conducted beats in the baseline period. She was able to increase to 11 per cent normal conduction with an increase in rate of only 2 beats per minute. The administration of atropine, on two different days, resulted in an increase in heart rate and conversion to 100 per cent normal conduction. She was unable to generate Wolff-Parkinson-White conduction during atropine administration. During base line with isoproterenol administration she exhibited 20 per cent normal conduction with a heart rate of 116 beats per minute. She decreased normal conduction to 9 per cent during the "increase" period and decreased normal conduction to 6 per cent during the "decrease" period. Heart rate were 124 and 121 beats per minute respectively.

During follow-up testing 10 weeks after initial training she was able to modify cardiac conduction differentially (Fig. 2).

DISCUSSION

Blockage of vagal tone increased heart rate and produced normal conduction. Vagomimetic effects of phenylephrine increased Wolff-Parkinson-White conduction and decreased heart rate. With faster heart rate during isoproterenol infusion or an exercise treadmill stress test, there was predominant Wolff-

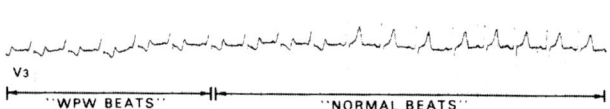

Fig. 2. Electrocardiographic rhythm strip taken 10 weeks after completion of training (WPW denotes Wolff-Parkinson–White). The patient was able to control differentially her heart rhythm away from the laboratory and without feedback.

Parkinson-White conduction. Since both atropine and either isoproterenol or exercise increase heart rate but have opposite effects on conduction, we conclude that heart rate alone is not the determinant of conduction in this patient. We hypothesize that learned modification of vagal tone to her heart is the mechanism by which she is able to modulate conduction.

A complete discussion of the behavioral mechanisms associated with learned control of cardiac function is beyond the scope of this report; however, we have discussed some of these factors elsewhere.[7] Other investigators have shown that learned control of cardiac changes is not necessarily mediated by respiratory or skeletal effects.[8] Our observations in this patient suggested that her control was not mediated by modifications of respiration or by modifications in skeletal-muscle activity.

This study integrates technics of behavioral training with the investigation of the physiology of cardiac conduction. Further studies in patients with the Wolff–Parkinson–White Syndrome are indicated to investigate physiologic and clinical applications of similar training. It would be especially worthwhile to carry out these studies in conjunction with pharmacologic agents, His-bundle recordings and epicardial mapping technics.

ACKNOWLEDGMENT

We are indebted to Dr. Gustav C. Voigt for advice in the care of this patient, and for helpful comments on this manuscript.

REFERENCES

1. Engel BT, Hansen SP: Operant conditioning of heart rate slowing. Psychophysiology 3: 176–187, 1966
2. Engel BT, Chism RA: Operant conditioning of heart rate speeding. Psychophysiology 3:418–426, 1967
3. Levene HI, Engel BT, Pearson JA: Differential operant conditioning of heart rate. Psychosom Med 30:837–845, 1968
4. Frazier TW: Avoidance conditioning of heart rate in humans. Psychophysiology 3:188–202, 1966
5. Weiss T, Engel BT: Operant conditioning of heart rate in patients with premature ventricular contractions. Psychosom Med 33:301–321, 1971
6. Bleecker ER, Engel BT: Learned control of ventricular rate in patients with atrial fibrillation. Psychosom Med (in press)
7. Engel BT: Operant conditioning of cardiac function: a status report. Psychophysiology 9:161–177, 1972
8. Miller NE: Learning of visceral and glandular responses. Science 163:434–445, 1969

Chapter 7: Raynaud's Disease

Introduction

RAYNAUD'S DISEASE, first described in 1862, has been defined as

> the primary or idiopathic form of paroxysmal, bilateral cyanosis of the digits, with or without local gangrene. The attacks are produced by cold or emotion and are relieved by heat . . . [The attacks are] due to complete interruption of local blood flow by tight constriction of the digital and palmar, or plantar arteries . . . .[1]

As for migraine, also a vascular syndrome (see Chapter 5), it is thought that serotonin may play an important role. Raynaud himself, even in 1862, recognized that excessive vasoconstrictor tone of central (i.e., CNS) origin must be responsible.

> The onset is usually gradual, the first mild attacks appearing in winter, or less commonly, during a period of emotional stress . . . . In a typical well developed attack from one to four digits . . . on each hand become deeply blue, or initially white then blue.[1]

With the attacks, of course, the fingers are cold, more or less numb, and achingly painful. In about half the cases, the hands alone are affected, and in most other cases the hands and the feet are affected. Rarely, the nose, cheeks, ears and chin may be involved, as in Case 1 reported by Dr. Surwit and treated by him personally. In rare (0.4%) very severe cases, it may become necessary because of gangrene to amputate the terminal phalanges. Medical treatment at best can be characterized as providing only partial relief, although the avoidance of smoking (which produces vasoconstriction) and of cold climates may help. Raowulfia drugs (which are serotonin antagonists) may occasionally bring symptomatic relief, and vasodilator drugs taken immediately before exposure to cold may provide some protection from attacks. Surgical treatment, by sympathectomy, effective through the removal of tonic vasoconstrictor impulses, may be indicated when more conservative management fails and the course becomes one of increasing pain, ulceration and gangrene. Even sympathectomy, however, does not insure against recurrences several years after surgery; and, as in the first case presented by Dr. Surwit, sympathectomy may not help symptoms in the hands, or in the face. Also, of course, sympathectomy is a major surgical procedure, which permanently abolishes sweating in those areas of skin deprived of sympathetic impulses.

Against this rather bleak therapeutic background, the clinical results summarized by Dr. Surwit in the five pilot cases reported in this chapter appear to be of some definite practical significance.

In this application (as in migraine), the target response is warming of the hands (or feet, or face); the measuring physiologic instrument is either a thermistor, measuring skin temperature, as in Cases 1, 2, and 3, or a photoplethysmograph, measuring digit volume, as in Cases 4 and 5 (Both digital skin temperature and digit volume are connected with the root measure digital blood flow.) The reinforc-

© 1973 by Grune & Stratton, Inc.

ing stimulus is feedback about success, delivered by means of a variety* of auditory and/or visual stimuli in the five cases.

Of the five cases reported, four appear to have benefited substantially, and the one who did not benefit was reported to be very ambivalent about treatment, and to have discontinued treatment after only approximately ten sessions.

Lee Birk, M.D.

REFERENCE

1. Beeson PB, McDermott W (eds): Cecil-Loeb Textbook of Medicine (ed 12). Philadelphia, Saunders, 1967, p 733

---

*Each case was treated by a different investigator or team of investigators.

Biofeedback: A Possible Treatment for Raynaud's Disease

Richard S. Surwit, Ph.D.

The physiology of Raynaud's disease and the efficacy of biofeedback in controlling various physiologic functions are reviewed. Five case studies are presented in which biofeedback was used as the primary mode of treatment of Raynaud's disease or Raynaud's phenomenon. The outcome of these studies is discussed in terms of the questions they raise for future research. It is suggested that although biofeedback cannot, at present, be considered a reliable treatment of Raynaud's disease, it might be preferable to more drastic surgical procedures.

RAYNAUD'S DISEASE, like essential hypertension, is a functional disorder of the cardiovascular system: that is, it involves no observable organic pathology in its early stages. Its symptoms consist of intermittent, bilateral vasospasms of the hands, feet, and rarely the face, which can be elicited by cold stimulation and/or emotional stress.[1] During an attack, the affected area usually goes through a three-stage color change, first blanching, then turning cyanotic blue, and finally becoming bright red as the spasm is relieved and reactive hypermia sets in.

While severe manifestations of this condition are not common, Lewis[11] estimated that it effects approximately 20% of most young people in its mildest forms. Clinical Raynaud's disease is found to occur five times more often in women than in men,[1] the time of onset occurring in the first and second decades of life.[4] When this syndrome results for an identifiable pathologic process, it is known as Raynaud's phenomenon.

The physiology of Raynaud's disease is not completely understood. While Raynaud himself[19] attributed the malady to sympathetic overreactivity, Lewis[11] maintained that the fault was primarily local. He collected evidence showing that changes in environmental temperature could have specific effects on the part of the digit stimulated by cold. In more severe cases, he felt that vascular pathology was also a contributing factor. Lewis did not believe that patients suffering from Raynaud's disease were abnormally "nervous," and therefore made the mistake of ignoring the effects of emotional stimuli upon the disorder.

Mittlemann and Wolff[16] demonstrated that emotional stress could reduce the digital blood flow, as measured by skin temperature in both normals and Raynaud's patients. In Raynaud's patients, however, these changes in temperature were accompanied by the blanching–cyanotic–edemic color change and pain typical of the vasospasmodic disorder. They reported that temperature changes were not, in themselves, a sufficient cause for the spasm. Rather, the attacks seemed to occur most reliably when emotional stress and low environmental temperature interacted. In addition, they failed to find emotional stimuli effective in producing this reaction after sympathectomy. Graham[6] was also able to

---

Reprint requests should be addressed to Dr. Richard S. Surwit, Harvard Medical School, Massachusetts Mental Health Center, 74 Fenwood Road, Boston, Mass. 02115.
©1973 by Grune & Stratton, Inc.

demonstrate the effects of disturbing interviews on skin temperature in both patients with Raynaud's disease and normals. In addition, he was able to isolate hostility or anxiety as the emotions most often responsible for this reaction. Also, Graham, Stein, and Winokur[7] were able to show that suggesting these emotions to normal subjects could produce vasoconstriction. This evidence strongly implies that emotional stimuli are at least a contributing factor in the elicitation of Raynaud's disease and that Lewis[11] was incorrect in concluding that the fault was local. However, as Mendlowitz and Naftchi[14] have suggested, Raynaud's disease might be dichotomized into two separate disorders, one in which the vasculature is normal and vasomotor tone is heightened by sympathetic overreactivity and another class with normal vasomotor tone but locally sensitive vasculature.

BIOFEEDBACK AND VOLUNTARY AUTONOMIC CONTROL

Since the latter part of the last decade, the literature on the voluntary control of various autonomic functions has expanded exponentially.[3,22,28] Despite recent difficulties in the replication of autonomic learning in curarized animals,[15] there is little doubt that humans can learn at least limited control of systolic blood pressure,[26] diastolic blood pressure,[25] heart rate,[3] electroencephalographic activity,[17] and electrodermal activity.[23] In addition, control of electromyographic activity, although not autonomically mediated, has been facilitated with biofeedback techniques.[8] In most cases, the procedures used to train people in the control of these responses are similar. Electrodes are attached to record the desired response and the subject is provided with some form of information as to his performance relative to a desired goal. This information can be some *continuous analogue* of the measured activity, such as a light whose intensity varies with the amplitude of the desired response or it can consist of a *dichotomous signal,* appearing only when the subject is responding correctly. In either case, subject motivation can be manipulated by the use of rewards contingent upon the subject's performance.

Because the peripheral vasomotor system is only sympathetically innervated, it is less complex than many of the response systems just mentioned. Therefore, it is somewhat surprising that the literature on voluntary control of vasomotor responses is so small. The first report of voluntary vasomotor control came from the USSR, in which Lisina[12] was able to demonstrate that subjects could learn to increase the blood flow in their arms if allowed to watch their plethysmographic record. Snyder and Noble,[27] using a dichotomous feedback procedure, were able to train subjects in vasoconstriction of the fingers independent of changes in heart rate, finger movement, muscle tension, or respiration. Volow and Hein,[31] using analogue and discrete feedback, trained subjects to both increase and decrease blood flow in their fingers. They reported, however, that constriction seemed to be easier to learn than dilation. Finally, Taub[30] was able to teach subjects to increase or decrease the skin temperature of their hands by an analogue feedback method.

Another line of research also presents evidence for voluntary control of peripheral blood flow. Barber[2] has reviewed the literature on the effects of "hypnosis" upon vasomotor functioning and cites four studies in which "hypnosis" or suggestion were found to allow subjects control over their peripheral blood flow. In a more recent report, Maslach et al.[13] demonstrated that subjects who were trained in hypnosis were able to change the skin temperature of their two hands in opposite directions. As in the biofeedback study of Volow and Hein,[31] the investigators found that vasoconstriction was easier to obtain than vasodilation. While the relationship between hypnosis, suggestion, and biofeedback is not immediately clear, these studies, taken as a whole, strongly imply that voluntary control might be used as a means of treating peripheral vascular disorders such as Raynaud's disease. This possibility is especially tantalizing in the case of the latter disorder, since there are few effective therapies for it.[1] That the following experimental treatments were attempted on somewhat tenuous theoretical grounds reflects the urgent need for a therapeutic alternative in the alleviation of this type of vascular problem.

CASE REPORTS

To date, there have been at least four cases in which biofeedback was successfully employed as the major mode of treatment of Raynaud's disease or Raynaud's phenomenon. Although these four reports involve the implementation of somewhat different methods and are probably not all dealing with Raynaud's disease *per se,* they have in common one essential point; in each case, patients reported achieving control of Raynaud's symptom they previously thought to be involuntary.

Case 1

Surwit et al.,[29] working at the Allen Memorial Institute of McGill University, have treated one such case for over a year. Upon referral, the patient, a 21-yr-old female, had been suffering from Raynaud's disease for about 5 yr. Initially, her symptoms included vasospasms in the hands and feet while her face was extremely sensitive to cold. Following both cervical and lumbar sympathectomies the patient experienced a complete remission of symptoms in the feet but vasospasms in the hands and face continued for 2 yr.

Prior to feedback training, the patient was given intensive instruction in relaxation and autogenic imagery. This was done in the hope of providing her with some sort of strategy that might facilitate her learning to control her peripheral blood flow. Training consisted of a temperature feedback procedure. A sensitive thermistor (time constant < 1 sec) was mounted on the patient's left hand. During each 10-min trial, the patient's temperature was monitored continuously by a polygraph. The output of the polygraph was fed into a small laboratory computer that sampled temperature at intervals of 0.1 sec. At the end of each 3 sec, the average temperature was compared to the previous 3-sec average. If there was a net increase in temperature in excess of $0.1°C$, the patient was given feedback. This consisted of a bell, a flashing light, and an increment in a cumulative graph displayed on the computer's scope. At the end of a trial, the scope would black out, and the computer teletype would print out the per cent of successful responses for that trial. The therapist would then verbally reinforce the patient for her success. Each session consisted of three 10-min trials separated by 5–10-min rest periods. Fourteen sessions were administered over a 3-wk period, after which time the patient stopped treatment for 1 mo to go on vacation. Upon her return, sessions were administered twice a week and consisted of two 10-min trials for each hand. This mode of therapy lasted for 4 mo and was supplemented by counseling and assertive training[33] for family problems. All therapy was then discontinued for 1 mo and then feedback training was resumed at weekly intervals for the next 6 mo.

After a year of training, this patient managed to increase her basal skin temperature (both hands) from an average of 23°C to 26.6°C. She was able to go outdoors in the Montreal winter without elaborate protective garments and had markedly decreased the number of Raynaud's attacks she experienced. Also, the color of her hands had changed from a pasty white to a more natural pink. However, the patient still complained of pain in her hands even when her skin temperature was normal. One year after the beginning of training, as feedback training was being phased out and termination of therapy was imminent, this patient suddenly lost all ability to control her skin temperature. She was seen for a consultation at the Harvard Medical School by the author, at which time she was again encouraged to try to control her skin temperature in a biofeedback situation. After failing to do so she spontaneously admitted that she was not paying attention to the feedback because she was bored. Although the entire reason for this sudden setback cannot be assessed at present, it does seem that a motivational deficit is involved.

Case 2

Two other investigators have employed temperature feedback in the treatment of Raynaud's phenomena or Raynaud's disease. Peper[18] has reported treating a 50-yr-old woman who had been suffering from what appeared to be Raynaud's disease for about 30 yr. As in the previous case report, this patient was first instructed in relaxation and autogenic techniques before the onset of biofeedback training. Biofeedback training, however, followed a different procedure. Thermistors were placed on both the temporal artery and on the finger of one hand. The net difference between the readings of these two thermistors was used to drive an analogue auditory feedback system. That is, the patient received an auditory signal that varied directly with the temperature difference between the reference thermistor placed on the temporal artery and the thermistor on her finger. The patient was instructed in the use of the auditory feedback device and told to practice with it twice a day for 10 min. After a month of training, the patient's basal skin temperature, as measured on the finger tip, had increased from 75°–85°F. In addition, she reported that for the first time in 30 yr she could hold on to the cold steering wheel of her car without gloves. No systematic follow-up data is available.

Case 3

Working with a similar technique, Jacobson and Hackett[9] have reported success in the alleviation of Raynaud-like symptoms in a 31-yr-old male. The patient had been experiencing these symptoms for the past 4 yr and claimed that they were increasing in severity during the year preceding treatment. The patient was first trained in autohypnosis for relaxation and then given four sessions of differential temperature feedback like that employed by Peper.[18] After this brief treatment, the patient was able to voluntarily produce increases in skin temperature of up to 4.2°C—even outside of the feedback situation. Corresponding color changes, suggesting increased blood flow, were also observed. As in the case reported by Peper,[18] the patient reported that for the first time in years he was able to grasp very cold objects without triggering a vasospasmodic attack. Seven and one-half months after treatment, the patient reported continued relief from Raynaud's symptoms.

Cases 4 and 5

Finally, Shapiro and Schwartz[24] have reported the successful application of biofeedback for a related circulatory problem. Their patient was a 60-yr-old man who had complained of chronic sensations of cold in his hands and feet for 2 yr. Although no signs of vascular disease or specific reaction to cold were found by the examining physician, this patient did complain of increased difficulty in winter months as found in Raynaud's disease. A treatment procedure was devised by using the DC component of a photoplethysmograph for feedback. The photoplethysmograph transducer was attached to the patient's large toes of each foot. Feedback training was conducted for ½-hr sessions four times a week for 3 wk. At first, feedback was given for increases in blood volume in the left toe (where he experienced the most severe discomfort), and later training was done for increases in blood volume in the right toe. One month later, five additional sessions were administered following the same procedure. Although the patient was given no direct autogenic instructions, he reported that he experienced the most success in increasing his blood flow while he imagined experiencing warmth. Through this surreptitiously arrived at strategy, this patient was able to obtain much relief and showed control of his symptoms for approximately a year. Recently, he has requested some further training because he feels he is losing the control he experienced earlier. Unfortunately, the same procedure failed to produce positive results with a second patient. This woman had more severe manifestations of vasospasms and was very ambivalent about this mode of treatment. Upon mutual agreement, treatment was terminated after approximately ten sessions because of lack of progress and sufficient motivation.

CONCLUSIONS

Persuasive though these reports are, it would be premature to conclude that biofeedback was the sole therapeutic agent responsible for improvement. In each case, relaxation and/or autogenic imagery were used by or suggested to the subject in the process of training. In addition, the large amount of attention given to each patient coupled with the enthusiasm of the therapists for this new treatment may have given these procedures considerable placebo value. It is noteworthy, however, that in two cases[9,29] patients specifically reported that they first had to abandon relaxation and autogenic strategies in order to control the feedback. As in biofeedback studies of other physiologic systems, these patients could not verbalize what, if any, strategy they used to control blood flow. Nevertheless, it is clear that carefully controlled investigations must precede any conclusions about the exact contribution biofeedback can provide in the treatment of Raynaud's disease and other peripheral vascular disorders.

As mentioned by Schwartz et al.[21] elsewhere in this symposium, the motivation of the patient is the most crucial variable in the success of any biofeedback therapy. While material extrinsic reinforcers are normally used in biofeedback studies employing normal subjects, the motivational value of the feedback stimulus in clinical application lies in the desire of the patient to improve. This point is well illustrated by an anecdote from the case of Surwit et al.[29] After several weeks of treatment, the patient spontaneously verbalized that she was ambivalent about giving up her symptoms because she had tailored her life-style around them. Counseling and assertive training were then instituted to help the patient acquire more adaptive ways of coping with social situations. Supplemental therapeutic procedures such as these may, therefore, be a necessary part of any comprehensive treatment program involving biofeedback; not only for insuring proper patient motivation, but for remolding the patient's life-style so that stimuli in the environment no longer reinforce the symptom. Although there exists some evidence to suggest that patients suffer Raynaud's attacks in lieu of more adaptive social responses,[6] further research is needed to clarify the importance of these relationships in the treatment of Raynaud's disease.

The optimal physiologic measures to use in a biofeedback treatment for Raynaud's disease would, of course, depend upon the precise physiologic mechanism involved in the disorder. Unfortunately, Raynaud's disease, like essential hypertension, is, by definition, of unknown etiology. Although it is known that during a spasm blood is initially absent in the capillaries,[11] it is not known whether the spasm occurs at the arterial, arteriolar, or capillary level.[32] Langer and Croccel[10] have suggested that arteriovenous anastomoses might play a central role in Raynaud's disease shunting the blood away from the outermost layers of the skin during an attack. If indeed this is true, then skin temperature would not be the measure of choice in a biofeedback treatment procedure. Rapid flow through the arteriovenous anastomoses might heat the finger but leave the affected layers deprived of blood. Indeed, the patient of Surwit et al. reported persistent pain even after her temperature had risen to normal ranges, confirming the earlier observations of Mittlemann and Wolff.[16] If arteriovenous shunting is involved in the production of Raynaud's disease, then a photoplethysmographic measure of surface blood volume might be a better response for feedback than skin temperature in the treatment of this vascular problem.

At our laboratory at the Massachusetts Mental Health Center, the relationship between skin temperature and both A.C. and D.C. photoplethysmographic measures is presently being explored. By recording these functions simultaneously at the same site while giving feedback for one measure at a time, it is hoped that a better understanding of the underlying physiology that governs their operation will emerge. This research, now being carried out with normal subjects, will eventually be extended to Raynaud's patients as well. It is also hoped that similar measurement techniques, employed during both thermal and emotional stimulation, might lead to meaningful diagnostic procedures able to identify the patients who might most benefit from biofeedback training. If, as Mendlowitz and Naftchi[14] have suggested, two groups of Raynaud's patients exist, it is conceivable that biofeedback training might benefit only one. Before these basic physiologic and methodologic problems are solved, one cannot intelligently advocate biofeedback as a reliable alternative to present methods in the treatment of Raynaud's disease. In evaluating the place of biofeedback in the treatment of Raynaud's disease, one must consider the record of conventional treatments now available. Medical-pharmacologic remedies have not been particularly effective in relieving this disorder.[1] Sympathectomy seems to have been equally unreliable, having the added disadvantage of permanent side effects.[20] It might therefore be preferable to attempt biofeedback in lieu of surgery when more conservative techniques have failed.

ACKNOWLEDGMENT

Preparation of this manuscript was supported by NIMH Grant MH-08853 to Dr. David Shapiro and by NIMH Training Grant MH-08934 to Dr. Elliot Mishler. I especially thank Dr. Shapiro for his guidance and helpful comments.

REFERENCES

1. Allen EV, Barker NW, Hines EA Jr.: Peripheral Vascular Diseases (ed 4). Philadelphia, Saunders, 1972, Chap 19
2. Barber TX: LSD, Marihuana, Yoga, and Hypnosis. Chicago, Aldine-Atherton, 1970
3. Barber TX, DiCara LV, Kamiya J, et al (eds): Biofeedback and Self-control 1970. Chicago, Aldine-Atherton, 1971
4. Blain A, Coller FA, Carver GB: Raynaud's disease: A study of criteria for prognosis. Surgery 29:387–397, 1951
5. Brener J: Heart rate as an avoidance response. Psychol Rec 16:329–336, 1966
6. Graham DT: Cutaneous vascular reactions in Raynaud's disease and its states of hostility, anxiety, and depression. Psychosom Med 17:200–207, 1955
7. Graham DT, Stern JA, Winokur G: Experimental investigation of the specificity of the attitude hypothesis in psychosomatic disease. Psychosom Med 20:446–457, 1958
8. Hefferline RF, Keenan B: Amplitude-induction gradient of a small human operant in an escape-avoidance situation. J Exp Anal Behav 4:41–43, 1961
9. Jacobson AM, Hackett TP: Personal communication
10. Langer P, Corccel L: Le Phénomène de Raynaud: Aspects cliniques, etio-pathogeniques et thérapeutiques. Paris, L'Expansion Scientifique Française, 1960
11. Lewis T: Vascular Disorders of the Limbs: Described for Practictioners and Students. London, Macmillan, 1949
12. Lisini MI: The role of orientation in the transformation of involuntary reactions into voluntary ones, in Voronin LG, Leontiev AN, Luria AR, et al (eds): Orienting Reflex and Exploratory Behavior. Washington, DC, American Institute of Biological Sciences, 1965
13. Maslach C, Marshall G, Zimbardo PG: Hypnotic control of peripheral skin temperature: A case report. Psychophysiology 9:600–605, 1972
14. Mendlowitz M, Naftchi N: The digital circulation in Raynaud's disease. Am J Cardiol 4:580–584, 1959
15. Miller NE, Dworkin BR: Visceral learning: Recent difficulties with curarized rats and significant problems for human research, in Obrist PA, Black AH, Brener J, et al (eds): Contemporary Trends in Cardiovascular Psychophysiology. Chicago, Aldine-Atherton, 1973
16. Mittlemann B, Wolff HG: Affective states and skin temperature: Experimental study of subjects with "cold hands" and Raynaud's syndrome. Psychom Med 1:271–292, 1939
17. Mulholland T, Evans CR: Occulomotor-function and the alpha-activation cycle. Nature (London) 211:1278–1279, 1966
18. Peper E: Case report presented at the Second Annual Meeting of the Biofeedback Research Society, 1972
19. Raynaud AGM: De l'Asphyxie Locale et de la Gangrène Symétique des Extrémités. Paris, Rignoux, 1862
20. Ruch TC, Patton HD, Woodbury JW, et al (eds): Neurophysiology (ed 2). Philadelphia, Saunders, 1965
21. Schwartz GE, Shapiro D: Biofeedback and essential hypertension: Current findings

and theoretical concerns. Semin Psychiatry 5:000, 1973

22. Shapiro D, Barber TX, DiCara LV, et al (eds): Biofeedback and Self-control 1972. Chicago, Aldine-Atherton, 1973

23. Shapiro D, Crider A, Tursky B: Differentiation of an autonomic response through operant reinforcement. Psychonom Sci 1: 147–148, 1964

24. Shapiro D, Schwartz GE: Biofeedback and visceral learning: Clinical applications. Semin Psychiatry 4:171–184, 1972

25. Shapiro D, Schwartz GE, Tursky B: Control of diastolic blood pressure in man by feedback and reinforcement. Psychophysiology 9:296–304, 1972

26. Shapiro D, Tursky B, Gershon E, et al: Effects of feedback and reinforcement on the control of human systolic blood pressure. Science 163:588–590, 1969

27. Snyder C, Noble ME: Operant conditioning of vasoconstriction. J Exp Psychol 77:263–268, 1968

28. Stoyva J, Barber TX, DiCara LV, et al (eds): Biofeedback and Self-control 1971. Chicago, Aldine-Atherton, 1972

29. Surwit RS, Bouchard C, Peloquin L, et al: Unpublished case report. McGill University, Montreal, 1972

30. Taub E, Emurian C: Autoregulation of skin temperature using a variable intensity feedback light. Presented at the Second Annual Meeting of the Biofeedback Research Society, 1972

31. Volow MR, Hein PL: Bi-directional operant conditioning of peripheral vasomotor responses with augmented feedback and prolonged training. Presented at the Eleventh Annual Meeting of the Society for Psychophysiological Research, 1971

32. Willerson JT, Thompson RH, Hookman P, et al: Reserpine in Raynaud's disease and phenomenon: Short-term response to intraarterial injection. Ann Intern Med 72:17–27, 1970

33. Wolpe J: Psychotherapy by Reciprocal Inhibition. Stanford, Calif, Stanford Univ Pr, 1958

Chapter 8: Hypertension

Introduction

THIS CHAPTER deals with a very important disorder that is both potentially serious and extraordinarily common, affecting for example 15%–30% of the population of the United States.

It is therefore especially dissappointing that the clinical results in patient trials have so far proven rather discouraging (see page 138), especially in the production of lowered diastolic pressures, which of course are the most important clinically. So far at least, biofeedback has simply not proven very helpful clinically in treating established cases of essential hypertension.

This is speculative, of course, but the results may turn out to be much better as work proceeds and as preventive rather than therapeutic techniques are emphasized. This area seems worthy of research, because it is probably the irreversible deteriorative anatomical changes that occur within the walls of blood vessels when hypertension has been long-established that limit success in the use of biofeedback training to combat essential hypertension. Combining a program of screening and early case finding with preventive biofeedback training for early cases, *before* deteriorative changes in blood vessels have occurred, may yet prove very helpful.

In this attempted application, the target symptom is elevated systolic and diastolic blood pressure, and the criterion response was reduction in systolic/ diastolic pressure. The measuring physiologic instrument is a constant cuff pressure sphygmomenometer. This instrument measures blood pressure by being systematically inflated to a level where 50% of heart beats exceed the cuff pressure. Systolic pressure is measured directly as the cuff pressure at which 50% of the heart beats produce audible Korotkoff sounds. Diastolic pressure is measured by the precise monitoring of cuff oscillations. Two kinds of reinforcing stimuli were used: (1) feedback-type stimuli, beat for beat, in binary (yes–no) form, signaled by specific lights and tones; and (2) reward-type stimuli, in the form of viewing a slide of interest.

The results of this applied to hypertensive patients* can be briefly summarized as follows. (1) Five out of five patients with essential hypertension and elevated systolic pressure levels showed decreases in systolic pressure; these averaged 22 mm Hg over a mean of 26 treatment sessions. (2) Only one out of seven patients with essential hypertension and elevated diastolic pressure responded positively at all to biofeedback training; this one patient showed a progressive reduction in diastolic pressure from 99 to 85 mm Hg.

These results, although somewhat encouraging, are not conclusive. The five patients who apparently responded to biofeedback training to lower their systolic pressures, as Drs. Schwartz and Shapiro point out, in fact might have simply been responding to a process of progressive acclimatization to the lab-

---

*The hypertensive patients in this study were also maintained on their prior drug treatment schedule during the study.

oratory situation over an extended period of time. What is needed for certainty is a demonstration, parallel to the methods of Dr. Engel (see Chapter 6) that biofeedback procedures can make the pressures go *up* as well as down, *and then back down again,* depending on whether feedback is used to reinforce increased or decreased pressures.

The one patient who did apparently respond to diastolic biofeedback training likewise might well be profitably studied with a down-up-down methodology. Also, it would be of interest to have data on the number of months or years he had had a diastolic elevation in comparison to the six patients who did not respond at all.

These early results, summarized above, plus the possibility of developing a useful preventive technique, warrant further research.

Lee Birk, M.D.

Biofeedback and Essential Hypertension: Current Findings and Theoretical Concerns

Gary E. Schwartz, Ph.D., and David Shapiro, Ph.D.

When normotensive and hypertensive subjects are provided with feedback for relative increases or decreases in blood pressure and rewarded for these changes, they can learn to exert some control over their pressure. Biofeedback research on self-regulation of systolic and diastolic pressure, heart rate, and patterns of these functions is reviewed, and a general model of pattern learning is described. Application of these techniques to the control of systolic and diastolic pressure in patients diagnosed with essential hypertension are presented and critically analyzed. Problems of expectancy and motivation, personality and life-style, and biologic constraints are emphasized. It is concluded that biofeedback techniques should be viewed as only one part of a combined behavioral treatment program for hypertensive patients.

ESTIMATED TO AFFECT between 15% and 30% of the U.S. population, high blood pressure is a serious medical problem. Concern with hypertension is largely due to its association with increased risk of coronary artery disease and cerebrovascular accidents,[20,21] the major causes of death in the U.S. today.[44] Between 90% and 95% of all cases of hypertension have no known etiology and are labeled "essential." The systematic application of behavioral theory and methods to the study of essential hypertension has occurred relatively recently, even though environmental factors have been long suspected of having an important etiologic role.[15]

For more than 6 yr our laboratories have been concerned with the application of feedback and reward procedures to the self-regulation of blood pressure and other cardiovascular responses in healthy human subjects and patients with essential hypertension. The purpose of this paper is to review and evaluate these data and also to consider current theoretical and practical issues in light of other findings. Included are new data on attempts to train patients with essential hypertension to lower their diastolic pressure using biofeedback techniques.

MEASUREMENT OF BLOOD PRESSURE

In order to provide subjects with feedback for small changes in blood pressure, it is necessary to be able to easily and reliably measure pressure on each beat of the heart. Direct arterial catheterization is not amenable for routine and repetitive laboratory training with human subjects, so alternative monitoring procedures are necessary. After evaluation of various sphygmomanometer techniques, a new system was developed using a constant cuff pressure proce-

---

Supported by the Milton Fund and the Spencer Fund of Harvard University; the Advanced Research Projects Agency of the Department of Defense and monitored by the Office of Naval Research under Contract N00014-70-C-0350 to the San Diego State University Foundation; NIMH Grant MH-08853; Research Scientist Award MH-20476; Office of Naval Research Contract N00014-67-A-0024; and USPHS Grant 5 R01 HL 14486-02.

Reprint requests should be addressed to Dr. Gary E. Schwartz, Department of Psychology and Social Relations, Harvard University, 1444 William James Hall, Cambridge, Mass. 02138.

© 1973 by Grune & Stratton, Inc.

dure.[38,43] The reader is referred to Tursky[42] and Benson[3] for recent reviews of blood pressure recording procedures in humans.

Briefly, a blood pressure cuff is wrapped around the upper arm and a microphone is placed at the distal end under the cuff over the brachial artery. If the cuff is inflated to approximately average systolic pressure and held there, whenever systolic pressure rises and exceeds the cuff pressure following a given heart contraction, blood will be forced through the artery under the cuff and a Korotkoff sound will be heard. Conversely, for those heart beats followed by a systolic peak pressure that is less than the occluding pressure of the cuff, blood will not flow through the artery and a Korotkoff sound will not be heard. Using regulated pressure sources and solid state programming equipment, it is possible to establish automatically the cuff pressure at which 50% of the beats are above the pressure in the cuff and 50% are below. This, by definition, is median systolic pressure and corresponds within 2 mm Hg to median pressures obtained using direct arterial catheterization.[43]

Typically, the cuff is inflated for 50 heart beats and then deflated for 30–45 sec to allow blood flow and eliminate discomfort and potential artifacts. The period of inflation consititutes a trial. If the subject raises or lowers his average systolic pressure in a given trial by more than 2 mm Hg, this will correspondingly increase or decrease the percentage of Korotkoff sounds by about 25%. The percentage of Korotkoff sounds in a trial determines how the pressure should be set for the next trial, thus making it possible to track median pressure over trials. Normally the cuff pressure is raised or lowered by 2 mm Hg for ± 25% changes in Korotkoff sounds, and 4 mm Hg for ± 50% changes. The system also provides information on relative changes in pressure on each successive beat of the heart.

In the studies, subjects are provided with binary (yes–no) feedback in the form of lights and tones whenever a coincidence (R spike of EKG plus Korotkoff sound within 300 msec) or anticoincidence (R spike and no Korotkoff sound) occur, depending upon the experimental condition. At median systolic pressure, a coincidence, or presence of Korotkoff sound, indicates a relative increase in pressure; an anticoincidence or absence of Korotkoff sound indicates a relative decrease in pressure. After producing a certain number of such "feedback stimuli," subjects earn a reward in the form of a slide. In normotensive subjects, depending upon the particular experiment, the slides have been landscapes of Boston, pictures from around the world, photos of nude females, and monetary bonuses. In working with hypertensive patients, motivation becomes an important problem, one not easily solved using simple extrinsic rewards.

Before considering the data, it is important to indicate how the concepts of feedback and reward, voluntary control and conditioning are used here, especially in view of previous confusion arising in the literature concerning definition of terms and theoretical interpretations (e.g., Crider et al.[11] and Katkin and Murray[22]). The distinction between feedback and reward is viewed more as a continuum involving the extent of intrinsic incentive value in the stimulus. In the binary feedback–reward procedure described above, the feedback and reward each contain comparable information value about changes in blood pressure. Whether the reward is more "rewarding" than the feedback depends on their relative degree of incentive value for a given subject. One can, however, experimentally separate information components from incentive. For example, in ongoing basic research in our laboratories, subjects receive binary feedback, but the reward is now contingent upon changes in cuff pressure rather than on the number of feedbacks *per se*. Hence the "feedback" reflects phasic (beat by beat) changes while the "reward" is for more tonic changes in pressure.

From a procedural point of view, operant conditioning is simply defined as an experimental technique where the information and incentive value are contained in the same stimulus (the reinforcer). However, to the extent that feedback terminology is more physiologic in nature and more consistent with control theory of biologic machines, it has definite advantages.[9,31]

The distinction between voluntary control and conditioning as *processes* may also be viewed in terms of a continuum, from self-directed to environmentally controlled behavior. From a clinical point of view, the general goal is twofold: to teach patients self-control of their pressure and ultimately have it become habitual and automatic. Therefore, this goal incorporates the common meanings of both voluntary control and conditioning.

SELF-REGULATION OF BLOOD PRESSURE AND HEART RATE: BASIC RESEARCH

Not knowing whether voluntary control of blood pressure was feasible, the initial studies were concerned with whether healthy college students could learn to increase and decrease their systolic blood pressure using the constant cuff pressure system.[38,39] To control for possible complications due to differential instructions and experimenter bias,[29] all subjects were given the same general instructions indicating that their task was to learn how to make the feedback occur as often as possible. They were not told the response was their blood pressure, nor were they told what direction it was to change. The data indicated that (1) subjects could learn to relatively increase or decrease their blood pressure with feedback; (2) systolic pressure changes appeared independent of heart rate, and (3) subjects could not consciously tell which experimental condition they were in, as indicated by interviews and questionnaires—that is, they revealed no consistent cognitive strategies reflecting, for example, a simple "relaxation-tension" dimension.

Although many questions were raised by these first studies, it became clear that the choice of "base-line" values was critical in evaluating relative degree of learned increases and decreases (see also Crider et al.[11]). It has often been assumed that resting values obtained at the beginning of a session will remain constant over the session. In some situations, however, increases will occur due to the arousing nature of the stimuli and the task itself. Or, subjects may habituate to the experimental situation, producing a natural decrease in blood pressure. For example, when a group was included that was given identical stimuli and instructions, but for whom the feedback was in fact randomly related to systolic pressure,[39] the correct feedback for increases or decreases led to *relative* control of blood pressure *vis-à-vis* the declining "base-line" values. While the initial curves had suggested that decreases in pressure were easier to obtain, an opposite conclusion may be drawn when correct base-line estimates are used.

The question of appropriate base lines and range of possible values per individual therefore becomes paramount in evaluating clinical effects.[31]

A follow-up study was designed to explore further the dissociation of blood pressure and heart rate and the nature of the subjective experience in self-regulation. Subjects were given the identical binary feedback and reward paradigm, except that feedback and reward was given for increases or decreases in heart rate, while systolic pressure was simultaneously monitored.[40] Under these conditions, subjects learned to increase and decrease their heart rate without differentially affecting their systolic pressure. Again, postexperimental interviews did not reveal any consistent cognitive or somatic processes that distinguished the groups. Subgroup analyses were made of the best learners in both the heart rate control study and in the earlier blood pressure study to further evaluate specificity of learning. Again there was no indication of simultaneous learning in both functions.

Although these data were encouraging from a clinical point of view in suggesting that biofeedback might be used to treat specific symptoms,[36] they did not explain why specificity should occur, nor what the possible constraints might be. A series of studies on the measurement and control of patterns of blood pressure and heart rate were undertaken to provide some answers to these questions.[32-34,37] Schwartz[32] hypothesized that when feedback is given for one response, simultaneous learning of any other response will depend on several factors. One factor is the precise nature of the relation of other responses to the response controlling the feedback (e.g., if two responses were always waxing and waning together, then feedback for one would result in identical feedback for the other as well, and therefore both should show learning and change and in the same direction). The other factor concerns potential biologic constraints that can affect the interrelation of the responses. This analysis suggests that learned specificity will occur to the extent that multi-responses are randomly related over time and that the systems are biologically capable of separating.

A system was developed for tracking both phasic and tonic patterns of blood pressure and heart rate in real time (e.g., isolating $BP^{up}\ HR^{up}$, $BP^{up}\ HR_{down}$, $BP_{down}\ HR^{up}$, $BP_{down}\ HR_{down}$ responses at each heart beat). To test the hypothesis that pattern learning is possible, subjects were given feedback and reward for each of the four possible patterns. The results showed that subjects readily learned to integrate these responses; in fact, feedback for $BP^{up}\ HR^{up}$ or $BP_{down}\ HR_{down}$ led to more rapid learning and produced somewhat larger effects in *both* responses than the earlier feedback for either one alone.[32,33] In addition, subjects were able to voluntarily differentiate these responses, although this proved to be more difficult, especially for the $BP^{up}\ HR_{down}$ pattern.[32] Analysis of the phasic patterns confirmed that each of the four patterns was equally likely, thus explaining the earlier specificity findings. In addition, by carefully analyzing the natural tonic reactivity in this situation, it was possible to predict the extent and time course of learning for each of the four conditions.

Interestingly, despite the fact that these subjects were relatively uninformed, analysis of the subjective report data showed that subjects became more relaxed as they learned to lower *both* their systolic pressure and heart rate.[32]

To the extent that general relaxation is a pattern of decreases in many physiologic systems simultaneously, it is reasonable to assume that decreases in both blood pressure and heart rate will be more associated with subjective relaxation than decreases in either one alone.

In current work on the voluntary control of diastolic pressure, the usefulness of this strategy has been supported. When subjects are given feedback and reward for changes in diastolic pressure, some learning in heart rate also occurs.[37] Analysis of natural phasic integration reveals that these two responses are partially, but not completely integrated. This can explain why heart rate shows some learning, but not as much as is obtained when only heart rate feedback is used. Taking into account base-line constraints and physiologic considerations, it has been possible to predict the degree to which subjects can learn to voluntarily integrate and differentiate their diastolic pressure and heart rate.[34]

Space does not allow a more detailed presentation of the theory and data (see Schwartz[30,31]). However, brief mention of their clinical implications is in order. First is that the simple notion of symptom treatment as employed in behavior therapy may be in error; more careful analysis of patterns reflecting underlying physiologic causes may be needed to utilize feedback more efficiently. For example, in disorders such as angina pectoris, where it is desirable to lower both blood pressure and heart rate,[8] direct feedback for BP_{down} HR_{down} patterns may be in order. Further, since blood pressure reflects the sum total of multi-cardiovascular factors operating at the same time, then exactly which component of the pressure is selected for feedback will influence the degree to which different underlying mechanisms are receiving contingent feedback. Therefore, if it is desirable for certain patients to reduce their peripheral resistance, but feedback is given for small, phasic changes in diastolic pressure, the patient may well be receiving feedback for heart rate-mediated changes, and therefore not learn to control the peripheral factors directly. If the patient becomes "confused" with partially inaccurate feedback, more direct feedback procedures may be required, either singly or in patterns.

On the side of biologic constraints, it is reasonable to assume that to the extent that chronic pathology is present (e.g., in atherosclerosis), self-regulation of neural and hormonal processes may have little effect, at least in the short run. One possible predictor of clinical success with biofeedback may be the extent to which the system is labile and biologically capable of change (e.g., by comparing responses during sleep, exercise, relaxation, and different conditions of environmental stimulation).

CONTROL OF SYSTOLIC PRESSURE IN ESSENTIAL HYPERTENSION

The jump from normotensive college students to hypertensive patients was stimulated in part by operant conditioning experiments with primates. High blood pressure was found to be associated with operant schedules that continuously exerted strong control over the animals' behavior.[16] Chronic high blood pressure was also achieved in other experiments where avoidance of shock was made directly dependent on increased arterial pressures.[4] Further, in these same experiments, blood pressure levels could be reduced to normotensive levels when avoidance of shock was made dependent on decreased pressure. In light of this research in monkeys, the constant cuff pressure feedback technique was applied to patients diagnosed with essential hypertension.[6] Seven patients were studied for five to 16 control sessions during which time stable median systolic pressure was obtained under quiet resting conditions. All patients then received daily feedback sessions for decreasing systolic pressure until no further reductions in blood pressure occured in five consecutive sessions. For the period of the study, all patients were maintained on their prior drug schedule. The results showed that the five patients diagnosed with essential hypertension responded positively to the treatment, showing decreases of 34, 29, 16, 16, and 17 mm Hg with 33, 22, 34, 31, and 12 sessions of training, respectively. Of the other two patients, one did not have elevated systolic pressure and the other had renal artery stenosis with normal renin levels; neither showed significant decreases in pressure.

Although these findings are encouraging, they are only a beginning, and many questions need to be answered before their clinical value can be decided. Despite the fact that extensive control pressures were taken before the feedback sessions, it could be argued that decreases might have also occurred if more resting sessions were used. Furthermore, the novelty of the experimental situation plus expectancy effects may have operated as a "placebo" treatment, and therefore the role of the feedback itself can be questioned. On the other hand, it is hypothesized* that expectancy effects, particularly in behavioral therapies where practice on the part of the patient is necessary for successful outcome, are an essential ingredient for effective therapy.[36] It is conceivable that feedback *plus* suggestion effects can act synergistically, thereby producing larger effects than either alone,[45] although this remains to be demonstrated in a clinical setting.

Other questions that can be raised include: (1) Can patients learn to control their pressure without feedback? Shapiro, Schwartz and Tursky[37] have provided some positive data for this in normal subjects. (2) Will their pressures be lower in the stressful environment outside of the quiet of the laboratory? Pressure taken outside the laboratory in two of the patients studied suggested that this was possible, although the data are not complete enough to draw conclusions at this time. Recently, Sirota, Schwartz, and Shapiro[41] have found that subjects can voluntarily lower their heart rate in anticipation of a stressful stimulus. Furthermore, heart rate slowing through biofeedback and instructions can reduce the perceived noxiousness of the stimulus. Whether hypertensive patients can learn to voluntarily lower their pressure under stressful conditions remains to be demonstrated.

As described by Shapiro and Schwartz,[36] motivation is an important component for success in any form of psychotherapy (both in and out of the therapy situation) and this particularly applies to patients with essential hypertension. Unlike patients who suffer from psychologic problems such as phobia or psychosomatic disorders such as tension headache, patients with

---

*Editor's note: This need not be merely hypothesized; rather, it has in fact been demonstrated, and even studied quantitatively, (see Chapter 3) by Dr. Stroebel, on the interaction of effects mediated by suggestion vs. those by autonomic learning.

essential hypertension typically experience little or no discomfort from their condition. Thus, motivation for change is based on physicians' "threats" that serious problems may arise *in the future* if they do not take care of themselves. Given the difficulty in getting patients to take medication reliably, it would not be surprising if prolonged biofeedback training in and of itself had little long-term clinical value. When the patient with a tension headache reduces his frontalis tension with biofeedback,[10] the reward in terms of relief from pain is relatively immediate and strong; unfortunately, the hypertensive patient experiences little of this.

Further discussion and examples of these and related issues can be found in Schwartz[30,31] and Shapiro.[35]

VOLUNTARY CONTROL OF DIASTOLIC PRESSURE IN ESSENTIAL HYPERTENSION

Based on the findings for systolic blood pressure, in collaboration with H. Benson at the Boston City Hospital, we have recently completed a study using biofeedback for diastolic pressure in seven patients diagnosed with essential hypertension. The basic constant cuff pressure system was employed, although the Korotkoff sound was replaced with cuff oscillations[3] to improve across-session comparisons within subjects. Each patient was studied for either 15 or 20 separate sessions. No instructions or feedback were given during the first five sessions (resting base-line period). During the next five sessions, the patients were asked to "think pleasant thoughts and relax" in order to lower their pressure and they were rewarded for total decrease in pressure at the end of the sessions. Again, no feedback was employed. However, during the next five sessions, information about the level of average blood pressure was fed back to the patients after *each* cuff inflation, and monetary reward was directly related to the decrease in median diastolic pressure. Hence, rather than giving feedback for phasic diastolic changes, tonic changes in level were used instead. In these five sessions, the patients were informed only about decreases in pressure. In the final five sessions, information about increases as well as decreases in tonic diastolic pressure was provided.

The results for these patients proved to be discouraging. Compared to the resting condition average of 102 mm Hg, the remaining three conditions of the experiment yielded average pressures of 104, 102, and 102 mm Hg, respectively. Only one of the patients responded positively, showing a progressive reduction in diastolic blood pressure from 99–85 mm Hg.

Although it is possible to argue that the feedback and reward procedure was not optimal, this is tempered by the fact that *within*-session decreases during the two feedback conditions yielded statistically significant decreases in diastolic pressure of 5 mm Hg. This is comparable to the within-session differences in systolic pressure found in the previous patient group.[6] The latter group showed across-session tonic effects as well. Further, the within-session decreases observed in patients given diastolic-level feedback were twice the magnitude as the within-session decreases observed in normal subjects given diastolic phasic binary feedback.[37] Although other hypotheses can be offered, the one favored at the moment is that in chronic hypertension, diastolic pressure becomes relatively fixed due to chronic changes in the vascular beds leading to increased peripheral resistance. To the extent that systolic pressure is still governed in part by sympathetic nervous system activity resulting in increased cardiac contractility, this neural component may be more readily self-regulated through biofeedback techniques. If substantiated by hemodynamic studies, this would suggest that biofeedback (and other techniques) aimed at lowering sympathetic activity in labile hypertensive patients with increased cardiac output may be the most fruitful direction in which to move.

THE PLACE OF BIOFEEDBACK IN ESSENTIAL HYPERTENSION TREATMENT

If biofeedback is conceptualized as but one possible procedure in therapy, then its potential role can be viewed in perspective. It is now apparent that the procedure is only as "powerful" as the patient allows it to be. Further, to the degree that hypertension is mediated by complex factors including genetics, diet, smoking, behavioral and social stress, plus maladaptive coping mechanisms on the part of the patient, it becomes clear that voluntary control of pressure *per se* will in most cases be limited.

Physiologically, early hypertension is associated with increased cardiac output.[13] From the behavioral side, Gutmann and Benson[15] suggest that the pattern of responses in labile hypertension reflects a repeatedly activated "fight or flight" reaction, related to stressful environmental events that require continuous behavioral adjustment. This preparation for somatic action is not unlike anticipation of active exercise,[27] and not surprisingly it involves increased muscle tension in preparation for aggression or withdrawal. Clinicians have noted that patients with essential hypertension appear as a group to be overly inhibited in expression of anger and anxiety,[1] and these individual differences continue to emerge in current personality research,[28] although writers disagree as to their etiologic significance because of the present lack of prospective studies.[15] Inducing attitudes of constantly being on guard for danger leads to increased pressure (see Graham[14]). Hokanson and colleagues[18] have empirically demonstrated that if normal subjects are angered, their pressure rises and remains high unless they are able to express their aggression. This observation is consistent with cardiovascular research showing that isometric tension leads to sustained elevations in pressure, while isotonic action has less of a pressure-increasing effect, and sometimes may lead to a relative decrease in pressure.[25] Also consistent with this is the common clinical observation that exercise programs (e.g., jogging) sometimes have beneficial effects on high blood pressure, although little systematic research has been performed to date evaluating these claims.

Based on these observations, it would seem fruitful to explore techniques attempting to (1) reduce sympathetic activity in aggressive–anxiety situations by teaching patients to relax somatically; (2) teach patients how to recognize anger–fear situations and express their feelings in a psychologically and physiologically adaptive fashion; and (3) teach patients how to possibly avoid such situations, or change their environment so as to minimize them. Concerning the first factor, techniques include progressive relaxation,[19] autogenic training,[26] certain forms of yoga,[12] and transcendental meditation,[5,7] all of which claim to produce general relaxation that leads to reductions in high blood pressure. In addition, techniques like transcendental meditation claim to reduce anxiety and aggressive tendencies as well, and Schwartz and Goleman have recently found evidence for these changes in the personality of meditators (unpublished data). Of course, direct biofeedback training for muscle relaxation could be very useful in lowering high blood pressure, as recently observed by Mueller and Love (unpublished data).

Concerning the second factor, desensitization procedures and particularly assertive training[46] might be efficiently used to help patients learn how to express their aggressive feelings. Modeling and role-playing situations[2] might also be used to extend this further. To the extent that meditation techniques actually improve one's ability to recognize one's feelings and those of others,[24] these procedures might provide additional benefits. As for the last factor, this requires a change in the patient's motivation and life-style, and various forms of behavioral and verbal psychotherapy might be useful.

Where then does blood pressure biofeedback *per se* come in? This becomes an empirical question. Our hypothesis is that a combined treatment approach (e.g., using both relaxation training *and* direct blood pressure control techniques) may be better than either alone to the extent that the latter directs one's attention to the aberrant system and possibly increases one's awareness and control of it,[9] although it is possible that relaxation alone may be sufficient. Here, the feedback is being used primarily in a "control" sense to help the person develop more direct control over his blood pressure.

On the other hand, biofeedback can also be used as information or as a "monitor," not to be directly controlled but rather as an indicant of success in other spheres. Schwartz[30] has noted that in the same way that a scale helps the obese patient and therapist evaluate success in controlling food intake and/or exercise in order to reduce weight, so can biofeedback be used for pressure changes. By means of the feedback, the patient can learn to recognize what kinds of thoughts, feelings, situations, and actions lead to increased pressure, and how successful he is in changing his life-style and/or environment in order to reduce the pressure. Although it is difficult and expensive to accurately measure pressures in ambulatory patients (e.g., Hinman et al.[17]), less sophisticated procedures might be usefully employed, such as having patients keep track of their pressures throughout the day using a simple self-administered sphygmomanometer procedure. In this way, the patient can learn to utilize any cognitive or somatic "mediator" at his disposal to help him control his pressure.

In his recent textbook, Lachman[23] suggests that some of the major goals of psychotherapy with psychosomatic disorders are as follows:

> (1) To help the individual recognize the role of emotion in the development and precipitation of illness generally and of his illness in particular.
>
> (2) To help the individual identify particular—or at least probable—emotion-arousing situations and conflicts that operate for him.
>
> (3) To assist the patient in acquiring control over overt activities associated with emotional arousal. This includes not only training the individual to recognize emotional situations, but also training him to avoid such situations and, if they are encountered, to deal constructively with them. It also includes directing overt behavior toward reducing or dissipating the energy

resources and other physiological products generated by emotional reactivity, and directing behavior toward constructive activities and away from destructive responses.

(4) To achieve modification in amplitude, duration, and frequency of deviations of autonomic reactions from pathogenic values to normal or optimal levels.

(5) To help the individual to acquire, insofar as possible, direct control of his own autonomic reactions. (pp. 177–178)

Traditionally, biofeedback has been seen as primarily affecting the fifth goal. It is suggested that feedback can be used in the other four goals as well. However, it would appear that for psychosomatic problems—especially for disorders such as hypertension—combined procedures attacking the problem at many levels will be necessary to produce meaningful and long-lasting clinical effects.

ACKNOWLEDGMENT

We thank H. Benson for his helpful comments and S. Cronan for typing the manuscript.

REFERENCES

1. Alexander F: Psychosomatic Medicine: Its Principles and Applications. New York, Norton, 1950

2. Bandura A: Principles of Behavior Modification. New York, Holt, Rinehart & Winston, 1969

3. Benson H: Methods of blood pressure recording: 1733 to 1971, in Onesti G, Kim KE, Moyer JH (eds): Hypertension: Mechanisms and Management. New York, Grune & Stratton, (in press)

4. Benson H, Herd JA, Morse WH, et al: Behavioral induction of arterial hypertension and its reversal. Am J Physiol 217:30, 1969

5. Benson H, Rosner BA, Marzetta BR: Decreased systolic blood pressure in hypertensive subjects who practiced meditation (abstract). J Clin Invest (in press)

6. Benson H, Shapiro D, Tursky B, et al: Decreased systolic blood pressure through operant conditioning techniques in patients with essential hypertension. Science 173:740, 1971

7. Benson H, Wallace K: Decreased blood pressure in hypertensive patients who practiced meditation (abstract). Circulation 46:II-130, 1972

8. Braunwald E, Epstein SE, Glick G, et al: Relief of angina pectoris by electrical stimulation of the carotid-sinus nerves. N Engl J Med 227:1278, 1967

9. Brener J: A general model of voluntary control applied to the phenomena of learned cardiovascular change, in Obrist PA, Black AH, Brener J, et al (eds): Cardiovascular Psychophysiology. Chicago, Aldine (in press)

10. Budzynski T, Stoyva J, Adler C: Feedback-induced muscle relaxation: Application to tension headache. J Behav Ther Exp Psychiatry 1:205, 1970

11. Crider A, Schwartz GE, Shnidman SR: On the criteria for instrumental autonomic conditioning: A reply to Katkin and Murray. Psychol Bull 71:455, 1969

12. Datey KK, Deshmuk SN, Dalvi CP, et al: "Shavasan": A Yogic exercise in the management of hypertension. Angiology 20:325, 1969

13. Eich RH, Cuddy RP, Smulyan H, et al: Hemodynamics in labile hypertension. Circulation 34:299, 1966

14. Graham DT: Psychosomatic medicine, in Greenfield HS, Sternbach RA (eds): Handbook of Psychophysiology. New York, Holt, Rinehart & Winston, 1972

15. Gutmann MC, Benson H: Interaction of environmental factors and systemic arterial blood pressure: A review. Medicine 50:543, 1971

16. Herd JA, Morse WH, Kelleher RT, et al: Arterial hypertension in the squirrel monkey during behavioral experiments. Am J Physiol 217:24, 1969

17. Hinman AT, Engel BT, Bickford AF: Portable blood pressure recorder: Accuracy and preliminary use in evaluating intradaily variations in pressure. Am Heart J 63:663, 1962

18. Hokanson JE, Burgess M, Cohen MF: Effects of displaced aggression on systolic blood pressure. J Abnorm Soc Psychol 67:214, 1963

19. Jacobson E: Progressive Relaxation. Chicago, Univ of Chicago Pr, 1938

20. Kannel WB, Dawber TR, Kagan A, et al: Factors of risk in the development of coronary heart disease. Ann Intern Med 55:33, 1961

21. Kannel WB, Schwartz MJ, McNamara PM: Blood pressure risk of coronary heart disease: The Framingham study. Dis Chest 56:43, 1969

22. Katkin ES, Murray EN: Instrumental conditioning of autonomically mediated behavior: Theoretical and methodological issues. Psychol Bull 70:52, 1968

23. Lachman SJ: Psychosomatic Disorders: A Behavioristic Interpretation. New York, Wiley, 1972

24. Lesh TV: Zen meditation and the development of empathy in counselors. J Hum Psychol 10:39, 1970

25. Lind AR, Taylor SH, Humphreys PW, et al: The circulatory effects of sustained voluntary muscle contraction. Clin Sci 27:229, 1964

26. Luthe W: Autogenic training: Method, research and application in medicine. Am J Psychother 17:174, 1963

27. Obrist PA, Webb RA, Sutterer JR, et al: The cardiac-somatic relationship: Some reformulations. Psychophysiology 6:569, 1970

28. Pilowsky I, Spalding D, Shaw J, et al: Hypertension and personality. Psychosom Med 35:50, 1973

29. Rosenthal R: Experimenter Effects in Behavioral Research. New York, Appleton-Century-Crofts, 1966

30. Schwartz GE: Biofeedback as therapy: Some theoretical and practical issues. Am Psychol 28:666, 1973

31. Schwartz GE: Toward a theory of voluntary control of response patterns in the cardiovascular system, in Obrist PA, Black AH, Brener J, et al (eds): Cardiovascular Psychophysiology. Chicago, Aldine (in press)

32. Schwartz GE: Voluntary control of human cardiovascular integration and differentiation through feedback and reward. Science 175:90, 1972

33. Schwartz GE, Shapiro D, Tursky B: Learned control of cardiovascular integration in man through operant conditioning. Psychosom Med 33:57, 1971

34. Schwartz GE, Shapiro D, Tursky B: Self-control of patterns of human diastolic blood pressure and heart rate through feedback and reward (abstract). Psychophysiology 9:270, 1972

35. Shapiro D: Operant-feedback control of human blood pressure: Some clinical issues, in Obrist PA, Black AH, Brener J, et al (eds): Cardiovascular Psychophysiology. Chicago, Aldine (in press)

36. Shapiro D, Schwartz GE: Biofeedback and visceral learning: Clinical applications. Semin Psychiatry 4:171, 1972

37. Shapiro D, Schwartz GE, Tursky B: Control of diastolic blood pressure in man by feedback and reinforcement. Psychophysiology 9:296, 1972

38. Shapiro D, Tursky B, Gershon E, et al: Effects of feedback and reinforcement on the control of human systolic blood pressure. Science 163:588, 1969

39. Shapiro D, Tursky B, Schwartz GE: Control of blood pressure in man by operant conditioning. Circ Res 26, 27:27 (Suppl 1), 1970

40. Shapiro D, Tursky B, Schwartz GE: Differentiation of heart rate and blood pressure in man by operant conditioning. Psychosom Med 32:417, 1970

41. Sirota A, Schwartz GE, Shapiro D: Effects of feedback control of heart rate on judgments of electric shock intensity (abstract), in Shapiro D, Barber TX, DiCara LV, et al (eds): Biofeedback and Self Control 1972: An Aldine Annual on the Self Regulation of Physiological Processes and Consciousness. Chicago, Aldine, 1973

42. Tursky B: The indirect recording of human blood pressure, in Obrist PA, Black AH, Brener J, et al (eds): Contemporary Trends in Cardiovascular Psychophysiology. Chicago, Aldine (in press)

43. Tursky B, Shapiro D, Schwartz GE: Automated constant cuff-pressure system for measuring average systolic and diastolic blood pressure in man. IEEE Trans Biomed Eng 19:271, 1972

44. United States Department of Health, Education and Welfare, Vital Statistics, vol 2, part A. Washington, DC, Government Printing Office, 1967, p 1

45. Walsh DH: Effects of instructional set, reinforcement and individual differences in EEG alpha feedback training (abstract), in Shapiro D, Barber TX, DiCara LV, et al (eds): Biofeedback and Self Control 1972: An Aldine Annual on the Self Regulation of Physiological Processes and Consciousness. Chicago, Aldine, 1973

46. Wolpe J: Psychotherapy by Reciprocal Inhibition. Stanford, Conn, Stanford Univ Pr, 1958

Chapter 9: Epilepsy

Introduction

LIKE CHAPTER 6, this unavoidably is a technically difficult chapter for the non-physician, or even the non-neurologist.

It is, however, of great theoretical and practical interest—of great theoretical interest because the target organ for biofeedback in this study is the brain itself; of great practical interest because all four of the epileptic patients in this very long and laborious pilot study improved quite significantly and remained improved while biofeedback training sessions continued. (They remained improved, however, only as long as the biofeedback training sessions were continued.)

Dr. Sterman (see page 164) expressed his surprise that continued biofeedback training turned out to be important to maintain the observed therapeutic effect, to a degree that is much more true than in the case of tension headache, for example, or migraine headache. One possible explanation for this might lie in the fact that seizure activity, and perhaps also even preseizure activity, seems frequently to be inherently reinforcing,* whereas the pain of headache in and of itself is punishing.

In this application, devised for the treatment of patients with epilepsy, the target symptom is reduction in the seizure and preseizure activity of the brain. The measuring physiologic instrument is an electroencephalogram, or EEG, measuring the electrical activity of the brain. An unusual feature is the use of the discrete, easily recognizable 12–14 cps† "sensorimotor rhythm" or SMR of the brain as a competitive response evidently inimical to seizure activity. The criterion response, then, was the production of the seizure-inhibiting 12–14 cps SMR activity. The reinforcing stimuli were complex mixtures of visual and auditory feedback; this was in the form of the illumination of one of a row (the top row) of ten lamps, plus the concomitant sounding of a single chime, after each criterion response. Also each ten criterion responses (which illuminated the entire top row of lamps) activated, successively, the lamps in the bottom row, accompanied by the sounding of a double chime. In addition, several other feedback modes were variably employed, depending on patient preference, so as to achieve optimal training from each patient: (1) a single large lamp display that glowed in intensity as a direct function of the amount of appropriate EEG signal generated; and (2) a slide projector that presented sequential pictures on a screen in front of the patient, one picture for each criterion response: the sequences either depicted nature scenes, or provided for the sequential completion of picture puzzles.

Dr. Sterman's results, even though he reports on the treatment of only four epileptic patients, are very impressive indeed, as even a brief inspection of Table 1 (page 155) will reveal. The fact that surprised him, namely that cessation of biofeedback training for all these patients within 6 wk resulted in a clinical

---

*It is not rare, for example, for some epileptic patients to self-induce seizures on purpose.
†cps, cycles per second.

regression toward pretreatment levels, reversible by the reinstitution of biofeedback training, only adds a feeling of certainty to the conviction that here we are dealing with a real demonstrable and repeatable phenomenon, as well as a phenomenon apparently of significant therapeutic value.

Lee Birk, M.D.

Neurophysiologic and Clinical Studies of Sensorimotor EEG Biofeedback Training: Some Effects on Epilepsy

M.B. Sterman, Ph.D.

THE ALPHA RHYTHM, once hailed as "the wave of the future," has proved somewhat disappointing as a bioelectric phenomenon in operant conditioning experiments. The so-called "alpha state," which was initially advertised as a unique and pleasant mind trip, has not been unequivocally endorsed, and at least some subjects have found it to be clearly undesirable.[2,24] Questions have been raised also in relation to the degree of learning achieved in biofeedback studies of the alpha rhythm. While evidence indicates that subjects can learn to increase or decrease the amount of alpha activity with feedback,[15,19] it has proved impossible, thus far, to produce levels exceeding those that occur spontaneously during intervening rest periods (Lynch and Paskewitz[18]). Additionally, it has been suggested that other physiological responses mediate the EEG changes observed, and that instructional set is just as effective as biofeedback in altering alpha production.[3,18] Moreover, it is clear today that there are at least three semi-independent foci of alpha rhythm activity on the human cerebrum that could each be related to a different brain process.[16] Some of the more subtle conceptual and technical problems in this area have been discussed in depth recently by Black.[4]

These problems need not dampen our enthusiasm about the eventual utility of EEG biofeedback training. In fact, it is possible to identify neuroelectric patterns that can be associated directly with specific neural processes. Furthermore, the use of biofeedback techniques can significantly increase the occurrence of these patterns, thereby modifying the behavioral functions they mediate. Our laboratory has been involved in studies of this nature for the past 6 yr. I will attempt to review some of our more salient findings in this regard, and to show how our basic animal research studies have led to a new approach in the treatment of epilepsy.

In the past, we had utilized electrophysiologic recording and stimulation techniques in the cat for the study of brain mechanisms related to sleep. In one particular investigation, pairs of small electrodes had been placed on the dura over several functionally defined cortical regions. Among these was the sensorimotor area, consisting of the region adjacent to the cruciate (central) sulcus in the cat. Recordings from these localized electrodes in the behaving animal disclosed several different rhythmic EEG patterns specific to a given cortical area, and associated uniformly with certain classes of behavior.[20] Of particular interest in this regard was a 12–14-cps rhythm appearing over sensorimotor cortex during the voluntary suppression of movement.[26,27,28] We felt that this rhythm

---

Reprint requests should be addressed to Dr. M.B. Sterman, Neuropsychology Research, Veterans Administration Hospital, Sepulveda, Calif. 91343.

© *1973 by Grune & Stratton, Inc.*

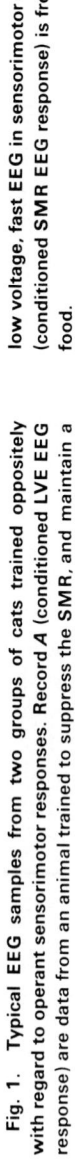

Fig. 1. Typical EEG samples from two groups of cats trained oppositely with regard to operant sensorimotor responses. Record A (conditioned LVE EEG response) are data from an animal trained to suppress the SMR, and maintain a low voltage, fast EEG in sensorimotor cortex, in order to receive food. Record B (conditioned SMR EEG response) is from a cat trained to produce the SMR for food.

might provide a bioelectric label for the neural process of motor inhibition and proceeded to examine the phenomenon in greater detail. Due to its origin, we had termed this activity the "sensorimotor rhythm" or SMR. The discrete nature of the SMR made it an excellent candidate for operant EEG conditioning. By providing food or positive brain stimulation as a reward for the production of SMR activity, we were able to train cats to control the rhythm with even greater ease than comparable conditioning of motor responses (Fig. 1).

The SMR-trained cats assumed stereotyped, motionless postures in order to produce the rhythm. It was clear from this study that the absence of movement was necessary but not sufficient for the production of the SMR. The essential motionlessness, however, provided an excellent opportunity for the study of other aspects of physiology. In trained animals, the SMR response was accompanied by a sustained decrease in tonic motor discharge and in cardiac rate (Fig. 2), while respiration became exceedingly regular.[6] We were interested also in the physiologic basis of this rhythm and carried out a series of studies to determine its origin.[12,13] The simultaneous recording of electrical activity in subcortical structures together with the cortical SMR quickly focused our attention on the ventrobasal area of the thalamus. Here, and particularly in the nucleus ventralis posterolateralis, we observed high voltage, 12–14-cps activity, which closely paralleled cortical SMR activity. Single unit recordings from cells in this nuclear group disclosed two fundamentally different patterns of discharge dur-

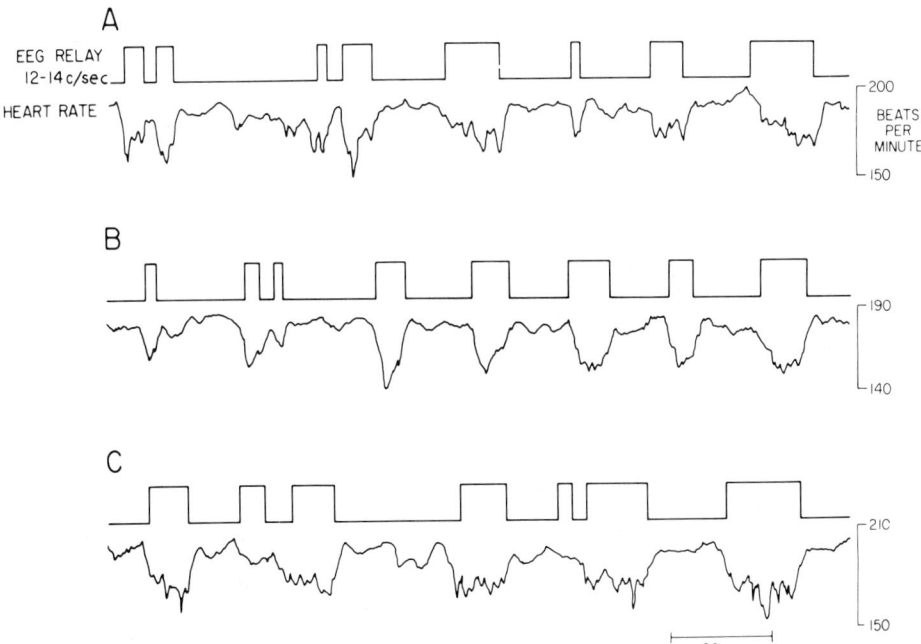

Fig. 2. Heart rate associated with sequential 12-14-cps EEG activity. Traces *A, B,* and *C* were obtained from different animals. Brief as well as long episodes of conditioned EEG activity were associated with a decrease in heart rate. The depression in heart rate was approximately the same during consecutive episodes of the conditioned EEG rhythm. (From Chase and Harper.[6])

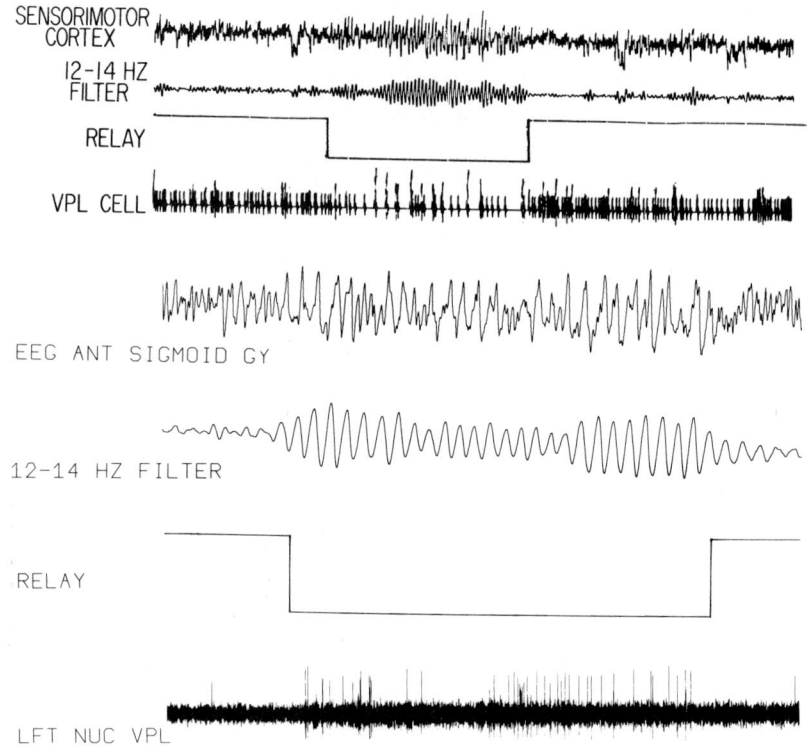

Fig. 3. Extracellular single-unit discharge patterns characterizing the two basic response types recorded from cells in the nucleus ventralis posterolateralis of the cat during trained SMR production. The record in the upper trace exemplifies the pattern change noted in approximately 80% of the units recorded and shows a shift from irregular high frequency discharge to a burst and silence configuration during SMR activity. The lower record, recorded at a slightly faster sweep speed, shows the response obtained in the remaining units studied, which was a shift from low base-line rates to a specific rapid discharge associated with the SMR. It is likely that the burst-silence pattern was characteristic of the larger transmission elements of VPL.

ing the SMR (Fig. 3). The most frequently observed change in relation to the occurrence of a conditioned SMR response was to a pattern of alternating bursting and silence. A smaller number of cells displayed a specific increase in discharge rate during the SMR. These and other observations were consistent with the well-documented electrophysiology of sensorimotor cortex and indicated that the SMR resulted from some form of gating or oscillation in thalamo–cortical–thalamic pathways, as suggested by the model of Andersen and Andersson.[1] The neural organization responsible for the rhythm represented a specific state of the central nervous system that followed the onset of motor quiescence but that was independent of that onset and of resulting motor postures. Other studies have shown that neuronal activity in a number of brain structures concerned with motor control is significantly dampened in relation to the occurrence of the SMR.

In addition to neurophysiologic studies we examined the *behavioral* consequences of SMR biofeedback training in cats. Utilizing untrained and oppositely trained control groups (Fig. 1), we established that sleep was significantly modified by SMR training. Sleep EEG spindles were enhanced and the number of motor disturbances (characteristic postural adjustments, etc.) during sleep diminished in the SMR-trained groups.[26] Moreover, the overall amount of time spent in sleep was reduced, due to a significant shortening of the recurrent sleep epochs in this polycyclic sleeper.[17] Perhaps the most dramatic observation of change related to SMR training was a surprising resistance to drug-induced seizures.[27] The convulsant studied was monomethylhydrazine, for which normative dose–response functions had been derived previously. This compound is highly toxic, producing convulsions in the cat at a dose of 7 mg/kg. It is thought to elicit generalized seizures by disrupting the metabolism of cerebral inhibitory interneurons, in much the same manner as strychnine.[7,11] Animals overtrained with SMR biofeedback showed a significantly prolonged latency to seizure at a dose of 9 mg/kg, and two of the tested animals failed to convulse at all, while clearly manifesting all other symptoms of toxicity related to this drug.

These observations led us to view EEG biofeedback from a somewhat different position than the rest of the field. The question of learning was not at issue and somatic mediation had been ruled out. What then could account for the apparent increase in seizure threshold observed in our trained animals? Could it be that this unusual opportunity for activation of motor inhibitory pathways had in some way altered the connectivity of these pathways? It is well known that denervation or disuse of neural components leads to profound changes in synaptic morphology and biochemistry.[8,22] These changes appear to be directed toward an increase in excitability at the expense of signal resolution. We hypothesized that *overuse* might produce opposite changes in synaptic organization leading to decreased excitability and greater signal specificity. Bliss et al.[5] were surprised and, in fact, disappointed to find that repeated stimulation of a central neural pathway led to a decrease in the probability of transmission, which was opposite to their expectations. But, indeed, this is precisely what one might anticipate if overuse produced cellular changes opposite to disuse, as suggested above. The implications of such a model were remarkable. Could EEG biofeedback provide a means of selectively overstimulating discrete neural networks and thereby decrease excitability in the mechanisms that they subserved? While continuing to seek neurophysiologic support for this concept, we were encouraged also to pursue similar biofeedback studies in man and to examine their utility in relation to epilepsy.

It should be noted that the human EEG is a good deal more complex than that of the cat. A number of classification systems have been evolved for the description of its component frequencies and rhythms, the most familiar of which are the waking alpha, beta, and theta rhythms and the slow wave (delta) and spindle (sigma) configurations of sleep. The human EEG is a sea of low voltage electrical activity in a constant state of flux. Our experience has indicated that functional pattern changes can occur not only in relation to the states of consciousness but, within a given state, in relation to a myriad of variables, such as time of day, time of month (in females particularly) and even events of the previous day or hour! Also, in man it is difficult to evaluate the nonspecific influence of cognitive variables and the specific influences of drugs, such as caffeine and nicotine, not to mention the plethora of patent medicines that one can encounter. Moreover, few studies have obtained substantial EEG samples over extended periods of time, so little can be said about the overall nature of individual variability in such important parameters as frequency, topography, and symmetry. Finally, what is seen is to a large extent determined by the equipment and analytic procedures utilized and the conventions of recording dictated by the history of electroencephalography. We have learned to appreciate these problems through our own experiences, and from them have developed a sense of caution in evaluating studies that appear to overlook these realities.

The techniques utilized originally in these studies were similar in principle to those used in our animal work. The equipment developed to detect SMR activity in cats consisted of a Neuro Feedback Instruments frequency analysis channel, made up of a calibrated precision attenuator and active frequency filter with a relay output. The relay output from the frequency analysis channel was directed to a feedback-logic channel. The unit was sharply tuned to respond to 12–14 cps activity (Fig. 4), and could be adjusted in its sensitivity-duration characteristics to provide for shaping of the desired EEG response.

Electrode placements and application techniques have evolved during the course of these studies. In our earlier work, a bipolar pair of cup electrodes was situated across the estimated central sulcus at sites approximately 1 cm anterior and posterior to C3, according to the international 10–20 system.[25] Currently, we are shifting placements to the medial–lateral plane, with one lead off vertex approximately 10% of the interaural distance and the other just lateral to C3 (see, for example, Fig. 9). Both needle and cup electrodes are used, depending on the patient, and bilateral recordings are uniformly obtained.

The basic EEG feedback unit consisted of a console containing two rows of ten small lamps. The logic channel activated an electronic counter that operated this unit. Each criterion response advanced illumination of the top row of lamps, which was accompanied in each instance by the sounding of a single chime. Each ten criterion responses (which illuminated the entire top row) activated, successively, the lamps in the bottom row, accompanied by a double chime. During the course of these studies, several new feedback modes were added to this system. One consisted of a single large lamp display above the basic console that glowed in intensity as a direct function of the amount of appropriate EEG signal generated. The discrete output of the basic unit was used, also, to operate a slide projector that presented pictures on a screen in front of the patient. These pictures consisted of sequences depicting nature scenes or providing for the completion of a picture puzzle. Different patients have preferred one or the other of these reward modes or a combination of several. This variable was manipulated so as to achieve optimal training from each patient.

We had chosen to study a small but select group of subjects. This strategy was dictated primarily by our model but was also consistent with our resources. Since we proposed that EEG biofeedback might alter neural organization through directed "exercise" of specific functional pathways, it was reasonable to assume that such an objective would require prolonged training. This approach could be compared more favorably with an attempt to create, through

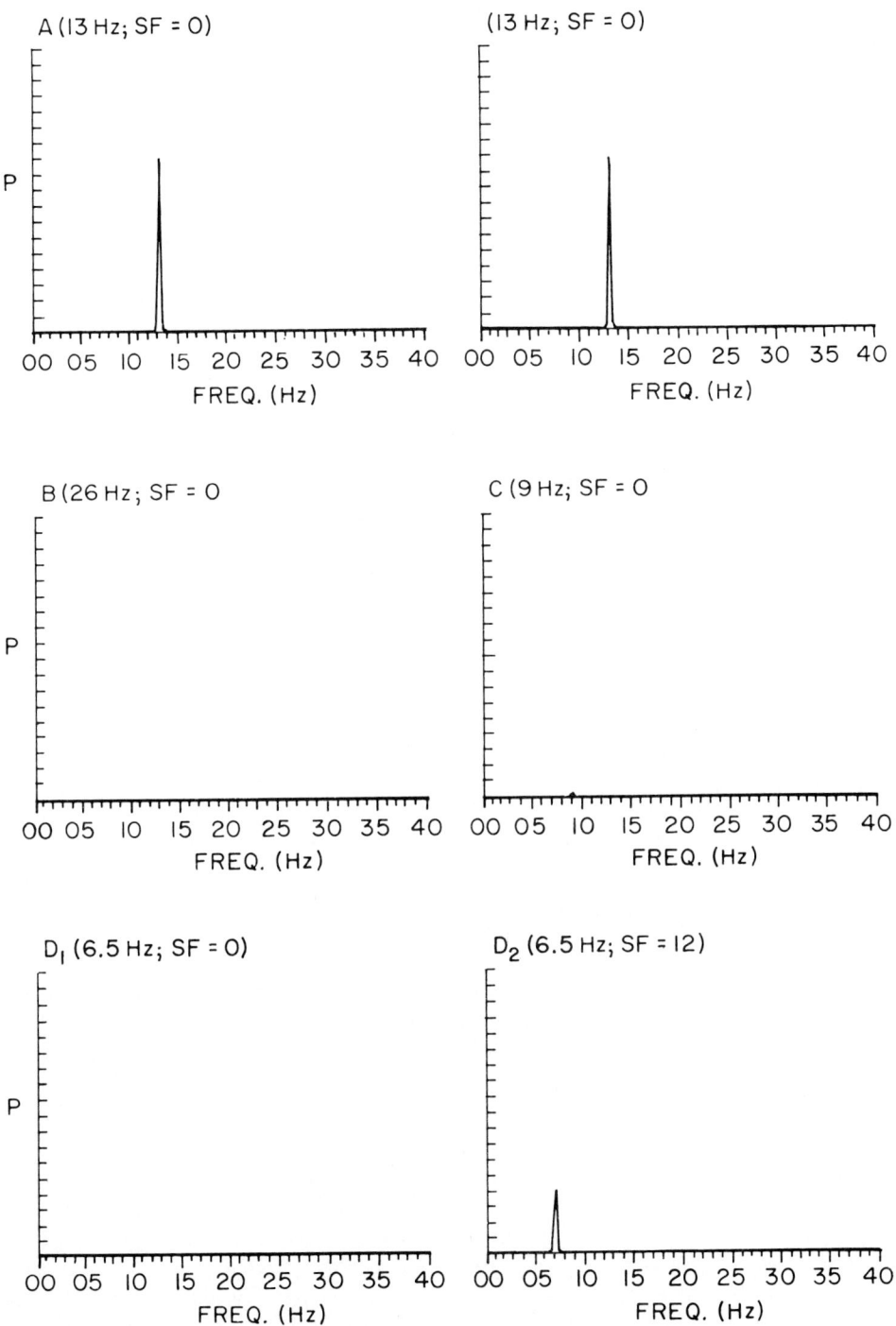

Fig. 4. Power spectral analysis of a 50μV oscillator signal at the frequencies indicated as recorded through our SMR feedback system. Note the specific response to the 13-Hz signal and the lack of response to harmonics of this frequency or to other frequencies.

training, a concert pianist or to retrain a disabled limb rather than with the objectives of most biofeedback studies. Accordingly, six patients were studied over periods ranging at this point from 6–20 mo. Four of these patients were epileptics and two suffered from spinal cord lesions. Four control subjects have been studied also, but these received less systematic attention. The epileptic patients selected in this initial study suffered from a variety of seizure disorders as indicated in Table 1. This situation was desirable, since it was possible that SMR biofeedback might prove more effective with some patterns than with others.

Each patient was familiarized with the apparatus and procedure in our biofeedback laboratory. They were then seated in front of the feedback unit and electrodes placed over appropriate cortical areas. EEG data were recorded on a ten-channel Grass Model 6 polygraph. The polygraphic display also included filter relay and reward outputs from the neuro-analyzer (see, for example, Fig. 7). A digital counting display provided the operator with a continuous update of the patient's progress. Extensive base-line EEG recordings were obtained where possible, but in all cases at least 3–5 min of data were gathered. At the end of the base-line recording period, the subject was instructed to relax and think positive thoughts in order to find the mental state that would produce activation of the feedback apparatus. This suggestion was based on previous experience with SMR feedback training.[24] Feedback was provided for a period of 20–40 min, depending on the state of the patient, and followed by a 3–5 min post-training baseline recording. Such training sessions were repeated a minimum of three times a week.

After 10 mo of training, one patient was provided with a portable home feedback unit and, thereafter, was recorded only several times per month in the laboratory. This unit contained an EEG preamplifier, a 60 Hz notch filter, a voltage amplifier, a frequency analysis channel and a single lamp display whose intensity directly reflected the occurrence of 13-cps activity. With the use of this unit the patient was able to obtain daily feedback training. Amplitude and frequency settings were calibrated during the intermittent laboratory training sessions.

The detailed description of our methods provided above was deemed important for those who wish to understand our approach. The results of our studies, however, will merely be reviewed here, since a comprehensive exposition of these new data is being prepared currently for the more appropriate context of a scientific journal. I wish also to acknowledge the collaboration of my associates, L. Macdonald and R. Stone, in this effort.

Data from four normal controls, two quadriparetics and four epileptics indicate that 12–14-cps activity can, indeed, be recorded over the rholandic or central cortical region in man. The amount, or operant level, of this activity prior to biofeedback training is low, with bursts occurring at widely spaced intervals. These bursts can usually be obtained only with the detection system set to respond to very low amplitude signals (3–6 μV) in this frequency band. When comparable recordings from other brain regions were passed through the detection system at the identical setting, little if any 12–14-cps activity was observed (Fig. 5). After at least 2 wk of training, the number and duration of these bursts

Table 1. Summary of Human SMR Studies*

Subject	Age	Pathology	Date Started Training	EEG	Post-Training Observations Clinical
K.H.	7	Mixed seizure disorder (major motor and PMV)	1/3/72	Significant decrease in polyspike and slow wave patterns; normalization	Significant reduction of major motor seizures, petit mal, and absence attacks (seizure-free for several periods of 2–4 mo)
M.F.	23	Major motor disorder (focal)	8/24/71	Significant decrease in focal spike discharge; normalization	Significant reduction in grand mal seizures from pretraining rate of 2/mo of 0.5/mo (seizure-free for several periods of 2–5 mos)
S.H.	18	Mixed seizure disorder (petit mal variant)	7/31/72	Significant decrease in polyspike and spike-wave discharge; normalization	Reduction of major motor seizures; decreased PMV manifestations.
D.K.	46	Adult petit mal	8/2/72	Unilateral suppression of 3/sec; spike-wave pattern	Frequent break-up clinical seizures; longest seizure-free periods in history of disorder
N.Y.	36	Quadriparetic (spinal cord compression)	3/29/72	Development of 6–8 Hz slow wave over central region (same true of all above patients)	
J.B.	24	Quadriparetic (spinal cord compression)	11/15/72	Development of profound 12–14 Hz; SMR pattern over central region	

*As of June 1, 1973.

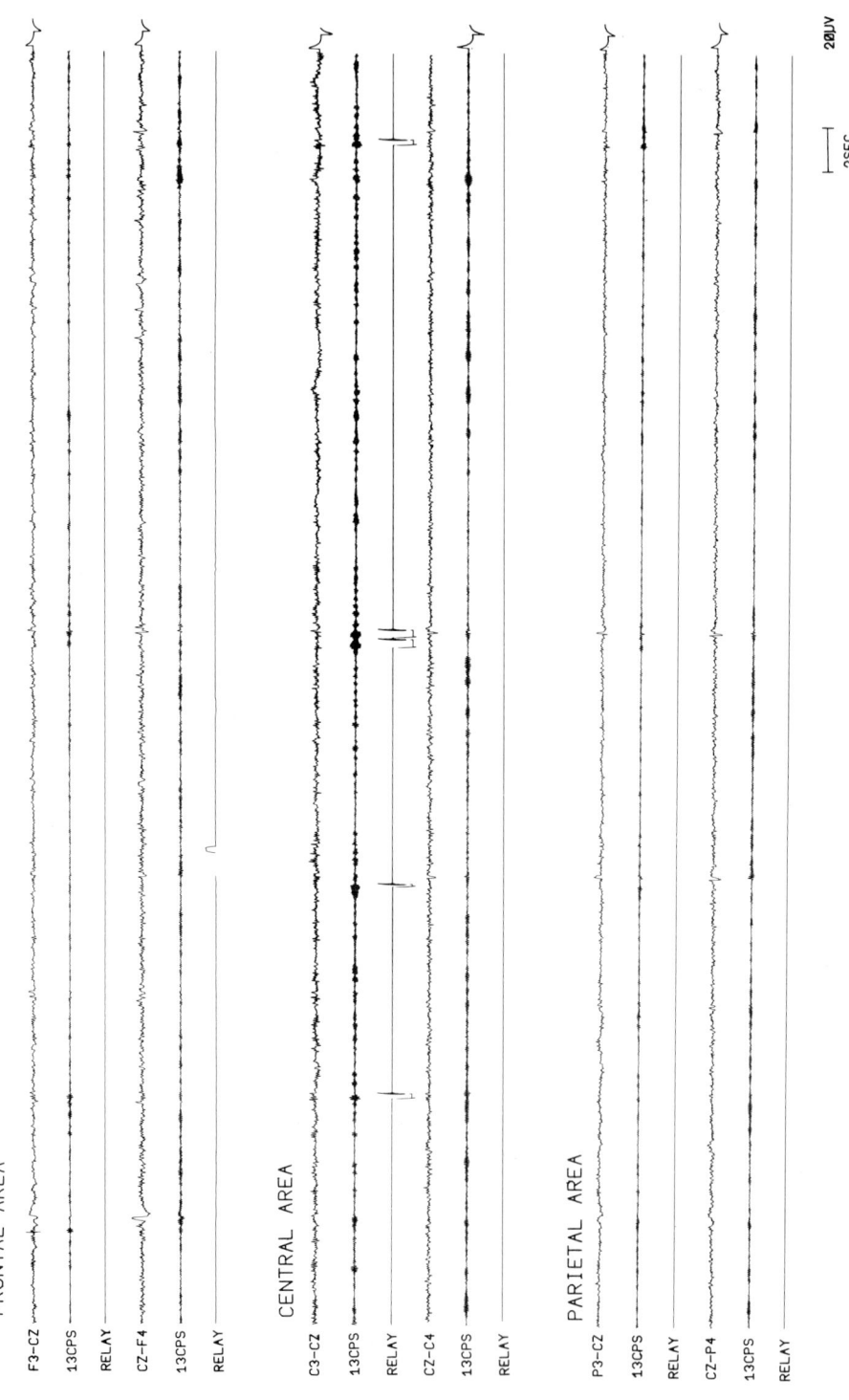

Fig. 5. One approach to localization and quantification of the human SMR involved the use of our feedback unit as a 12-14-cps detection system. Shown here are simultaneously recorded bipolar EEG tracings, equated for voltage and fed through the unit with all settings kept constant. These recordings were taken from frontal (Fz-F3), central (Cz-C3), and parietal (Pz-P3) leads of the left and right hemispheres in a naïve subject during the initial SMR training session.

began to increase, and several months later identical recordings showed a marked enhancement of this localized activity (Fig. 6). At the same time, detectable changes gradually emerged in the visually analyzed EEG. In all subjects, some increase in SMR amplitude was observed. However, the ultimate voltages achieved appeared to depend on the category of subject involved (Fig. 7). Our epileptics showed the smallest increase in amplitude (the bulk of rewarded bursts still occurring with low voltages which, to our surprise, appeared often to reflect an activation of the EEG); one of the quadriparetic patients showed the greatest increase ($>20~\mu v$), and normals were intermediate. These differences will be discussed below.

In addition to visual analysis of EEG patterns during training, these data were recorded on magnetic tape once per week and subjected to computer evaluation. Sequential 17-sec epochs of sensorimotor cortex EEG activity were subjected to Fast Fourier transform and plotted isometrically, so as to provide a continuous analysis of spectral density for periods ranging in duration from 3–10 min. In the initial phase of the study, such analyses were limited to central cortical activity on the side of the brain providing signals for the feedback device. Occipital leads were also recorded at this time. During the summer of 1972, this procedure was modified to provide for bilateral central cortical monitoring, and thereby a longitudinal analysis of EEG symmetry. These techniques allowed us to determine extant periodicities in the patient's EEG prior to, during, and after SMR training. They were extremely useful in demonstrating the abnormal EEG patterns of our epileptic patients as well as the ongoing modulation of such well-known EEG patterns as the alpha and theta rhythms. Because of the low voltages characteristic of the SMR and its intermittent occurrence during training sessions, power spectral analyses seldom reflected activity in this frequency range.

In all subjects studied significant changes were seen in the distribution of EEG frequencies during training. Normal subjects showed a reduction in occipital and central alpha activity during SMR performance. Epileptic patients all showed a decrease in abnormal low frequency discharge patterns with training. This decrease was progressive and sustained throughout the period of training. Additionally, these subjects showed a slowed central cortical alpha pattern (6–8 cps) during performance. With continued training, this theta activity was also diminished. In some patients, these changes were clearly more profound on the side of the brain where EEG patterns were being reinforced (Fig. 8). A 9-wk discontinuation of training was initiated in three patients at the end of 1972. Seizure manifestations in these patients were clearly exacerbated during this period, after a delay of 4–6 wk. This change in clinical condition was profoundly reflected in the power spectral analysis by a recurrence of abnormal frequencies and a decay of previously developed higher frequency activity (Fig. 9). EEG pattern characteristics in quadriparetic patients will not be elaborated here.

During the course of operant conditioning, our epileptic subjects showed significant changes, also, in clinical seizure manifestations. All patients experienced an improvement in their particular clinical patterns. Both grand mal

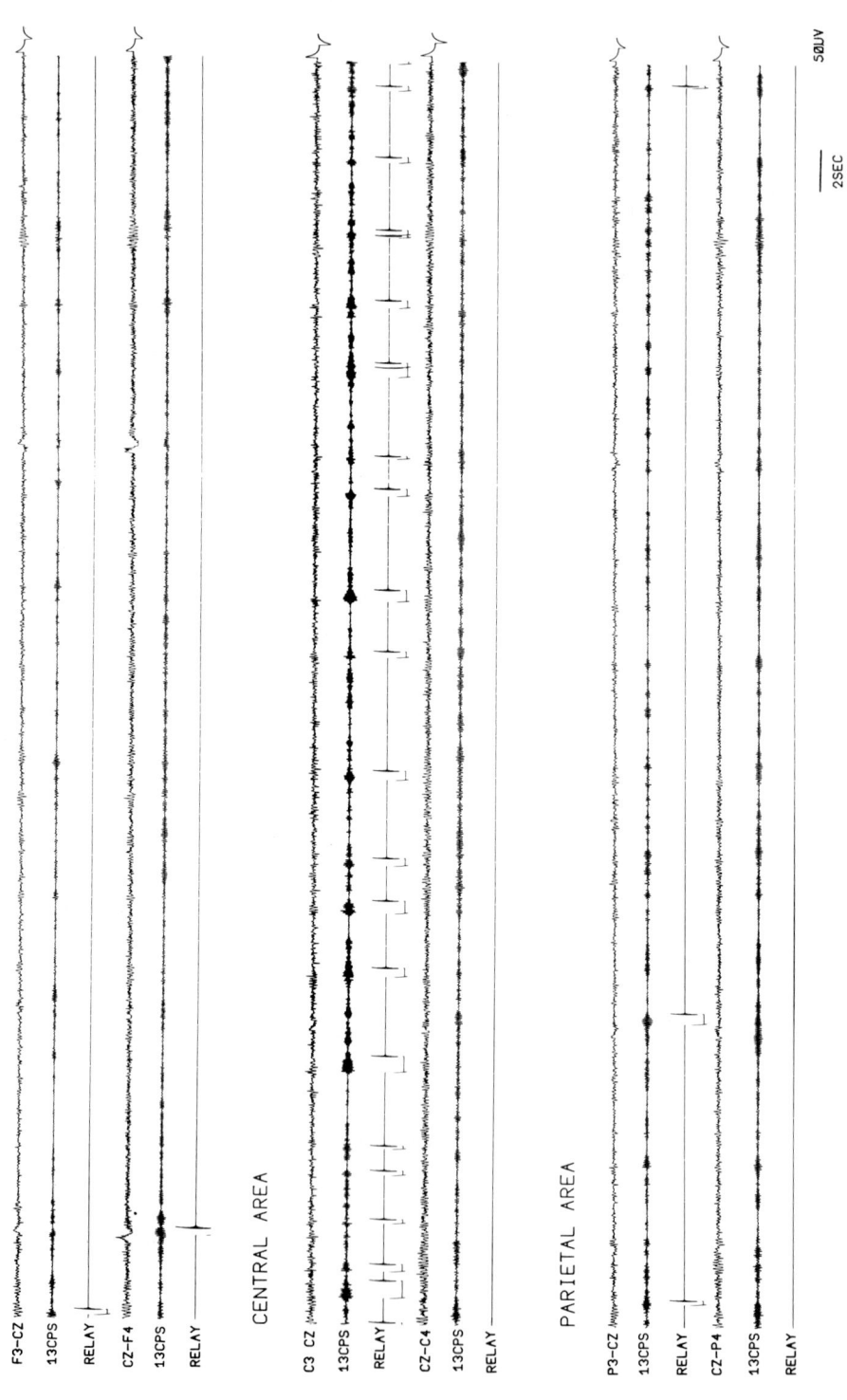

Fig. 6. This is an identical evaluation of SMR localization and quantity as shown in Fig. 5. In this case, however, the subject was well trained in SMR operant performance. Note the specificity of 12-14-cps activity from rholandic cortex and the marked increase in production resulting from training.

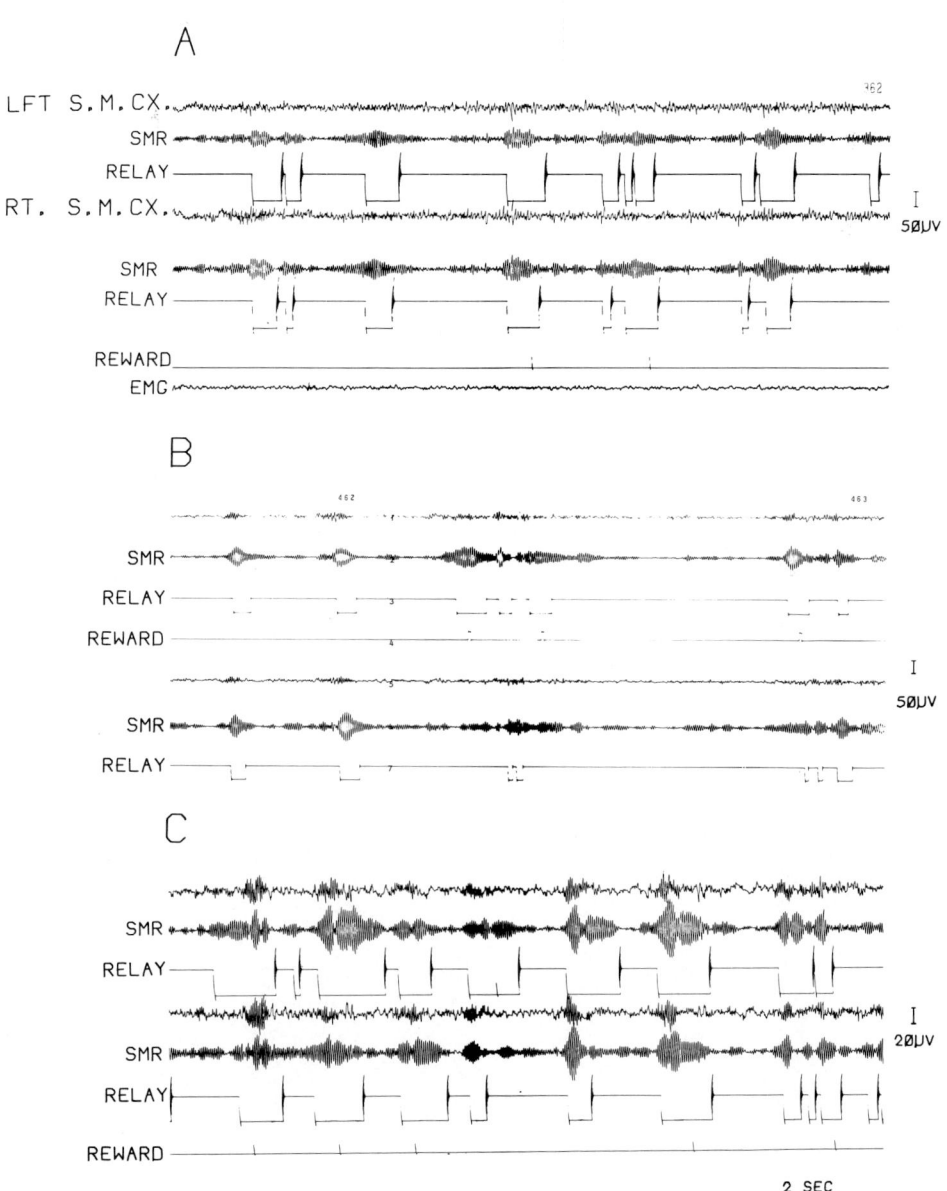

Fig. 7. Typical EEG recordings during SMR performance in three trained subjects. In each case, left and right sensorimotor cortex EEG tracings are shown together with associated 12-14-Hz filter activity, depicting the presence of this frequency independently of its amplitude, and relay activation when feedback criteria are achieved. Feedback is indicated by the reward maker. In *A*, the record was obtained from a patient with focal grand mal epilepsy, in *B*, from a normal control subject, and in *C*, from a quadriparetic patient. Note the relationship between SMR amplitude in the EEG tracings and the dimension of phasic motor excitability, extending from abnormal sensitivity in the epileptic to pathologic depression in the quadriparetic.

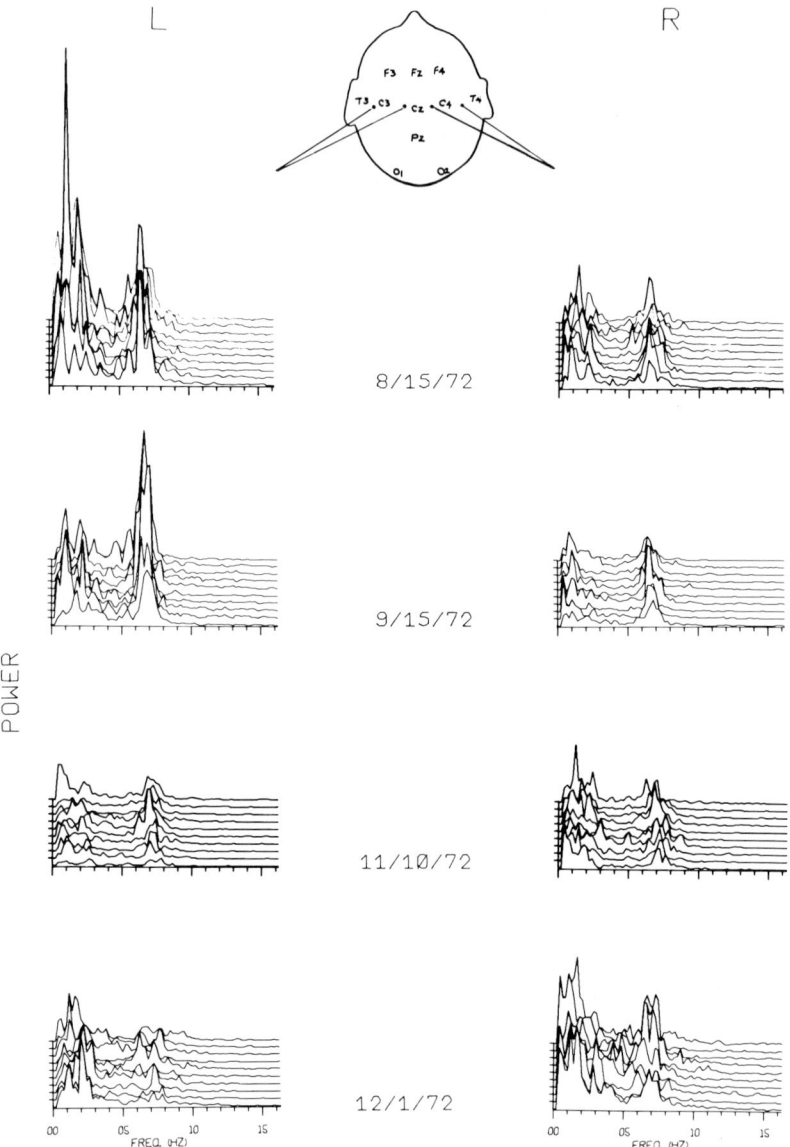

Fig. 8. Power spectral analyses of EEG data from left and right sensorimotor cortex are shown here as obtained over a 5-mo period of training in an epileptic patient. Each graph consists of sequential 17-sec epochs plotted isometrically, providing data from a continuous 3-min period of record. Note that this subject showed abnormally slow frequencies bilaterally that were most marked from the left sensorimotor cortex. In addition, a peak at 7 Hz, characteristic of epileptics, is seen. During the course of training, there were significant decreases in these abnormal frequencies on the left hemisphere, from which EEG signals were operantly reinforced, while frequency patterns from the right hemisphere did not change significantly during this same period. The records evaluated here were obtained during regular biofeedback training sessions and were not disrupted by any sustained seizure discharge. After several months of training, this patient would occasionally show unilateral subclinical seizures limited to the right hemisphere and not accompanied by a loss of consciousness. The occurrence of these seizures was consistent with the EEG asymmetry that had developed.

Fig. 9. The power spectral analyses shown here are similar to those presented in Fig. 8, but are compressed so as to present frequency analysis from continuous 10-min epochs of EEG recordings. In each instance, the records analyzed represent the first 10 min of training in a particular session. This subject had begun training in January 1972; however, bilateral recordings were initiated for the first time in August. The data presented here show the progression of change in component frequencies during the subsequent 4-mo period. They indicate relatively normal EEG frequencies, contrasting sharply with the grossly disordered patterns characteristic of this patient prior to training. The high density peak at 6–8 cps was characteristic of our epileptic subjects. Note the absence of any alpha manifestation and the gradual decrement of central 6–8 cps activity with continued training. There was an indication, also, of more marked change in the reinforced left hemisphere. Two months after the experimental termination of training, this subject showed exacerbated epileptic symptoms. His altered condition was clearly reflected in the power spectral analysis obtained on return to the laboratory.

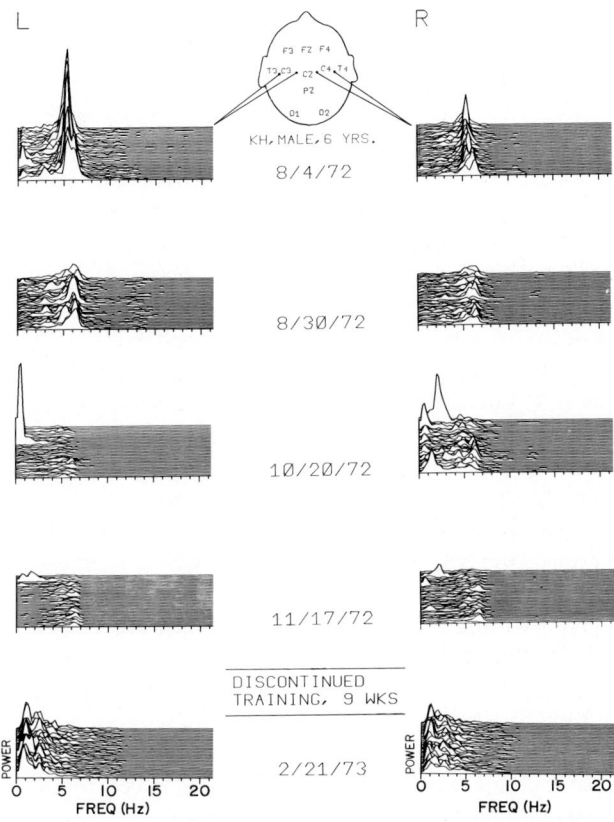

and petit mal manifestations were reduced. The lowest rates of clinical seizure activity in the history of their respective disorders were uniformly achieved within several months of the initiation of training. The best results were obtained in this regard from a 23-yr-old female patient suffering from focal grand mal epilepsy, and a 7-yr-old male patient with serious brain damage resulting in generalized and mixed seizure patterns (Table 1). Less remarkable changes were observed in patients with absence and petit mal variant disorders. All three of the subjects whose training was discontinued in December of 1972 experienced a return to pretraining levels of seizure activity within 6 wk. Upon the reinitiation of biofeedback training these subjects returned rapidly to the previous condition of improved control.

We have less systematic data on the behavioral effects of SMR biofeedback training. Subjects have consistently reported increased general awareness and an improved ability to sustain attention, in accordance with the typical reports of a relaxed, but alert and focused state of mind during successful performance. All subjects found the SMR training experience to be pleasant in nature. Two of the epileptic patients, whose clinical condition made education difficult if not impossible, demonstrated a marked improvement in school performance. In our 7-yr-old subject, severe problems of hyperactivity had compounded his seizure condition. A marked improvement in behavior control was reported by his parents and teachers, as well as by our laboratory staff, after several months of training. Finally, subjective reports during the course of training also suggested that the quality of sleep was improved during this period.

These briefly described observations indicate that 12–14-cps activity can be recorded over the central cortical region in man during wakefulness, that biofeedback techniques can successfully facilitate the occurrence of this activity, and that epileptics can benefit from extensive training in its production. While these statements are clearly substantiated by our findings, there are still many primary questions which must be dealt with. Why is the SMR difficult to observe in some subjects, and why is it manifest at such low voltages in man compared to the cat? Is the SMR indeed a separate EEG entity, or is the 12–14-cps designation inappropriate, the rhythm being of broader range and relating to previously described motor cortex EEG patterns? To what extent might alternative aspects of the biofeedback situation account for the observed improvement in EEG and clinical epileptic manifestations? Finally, why did our epileptic patients demonstrate a return to their previous clinical conditions following discontinuation of training?

Recordings in our animal preparations were obtained directly from the surface of the brain, while those in our human subjects were obtained from the surface of the skull. The presence of a laminated, bony calvarium results in higher resistance and, therefore, lower voltage recordings from humans. We have some reasons to believe that the SMR is obscured under these circumstances, and overshadowed by the relatively high voltage alpha and theta frequencies characteristic of man. However, in some patients, waking 12–14-cps activity may occur at relatively high voltages. We observed this in one man who suffered from a spinal cord compression leading to quadriparesis. After several training sessions this subject showed prominent bilateral SMR bursts over central and frontal cortical areas. In sleep recordings obtained from this patient, it was noted that spindle burst activity, associated with sleep EEG patterns, was also markedly enhanced. It is interesting to note that a similar enhancement of spindle activity has been reported from a teenage girl who had been isolated and restrained during development.[23] Moreover, this child demonstrated high-voltage SMR bursts in the waking state, according to the authors. The significance of these observations may be revealed if we consider certain other facts. In the few normal subjects we have trained, a clear 12–14-cps EEG pattern became apparent after several weeks of performance. While lower in voltage than in the quadriparetic patient, SMR activity in these subjects was nevertheless clearly observed. Also, with extensive training many of our epileptic subjects have shown repeated clear-cut bursts of rhythmic 12–14-cps activity. If one considers the behavior of these various subject groups in relation to corresponding EEG patterns, it is possible to hypothesize a relationship between general level of motor activity and the occurrence of the SMR. Individuals in whom motor behavior was curtailed, either actively or passively, showed high voltage SMR discharge. Conversely, subjects characterized by decreased thresholds for motor discharge (for example, epileptic and hyperkinetic patients) showed a minimal expression of SMR activity in the EEG. Normal subjects appeared to be intermediate between these extremes in terms of SMR manifestations. The motor mechanisms that underlie the appearance in the EEG of the SMR may be facilitated by inactivity and suppressed by somatic hyperactivity. It is interesting to note in this regard that the cats utilized in our experiments are normally maintained in standard laboratory cages, which, by their nature, substantially limit motor behavior. The profound SMR recorded in the cat may result, in part, from the restricted life space of this animal and his consequent inactivity.

These facts suggest that the SMR may indeed be a specific and functionally meaningful EEG phenomenon related to brain mechanisms that mediate motor suppression. However, it is also possible that such mechanisms are less specific than we suppose and are reflected by rhythmic activity of a broader frequency range. Thus, the so-called "en arceau" or "wicket rhythm,"[9] a somewhat slower rhythm that is blocked by movement in man, may likewise reflect the activity of this same motor suppression process, as we have suggested previously.[13] If so, training of this frequency from sensorimotor cortex may produce effects similar to those reported here. This is an empirical problem that can be resolved with further investigation.

It is a well-known fact that certain epileptics show clinical improvement associated merely with admission to a hospital. Extensive attention and concern, as well as the unique characteristics of a research laboratory, could produce similar "secondary gain" effects. The epileptics who have come to our program are seeking desperately to find a solution to their substantial medical problem. In at least one instance, an attempt to retain such a patient in our study for control procedures was not successful; the lack of positive results after several months led to his withdrawal from the program. Efforts to explain the need for control data did not impress this individual. For this reason, and due to limited resources in our laboratory, we have not established a control training group of epileptics. Ultimately, such an addition will be essential. However, there are some reasons to believe that such controls would be useful only from a technical point of view. Most of our epileptic patients have shown progressive clinical improvement, even after periods of training in excess of 1 yr. One might expect that secondary gain related to attention and novelty would be dissipated after so long a period of involvement. This progressive improvement has been apparent, also, in the objective EEG records obtained from these patients. As mentioned before, in several patients there is evidence of a unilateral EEG change in the hemisphere from which EEG signals were led to our feedback unit. Since both sides of the brain have experienced all other variables, one can conclude that the significant variable here was the biofeedback training. Additionally, one patient has been working at home with a portable unit for approximately 1 yr. This subject has demonstrated an even greater improvement in her clinical condition during this period of training out of the laboratory.

Conceivably, any situation that provided for sustained periods of relaxation and the focusing of attention on cerebral activities could produce effects similar to those noted here. We have found, however, that other EEG rhythms are diminished in the course of SMR biofeedback training. Thus, the alpha rhythm is clearly suppressed during SMR performance in a well-trained subject. The final answer to this question awaits studies in which other EEG and behavior phenomena are reinforced and the influence upon epileptic manifestations determined. From the data available we are encouraged to believe that the SMR effects are specific.

Finally, the model that we used to think about our biofeedback efforts rests upon the assumption that such changes would occur due to neuronal reorganization and that they might be long-lasting in nature. However, we have found that discontinuation of training after 6 mo in three patients resulted in a reversal of benefits previously achieved. It was difficult to determine the precise time course leading to exacerbation of symptoms. The three patients notified our laboratory of their worsened condition almost simultaneously, within a period 4–6 wk after training had been discontinued. This "withdrawal" effect came as a surprise to us. In accordance with our model, we could attribute this change to a kind of neuronal supersensitivity following upon a period of reduced activation of the SMR-related motor circuits. The time course of events associated with development of disuse supersensitivity in isolated cerebral cortex has been estimated at 2–4 wk.[21,22]

Our findings with SMR biofeedback in epileptics have been very encouraging thus far. We are cognizant of the fact that many interpretations of these results are possible, and that the mechanism of neural reorganization that we propose will be difficult to establish. Nevertheless, results have indicated a change in the epileptic process in all patients. Our future objectives in these studies will be to carry out some of the controls mentioned above, to evaluate the suggested relationship between EEG and behavior restriction, and to seek better and more efficient methods to accomplish SMR biofeedback training. While this approach may never provide a "cure" for epilepsy or other disease states of neural origin, it does suggest a desirable alternative to current chemical therapies.

REFERENCES

1. Andersen P, Andersson SA: Physiological Basis of the Alpha Rhythm. New York, Appleton-Century-Crofts, 1968, pp 1–235
2. Beatty J: Operant conditioning of the alpha rhythm. Presented at Learned Control of Physiological Functions (workshop) Winter Conference on Brain Research, Vail, Colo, 1972
3. Beatty J: Similar effects of feedback signals and instructional information on EEG activity. Physiol Behav 9:151–154, 1972
4. Black AH: The operant conditioning of central nervous system electrical activity, in Bower GH (ed): The Psychology of Learning and Motivations, vol 6., New York, Academic Press, 1972
5. Bliss TVP, Burns BD, Uttley AM: Factors affecting the conductivity of pathways in the cerebral cortex. J Physiol 195:339–367, 1968
6. Chase MH, Harper RM: Somatomotor and visceromotor correlates of operantly conditioned 12–14 c/sec sensorimotor cortical activity. Electroenceph Clin Neurophysiol 31:85–92, 1971
7. Clark DA, Bairrington JD, Bitter HL, et al: Pharmacology and toxicology of propellant hydrazines. Review 11-68, USAF School of Aerospace Medicine, Brooks A.F.B., Texas, 1968
8. Colonnier M: Experimental degeneration in the cerebral cortex. J Anat 98:47–53, 1964
9. Gastaut H, Terzian H, Gastaut Y: Etude électro-corticographique de la reáctivité des rythmes rolandiques. Rev Neurol 87:176–182, 1952
10. Globus A: Neuronal ontogeny: Its use in tracing connectivity, in Sterman MB, McGinty DJ, Adinolfi AM (eds): Brain Devel-

opment and Behavior, vol. 13. New York, Academic Press, 1971, pp 253–263

11. Goff WR, Allison T, Matsumia W, et al: Effects of 1, 1-dimethylhydrazine (UDMH) on evoked cerebral neuroelectric responses. AMRL-TR-67-67, Aerospace Medical Research Laboratories, Wright-Patterson Air Force Base, Ohio, September, 1967

12. Harper RM, Sterman MB: Subcortical unit activity during a conditioned 12–14 Hz sensorimotor EEG rhythm in the cat. Fed Proc 31:404, 1972

13. Howe RC, Sterman MB: Cortical-subcortical EEG correlates of suppressed motor behavior during sleep and waking in the cat. Electroenceph Clin. Neurophysiol 32:681–695, 1972

14. Howe RC, Sterman MB: Somatosensory system evoked potentials during waking behavior and sleep in the cat. Electroenceph Clin Neurophysiol 34:605–618, 1973

15. Kamiya J: Operant control of the EEG alpha rhythm and some of its reported effects on consciousness, in Tart C (ed): Altered States of Consciousness: A Book of Readings. New York, Wiley, 1969

16. Lehmann D: Multichannel topography of human alpha EEG fields. Electroenceph Clin Neurophysiol 31:439–449, 1971

17. Lucas EA, Sterman MB: A polycyclic sleep–wake cycle in the cat: Effects produced by sensorimotor rhythm conditioning. Exp Neurol (in press)

18. Lynch JJ, Paskewitz DA: On the mechanisms of the feedback control of human brain wave activity. J Nerv Ment Dis 153(3):205–217, 1971

19. Nowlis DP, Kamiya J: The control of electroencephalographic alpha rhythms through auditory feedback and the associated mental activity. Psychophysiology 6:476–484, 1970

20. Roth SR, Sterman MB, Clemente CD: Comparison of EEG correlates of reinforcement, internal inhibition and sleep. Electroenceph Clin Neurophysiol 23:509–520, 1967

21. Rutledge LT, Ranck JB Jr, Duncan JA: Prevention of supersensitivity in partially isolated cerebral cortex. Electroenceph Clin Neurophysiol 23:256–262, 1967

22. Sharpless SK: Isolated and deafferented neurons: Disuse supersensitivity, in Jasper H, Ward AA, Pope A (eds): Basic Mechanisms of the Epilepsies. Boston, Little, Brown, 1969, pp 329–348

23. Shurley JT, Natani K: Sleep EEG patterns in a fourteen-year-old girl with severe developmental retardation. Presented at the 80th Annual American Psychological Association Convention, Honolulu, 1972

24. Sterman MB: Studies of EEG biofeedback training in man and cats. Highlights of 17th Annual Conference: VA Cooperative Studies in Mental Health and Behavioral Sciences, St. Louis, 50–60, 1972

25. Sterman MB, Friar L: Suppression of seizures in an epileptic following EEG feedback training. Electroenceph Clin Neurophysiol 33:89–95, 1972

26. Sterman MB, Howe RC, Macdonald LR: Facilitation of spindle-burst sleep by conditioning of electroencephalographic activity while awake. Science 167:1146–1148, 1970

27. Sterman MB, LoPresti RW, Fairchild MD: Electroencephalographic and behavioral studies of monomethyl hydrazine toxicity in the cat. Technical Report AMRL-TR-69-3, Air Systems Command, Wright–Patterson Air Force Base, Ohio, 1969

28. Sterman MB, Wyrwicka W, Roth SR: Electrophysiological correlates and neural substrates of alimentary behavior in the cat, in Morgane JP, Wayner M (eds): Neural Regulation of Food and Water Intake. Ann NY Acad Sci 157:723–739, 1969

III. The State of the Art: General Remarks

Chapter 10: Biofeedback and Psychotherapy

Introduction

IN THIS CHAPTER, a traditionally trained psychotherapist tells of his experience in combining psychotherapy with biofeedback, using as illustrative cases two patients who would have been thought to have a very poor prognosis with conventional psychotherapy: one an unmarried, self-punitive, migraine-headache-ridden woman inimical to psychotherapy and psychologic-mindedness, and the other a man with a rigid personality structure, a bizarre developmental history, several years of prior unsuccessful psychotherapy, and chronic treatment-refractory insomnia.

The fact that both these patients became symptom free (of headache and insomnia) in the early months of treatment is somewhat impressive in itself, but the point of real interest is that their participation in biofeedback training seemed clearly to contribute to their involvement in concomitant psychotherapy, and to continue to catalyze their work in psychotherapy in a truly synergistic way.

Lee Birk, M.D.

© *1973 by Grune & Stratton, Inc.*

Biofeedback and Psychotherapy

Charles N. Legalos, M.A.

BIOFEEDBACK TRAINING tends to be regarded by many psychotherapists—if they are familiar with it at all—as a mechanistic technique felt to be inimical to the development of the warm, positive, patient–therapist relationship so essential for effective psychotherapy. Another concern is that biofeedback training might actually potentiate patients' resistance to psychotherapy. That is, the lure of a physically and emotionally painless treatment might seduce patients away from the often difficult and upsetting hard work of facing their feelings in psychotherapy.

That these objections come so readily to mind reflects the author's training and professional bias. Four years as an undergraduate in a psychology department chaired by a student of Anna Freud, followed by graduate school research on the mechanism of repression predicted skepticism for nonanalytical therapies.

Although at the outset the author held serious misgivings about biofeedback therapy, he is taking this opportunity to report on two cases that have gone surprisingly well.

CASE 1

Introduction

The first of the two cases to be presented is that of an unusually attractive 53-yr-old unmarried, professional woman. The presenting complaint was migraine headache; these were frequent (about 10 per mo) and severe; they had been a trying problem for about 30 yr.

She came to me for therapy after reading in a local newspaper article about the biofeedback therapies offered by our clinic. It may also be that the timing of her seeking medical help again was influenced by her life situation at the time, to wit, the plans of her brother as executor of her father's estate to sell the family home where they both lived, leaving her to make other arrangements for herself.

Following exhaustive efforts with medical specialists, the patient was reluctantly referred by her internist for biofeedback training. Upon learning that a comprehensive treatment plan including both palmar temperature control training and psychotherapy had been proposed, the patient's internist attempted to dissuade her from beginning therapy.

Given the chronicity and severity of the presenting symptom—intractable headache—in conjunction with the patient's subjective and medically supported resistance to psychotherapy, the prognosis was anything but positive.

Reprint requests should be addressed to Charles N. Legalos, 60 Dalby Street, Newton, Mass. 02158.
©*1973 by Grune & Stratton, Inc.*

History

This patient is one of four sibs in a maternally dominated, upper-class eastern family.

The patient described her mother with considerable ambivalence and confusion. She feels her mother to have been warm and loving, yet "very cool" and sarcastic; easy-going, yet stubborn and domineering; loving and good-natured, yet able to hold grudges, sometimes of a decade's duration. College educated, wealthy, and aggressive, the patient's mother had as disparate a background as possible from that of the patient's father. Destitute and a victim of parental desertion at age five, her father had managed to obtain only a grade-school education.

Progeny of this unlikely alliance include a World War II hero, the patient, her intellectually gifted twin brother, and a younger sister. Throughout her school years, the patient felt outdistanced by her brothers, yet, until recently, she resolutely maintained that she never felt hurt by them or angry toward them.

Therapy

Treatment has consisted of biofeedback training plus psychotherapy. The biofeedback training was completed within 3 mo, and required about 12 hr in all. One-half-hour palmar temperature control training sessions were held twice weekly, while the patient was concomitantly beginning psychotherapy. The psychotherapy was also twice weekly: 1 hr of individual therapy and 1½ hr of group therapy in a mixed group. Seven months after beginning, she still is in treatment in psychotherapy, having finished the biofeedback training sessions approximately 4 mo ago.

Biofeedback therapy was phased out during the third month because the frequency of migraine episodes had been reduced from about ten a month to one a month and because even this one attack was much less severe than usual, and unaccompanied by nausea.

It is noteworthy that nearly complete symptomatic relief was achieved *prior to* the occurrence of significant progress in psychotherapy. Only subsequent to this did the patient begin to gain meaningful insight into her self-punitiveness and its relationship to past, as well as ongoing events.

Anamnesis revealed that her first two serious physical crises coincided with her eldest brother's departure for and return from combat during World War II, which led the patient to the as yet hazy realization that she might be punishing herself symptomatically for angry feelings harbored toward this sibling. (The first of these crises was an appendicitis attack that was found upon operation to have been spurious, the second was her initial migraine headache).

Another source of suppressed rage has been the patient's felt need to be the "fall guy" for her father. That is, even though her IQ is 167, she compliantly adopted the appearance of ineptitude, clumsiness, and dull-wittedness as a ploy to draw attention away from the *faux pas* of her uneducated, lower-class father, and as a way of compliantly but angrily being the girl twin and the least favored of the three oldest siblings.

Currently, (and for the first time!) in most instances in which headaches occur, the patient is able to clearly label the antecedent feelings. Further, she is successful in aborting most of the headaches.

In the biofeedback work, this patient did well at preliminary relaxation training, but was *not* particularly adept at learning to produce palmar warming. (Some patients learn to increase the temperature of their fingers, vs. their foreheads, by 4-6° F in even a few training sessions; she achieved only very small changes, and these only during the last several sessions). Nevertheless, the special attention she paid to the headaches as a symptom, and the feelings and thoughts she had at the time, in the context of being concurrently in psychotherapy and biofeedback therapy seems to have been very successful.

This was dramatically demonstrated once, when after several months in psychotherapy, the author announced to the group patients that he would be away and wanted to reschedule the following week's meeting time. Upon leaving this session, the patient stage-whispered, "I hope your plane crashes." The afternoon prior to the author's departure she telephoned to say she was in bed with one of the most severe headaches she had ever experienced and she wished to apologize for her angry feelings. A brief conversation acknowledging the reality and legitimacy of both her positive and negative feelings was succeeded by almost immediate symptomatic relief.

It is significant that one of the only occasions in this woman's life when she openly expressed anger toward her elder brother was immediately followed by a telephone call informing her that her father had died.

Group psychotherapy has been especially beneficial in helping this patient become more self-observant and understanding of the significance of her maladaptive behavioral patterns, especially where the handling of angry feelings is concerned.[1,2] For example, in group it was noted that she frequently pinched her skin or bit her finger when angry. This led associatively in the group work to the revelation of her self-penalizing style of expressing anger, going back to early childhood. In her early years, typically angry responses included bedwetting, appearing clumsy, grimacing in family photographs. In many such ways, she vented her hostility, but simultaneously and self-punitively subjected herself to the ready ridicule of her family.

Obviously, this patient has made, and continues to make remarkable progress, not only in overcoming her problem, of three decades' duration with severe headaches, but also in moving toward a richer, freer life, without so much need for self-punishment. Much credit is due the biofeedback approach, not only for the symptomatic recovery, but also for introducing her to and catalyzing her involvement in psychotherapy. A few weeks after she and her biofeedback therapist mutually agreed to discontinue their work together, the patient remarked to the author that "had it not been for the biofeedback therapy I would never have done any of this."

CASE 2

Introduction and History

The following case is that of a 29-yr-old bachelor engineer. The patient's presenting problem was marked insomnia and general tension. Prior to the present treatment experience, he had had a total of 3 yr of psychotherapy with three different therapists.* The last of these three prior therapists, also experiencing no success in working with him, referred him for biofeedback and relaxation training. The patient, as well as the author, was counselled by this therapist: "Try it a couple of times and if it doesn't work, forget it."

Soon after being referred, the patient terminated his work with the referring therapist, and began a combined program of relaxation training with electromyograph feedback and group and individual psychotherapy.

Upon initial interview this man appeared as if carved from wood. He sat and moved with unusual restraint and evinced little or no affect. In light of this and his childhood experience with a psychotic psychoanalyst father, an institutionalized paranoid schizophrenic mother, and many years of therapy, the prognosis was decidedly negative.

After a few months of relaxation training the patient's progress plateaued. This was accompanied by marked anxiety, increasing with self-application of the relaxation methods. Despite the patient's newly learned ability to control skeletal muscle tension, insomnia continued to be a problem. He described his feeling that "my body is relaxing, but my mind is racing a mile a minute." Further biofeedback training did not result in either deeper relaxation or symptomatic relief and was consequently discontinued.

As in Case 1, however, only more dramatically so, the data suggests that the process of working specifically on the target symptoms of excessive muscular tension, (presumed to be interfering with sleep), in the context of combined biofeedback therapy and psychotherapy, led him to some important and catalytic recognitions. He learned that he could relax his muscles, yet he still felt tension, fear, and a need for watchfulness. It was this insight that, in turn, led him to associate to his fear of his father and to a specific, frighteningly bizarre sexualized threat his father had made against him: "Some day you and I are going to tangle assholes." Though his father had repeatedly threatened him with this strange phrase, he apparently had, prior to beginning combined biofeedback therapy and psychotherapy, completely repressed this fact and its crucial importance.

With this came a flood of affect—primarily fear—and an emergence into consciousness of the need to maintain vigilance throughout the night. Within a few weeks, insomnia ceased to be a problem and the patient reported being able to enjoy sleep and waking up more relaxed.

As for his "woodenness" and lack of affect, he has gained during the past 7 mo a nearly complete, although guarded, repertory of emotional expression. Topical progression in psychotherapy has been from discussions focused exclusively on symptoms to voicing of new-found interests in women, friends, and social activities. This until recently reclusive, frightened, and unemployed man now holds a responsible position involving international travel with a major corporation and is actively dating a number of women.

---

*Actually, his father considered himself to be this patient's first therapist; his father had ordered an electroencephalogram and psychologic tests done on his son when he was seven. For obvious reasons, his father is not, however, counted as one of the three previous therapists.

DISCUSSION

The foregoing case histories represent two very different types of patients—one well-nigh phobic of psychotherapy and of feelings in general; the other, the son of a disturbed psychoanalyst and the veteran of several years of therapy. Both cases were very difficult and carried a poor prognosis, although for quite different reasons. Case 1, the woman with migraine headaches, was patently skeptical of psychotherapy, and this feeling of hers was sanctioned and reinforced by her physician. The opposite was true of Case 2, the man with insomnia. However, he was also very difficult because of the crucial early negative experience with his first "therapist," his analyst father.

Despite the negative prognoses, while receiving biofeedback therapy in combination with psychotherapy, both these patients made rapid and dramatic progress. Further, the depth of these patients' motivation and involvement in psychotherapy came as a pleasant surprise to the author, whose concerns regarding the "mechanistic" and possibly resistance-potentiating nature of biofeedback training proved unfounded.

While two cases—notwithstanding the strikingly positive outcomes—certainly cannot establish the efficacy of a treatment method, the author feels that these two cases do at least illustrate the compatability and perhaps synergism of two very disparate therapeutic modalities.

ADDENDUM

Shortly after this paper was written, the subject of Case 2 discovered that his father's threat of "tangling assholes" had, in fact, been actualized. He recalled—for the first time since it occurred over 20 yr ago—that his father had actually raped him during a quarrel with his mother. That this is merely a classic paranoid-homosexual fantasy seems unlikely, since several important and previously inexplicable events in his life fall into place both temporally and logically around this tragedy.

Within 2 wk of recall and the start of the painful working through of the feelings associated with this memory, the patient had his first—and very enjoyable—sexual experience with a woman.

ACKNOWLEDGMENT

The author wishes to thank Mr. William Peyser, the biofeedback therapist for the two cases reported, and Dr. Lee Birk, Clinical Director of Learning Therapies, Inc., where the patients were treated, for their helpful suggestions in the preparation of this paper.

REFERENCES

1. Guttmacher J, Birk L: Group therapy: What specific therapeutic advantages? Compr Psychiatry 12:546–556, 1971
2. Birk L: Intensive Group Therapy: An Effective Behavioral-Psychoanalytic Method. Invited paper presented at a joint session of the American Academy of Psychoanalysis and the American Psychiatric Association, May 1973, Honolulu. Am J Psychiatry (in press)

Chapter 11: Biofeedback Procedures in the Clinic

Introduction

IN THIS CHAPTER, Dr. Budzynski, as one of the most experienced and versatile therapists in the new field of using biofeedback together with other treatment modalities, attempts to lay before the reader some of his still-accumulating clinical observations and generalizations relating to this enterprise. He comments, for example, on strategies for enhancing transfer of control to the real-life situation, (see page 178) and on techniques for potentiating the catalytic effects of self-perceived progress (see page 179). He also describes his experience with the use of biofeedback in quite a variety of clinical problems: drug dependency (see page 182); treatment-refractory anxiety and treatment-refractory insomnia (see page 183); and circumscribed and generalized phobias (see pages 183–184).

Finally, in his concluding remarks he speculates that biofeedback may have uses as a preventive technique, through "the development of self-control of internal functions at an early age." While this seems utopian, such a preventive format (as already mentioned—see Chapter 8) might be applicable to essential hypertension, for example, if used with an effective screening, detection, and early case-finding system.

Lee Birk, M.D.

Biofeedback Procedures in the Clinic

Thomas H. Budzynski, Ph.D.

A host of researchers and clinicians are exploring the clinical possibilities of biofeedback techniques. However, unwarranted claims and expectations, as well as strong placebo effects, render a proper evaluation of these procedures somewhat difficult. Nevertheless, certain approaches would appear to be quite effective. Applications to tension and migraine headache, anxiety, and insomnia can now be described. There is a suggestion that biofeedback training may be helpful as a preventive program with regard to stress-related disorders.

THE CLINICAL APPLICATION of biofeedback is such a rapidly evolving field that the techniques described in this paper may well be revised beyond recognition before another 12 mo have passed. However, if this flurry of activity could be "frozen" at this time, one would no doubt find a continuum of emphasis on biofeedback in clinical settings that ranged from heavy to none at all. The fact that biofeedback in general has captured the imagination of both the layman and the professional has made a determination of its efficacy quite difficult. Preliminary research results, often amplified in significance by the popular press, become "fact" before being tested in the crucible of professional criticism. Poorly designed biofeedback equipment and quality units misused by inexperienced but eager clinicians have contributed to the confusion regarding the effectiveness of these procedures. And, finally, it is getting more difficult to find naïve subjects who do not bring a host of expectations to each biofeedback study, thus contributing to strong placebo effects.

Even though unrealistic expectations and inadequate or misused equipment continue to cloud the picture somewhat, it is possible nevertheless to point out several bright spots in the application of biofeedback to clinical disorders. For example, normative data slowly are becoming more available as system parameters are standardized. Certain types of biofeedback appear to be more useful than others. Clinicians are discovering how to use biofeedback in the context of existing therapies. Reliable equipment manufacturers are responding to the needs of both researcher and clinician in providing systems that vary in complexity, yet give accurate quantified results as well as precise information feedback. In addition, it is a fact that biofeedback procedures are being explored in a variety of clinical settings including medical centers, hospitals, mental health clinics, behavior therapy clinics, private practice, and a few professionally staffed clinics specializing in biofeedback therapy.

WHAT CAN BIOFEEDBACK PROVIDE IN A CLINICAL SETTING?

Biofeedback training essentially has three main goals: (1) the development of increased awareness of the relevant internal physiologic functions or events;

Reprint requests should be addressed to Dr. Thomas H. Budzynski, University of Colorado Medical Center, 4200 E. Ninth Avenue, Box 2621, Denver, Colo. 80220.
© *1973 by Grune & Stratton, Inc.*

(2) the establishment of control over those functions; and (3) the transfer or generalization of that control from the training site to other areas of one's life.

Awareness of the Event

Before voluntary control can be established over some aspect of one's physiology that ordinarily functions below the level of awareness, relevant knowledge of the event must be made known to the subject. Relevant knowledge may include the presence or absence of the event, as is the case with some EEG feedback systems, or an indication of the level of the event, as is the case with EMG; or both, as provided by certain sophisticated EEG feedback systems. Thus, the tracking system should be sensitive, accurate, artifact-free, and it must provide meaningful information feedback.

Voluntary Control Over the Function

Gradually, through a process of trial and error and hypothesis testing, the patient evolves strategies for controlling the feedback and thus the response. As he becomes more successful he learns to associate certain thoughts, as well as proprioceptive and interoceptive sensations, however subtle, with changes in the feedback. It is an interesting fact nevertheless, that a patient may develop some degree of control even before he is able to verbalize what it is that he is, or is not, doing. With continued training he is able to express what he is *not* doing, and finally, what he *is* doing, e.g., producing sensations of floating, or heaviness, or warmth in his limbs, and excluding certain thoughts.

Transfer of Control

The ability to verbalize control strategies enhances transfer from the clinic or laboratory to "real life." Therefore, the patient should be encouraged during the training phase to describe his sensations, as well as his successful and unsuccessful strategies. Often the patient will use a phrase or series of phrases that will become conditioned to the desired physiologic pattern. The autogenic training formulae of Schultz and Luthe[17] are very useful for this purpose. In fact, Green et al.[8] were the first experimenters to combine autogenic training phraseology and biofeedback. Other researchers who have employed autogenic-type phrases to enhance biofeedback learning and transfer are Budzynski and Stoyva[2] and Love.[13]

Jacobson's progressive relaxation exercises[10] are also helpful in the initial stages of biofeedback training. These exercises, along with certain of the autogenic formulae, and other specialized instructions, can be placed on cassette tapes for use in the clinical setting, as well as for home practice. For the past 8 mo we have used clinic and home practice cassette tapes at the Applied Biofeedback Institute. They are now an integral part of the therapy programs. It appears that a patient is more inclined to do the home practicing if he can listen to a tape recording. The patient's progress from one tape to another is based on his ability to demonstrate a certain level of control over a particular function. Home practice cassettes also ease the transition of the patient away from the biofeedback equipment. Of course, the transfer is never completed until the patient can successfully demonstrate his newly developed ability under real-life aversive conditions.

Self-perceived Progress

If the successful pursuance of the three goals can be implemented, then biofeedback training can be of great value in clinical settings. For example, the use of feedback equipment with adequate quantification capability allows the therapist to specify target behaviors in terms of desired physiologic parameters at each stage of training. Thus, the patient perceives that he is progressing as he meets each criterion in turn.

Moment-to-moment knowledge of results provided by the feedback, as well as charts and graphs illustrating longer-term changes, provide objective evidence of progress. The confidence gained from this illustration of increasing control seems to generalize to other areas of the patient's life. Leitenberg,[12] for example, have shown that providing a subject with information about his performance has therapeutic effects.

WHAT BIOFEEDBACK CANNOT PROVIDE IN A CLINICAL SETTING

Although biofeedback training alone can result in positive change, it may be made more effective when used in conjunction with other therapy procedures. This is especially true if factors in the patient's environment appear to be contributing to his problem. These trouble areas of the patient's day-to-day existence may never be brought to light if he interacts only with a biofeedback machine. It is true that biofeedback training alone may help him to cope with these difficulties, however, the problems themselves can act to prevent progress with the training. The patient may find himself dwelling on problem-related thoughts during the training sessions, or he may find it difficult to practice at home.

A more troublesome situation for the therapist occurs when the patient is getting positively reinforced for maintaining his maladaptive behavior, or when he uses his symptoms to avoid certain feared situations. This may also manifest itself as an inability to progress in training and/or a reluctance to practice at home. A good relationship between therapist and patient can reduce, or at least help uncover, some of these motivational problems.

In short, biofeedback is simply a mirror reflecting some aspect of physiology. The patient really must want to learn to use the mirror in developing control over this response. An important part of the therapist's task is to maintain this motivation.

SPECIFIC BIOFEEDBACK THERAPY PROCEDURES

Since biofeedback is useful for altering and bringing under control physiologic responses, this training would seem to be particularly suited to disorders characterized by maladaptive physiologic patterns such as are evident in cases of tension and migraine headaches, essential hypertension, certain types of epilepsy, Raynaud's disease and cardiac arrhythmias. However, only a few of the possible clinical applications have been adequately researched. Requirements such as lengthy base lines, proper control conditions to guard against habituation and placebo effects, control of medication, and meaningful evaluation procedures, render such research with humans a gruelling and time-consuming task.

With equipment design and training procedures evolving at a rapid rate, it is often difficult for the researcher to "freeze" design and training for the length of time it takes to complete an adequate experiment. For example, the tension headache studies carried out at the University of Colorado Medical Center[4,5] involved a "bare bones" procedure. Patients in the second of these two studies were given only EMG (electromyographic) feedback from the forehead musculature for 16 sessions of 20 min each. They were asked to practice relaxing twice a day at home but were told only to do what they had learned in the training sessions. In spite of this simplified procedure approximately 70% of the patients showed significant reductions in headache activity.

Following the completion of the study, the control group patients were offered the real training. In this instance the "bare bones" procedure was augmented by cassette tape relaxation instructions, as well as portable EMG feedback units for home use. These additional measures seem to provide a greater incentive for practicing outside the laboratory.

The transfer of control to real life is enhanced not only by the daily home practice periods but also by reminding the patient to make frequent checks of his general tension level during the day. If he found himself tense, he was to attempt to relax for a short period (30 sec to 3 min). This practice can be implemented by placing a small sliver of brightly colored tape on the wrist watch dial. Thus, each time the patient looks at his watch the tape reminds him to scan around for tension spots. Incidentally, we have found that the color and shape of the tape reminder should be changed at least once a week; otherwise, people tend to habituate and subsequently ignore it. Since we ask our tension headache patients to chart headache intensity every hour, the wrist watch tape serves also as a reminder to complete this task.

Clinical Procedures for Headache Conditions

One of the more interesting conclusions arising from the work with tension headache at the University of Colorado Medical Center and the study of migraine headache at the Menninger Clinic[16] is that EMG feedback alone is quite effective for tension headache but not for migraine, whereas peripheral temperature feedback is effective for migraine but not for tension headache. Consequently, a careful differential diagnosis should be made prior to biofeedback training. Following this, an attempt should be made to determine the circumstances associated with the onset of the headaches as well as the present environmental contingencies that may be maintaining the headaches. The patient is told that he will have to maintain an hourly (if he has tension headaches) or daily (if he has migraine headaches) record of the headache intensity. He is also told that he must practice relaxing at home or at work twice daily, and that the degree of relaxation for each of these sessions must be charted. The patient is taught also to record the type and amount of medication on the headache intensity chart.

It is very important to ascertain from the patient when during the day he feels he can take time to relax. Although most patients will have agreed to follow all the instructions to this point, some patients balk when asked to be specific about home practice times. The therapist may have to review with the patient each day's activities, hour by hour, in order to find appropriate times for the relaxation practice. The patient is also instructed to inform his immediate family of the necessity for privacy and quiet during the home practice periods. If he has a private office at work he is told to have his secretary hold all calls and visitors during the 20-min practice periods.

In most instances a 2-wk base line of charting headaches and medication is taken before training is begun. Following the base-line period, training is initiated with twice-a-week sessions. An abbreviated form of Jacobson's tense-relax procedure is used during the first two or three sessions in order to provide the patient with at least a gross awareness of differing levels of tension in his muscles. A measure of arm and frontalis EMG levels is taken before and after each session. The patient is given a cassette tape with tense-relax instructions for home use. He is told to practice twice a day and to rate the degree of relaxation achieved on a scale of 0 to 5.

The next phase of training involves EMG biofeedback from the forearm extensor. Autogenic-type phrases are coupled with the physiologic changes resulting from the feedback training. These auto-suggestive phrases also help to bring about the desired changes signalled by feelings of heaviness and warmth in the limbs. A cassette tape with the autogenic formulae allows the patient to practice at producing the changes outside the clinic.

When the patient can maintain his forearm tension below a certain level ($3\mu V$), and when he can feel the heaviness and warmth sensations in his limbs, the feedback can be transferred to the forehead. Surface bioelectric activity in the forehead area is reflective of not only frontalis tension but jaw (masseter and temporalis) muscle tension, eye movements, and eye muscle tension. The diminution of all these signals contributes to a general decrease in arousal level.[7,9] A third cassette tape, building on the prior learning, is used for home practice during the forehead-training phase.

Eventually, the patient learns to reduce forehead bioelectric activity below $3\mu V$ while sustaining the warmth and heaviness sensations in his limbs. The patient then practices at keeping the forehead EMG low with his eyes open in an upright sitting posture. The feedback can be withdrawn gradually at this point to check the patient's ability to maintain relaxation in the absence of feedback.

A final phase of the biofeedback training for tension headache involves a "stress management" procedure. While receiving forehead EMG feedback, the patient visualizes, as vividly as possible, a variety of stressful situations. While doing so, he attempts to maintain relaxation, or, at least to recover quickly if aroused momentarily. As in the prior phase of training the feedback is gradually removed as the patient learns to sustain a relaxed physiology in the presence of stressful thoughts. At this point, the patient is encouraged to attempt to maintain an *optimal* arousal level in the face of real life stressors, and to try relaxing *after* the stressful situation is over (see Stoyva and Budzynski[19]).

Typically, the duration of training to this point is approximately 15 1-hr sessions or 8 wk.

Migraine patients receive training similar to those with tension headaches except that peripheral temperature feedback is introduced after the EMG feedback training. It has been our experience at the clinic that migraine patients quite often have cold hands (70°–80°F). They also tend to have somewhat lower forehead EMG levels than tension headache patients. Consequently, a shorter EMG training period is required before temperature feedback is initiated. The rationale for the EMG training with migraine cases is that the response of painfully dilated blood vessels in the head represents a rebound phenomenon occurring as a result of an initial over-reaction to stress. If this initial response to the stressor can be modified through relaxation training, then perhaps the rebound response will be weaker. Feedback of temperature information from the hand, a technique pioneered by Sargent et al.[18] appears to be effective in the postponement, alleviation, or prevention of migraine headaches.

For this phase of training, the patient hears an auditory analog of the skin temperature of the hand. When he can maintain regularly a temperature greater than 90°F, the patient is asked to do this with visual feedback only. He will next attempt to do so without feedback. A final phase of training for migraine patients involves the same stress management procedure as employed with the tension headache patients, except that finger temperature is used as the feedback information source.

BIOFEEDBACK USED TO FACILITATE BEHAVIOR THERAPY (SYSTEMATIC DESENSITIZATION)

Drug Dependency Problems (With Migraine Patients)

Even after they have learned to control their muscle tension and temperature responses, some migraine patients find it all but impossible to give up or even decrease their daily drug intake. These are patients who tend to have particularly severe headaches if they fail to take rather large amounts of drugs, such as three to four cafergot suppositories, some valium, and a number of aspirin each day. Rather than risk getting an extremely painful headache, these patients begin taking their medication at the first sign of such an event. Some patients maintain a daily prophylactic dosage and then augment this with additional amounts as a headache seems imminent. Unfortunately, through the years many events become conditioned to the headache pain. Thus, a heightened irritability, a slight feeling of depression, a tense neck musculature, a weather change, an argument with a friend or relative, or a party can signal the onslaught. The response of taking large amounts of medication at this point avoids the headache pain and thus strengthens the response. When asked to give up their medication (even a little at a time), and substitute their newly developed ability to control peripheral warmth, these patients may become very anxious, and therefore, more disposed to headaches.

Consequently, a period of systematic desensitization is required to reduce this anxiety before the medication reduction can begin. The desensitization hierarchy includes scenes in which the patient visualizes himself giving up a progressively greater amount of medication. Upon completion of the hierarchy, the patient is encouraged to begin a very gradual withdrawal from his medication.

Eventually, migraine patients find they can exist without medication except in extreme circumstances or in cases of menstrual cycle headaches that occur once or twice each cycle. Typically, the patients find that they can accomplish the hand-warming in the face of headache onset cues. However, if they are unable to accomplish this warming in 15 min, it is an indication that the headache onset has progressed too far and they will need some medication. This procedure gives the patient a chance to try altering his physiology before giving in to medication. In three cases of menstrual cycle migraine headaches, the hand-warming was difficult to accomplish and the patients usually resorted to medication at these times.

Treatment-refractory Anxiety

Although the research and clinical results with headache conditions appear somewhat compelling, such is not quite the case with biofeedback applied to anxiety problems. A recent study by Raskin et al.[15] indicated that three of ten chronically anxious patients improved moderately, and one showed marked improvement as a result of frontalis EMG feedback training.

Treatment-refractory Insomnia

In this same group of patients,* greater changes were seen in insomnia: of a total of six, four moderately improved and one markedly improved. Since all ten of these patients were considered to be treatment refractory (they had remained symptomatic despite 2 yr of treatment with individual psychotherapy and medication), and considering the fact that the biofeedback training was not augmented by other relaxation training, the results are indeed promising.

Circumscribed Phobias

After some 5 yr of experimentation at the University of Colorado Medical Center with a variety of biofeedback procedures for anxiety, we have evolved certain programs based on the type of anxiety response shown by the patient. As a general rule, the more specific the anxiety stimulus, the shorter the relaxation training and desensitization time required.[2,3] Experience with some 60 patients has led us to the conclusion that relaxation training may not be required for patients with very circumscribed phobias. Typically, the desensitization can be completed before the patient faces an in vivo phobic stimulus. In most instances he can confront it at a time of his own choosing.

Social Phobias

However, anxiety disorders in which the precipitating stimuli are more common in the environment, such as with social phobias, appear to be charac-

---

*Of these ten patients, four also had headache symptoms. Here the results were much better: three improved markedly and one moderately.

terized by higher arousal levels, and require a thorough period of relaxation training and desensitization.

Generalized Phobias

Lader and Mathews[10] have explored the relationship between the diffuseness of the anxiety and arousal level. Using spontaneous fluctuations of the galvanic skin response (GSR) as a measurement of arousal, they discovered that patients with more generalized phobias exhibited a significantly greater number of fluctuations than did normals or specific phobia patients. These researchers also discovered that those patients with generalized anxiety took much longer to habituate to an auditory stimulus than did normals or the specific phobia group. These conclusions are particularly interesting if the behavior therapy procedure known as systematic desensitization is considered to be an habituation phenomenon.

Thus, Lader and Mathews would view a patient with diffuse anxiety as manifesting a high level of arousal that may be maintained by a wide variety of stimuli, or by stimuli that are prevalent in the patient's environment. Lader and Mathews also predict that any improvement following desensitization would be short-lived in the absence of a *relatively permanent* decrease in arousal.

Agoraphobia

Lader and Wing[11] made the observation that agoraphobic patients have much anxiety even under resting conditions. They suggested that this condition may trigger episodes of positive feedback that are seen clinically as panic attacks. Furthermore, Marks[14] noticed that agoraphobic patients who had recently overcome their fears through systematic desensitization could experience a panic attack that would undo the effects of weeks of treatment. Raskin et al. stated that, "In order to achieve satisfactory results with chronic anxiety it appears necessary for the patient to incorporate relaxation into his daily activities."[15]

From the above observations, it has become apparent that patients with chronic generalized anxiety should be given thorough training in the achievement of low arousal states, and, furthermore, that they should be taught to maintain a normal arousal level in the face of everyday stress. If these goals are not achieved, the diffuse anxiety patient may become resensitized after completing systematic desensitization.

Achievement of Low Arousal

The concept of altering one's physiology in order to decrease the experience of anxiety has physiologic concomitants, however difficult they may be to measure. It is generally agreed that these physiologic correlates of anxiety are in the direction of heightened arousal. However, the arousal pattern, or profile of responses, for one individual may differ from that of another. Thus, the profile for one patient may be characterized by a large increase in frontalis EMG, and in another patient by a decrease in hand temperature. A third may show a suppression of the alpha EEG brain wave rhythm. Individuals tend to maintain their profiles across different stress conditions—a tendency labelled response sterotype or response specificity.[6] It simply means that a given individual, on different occasions, probably will show the greatest response to stress or anxiety in one particular system.

Perhaps the most efficient approach to biofeedback training for anxiety would involve the monitoring of several physiologic systems while the patient is made to feel slightly anxious or under stress. In this situation, that system (cortical, autonomic, or skeletal muscle) found to be most reactive would be the best prospect for the application of biofeedback. For example, if the patient is asked to think about an anxiety-arousing situation, or is asked to do mental arithmetic, his physiologic responses will change in the direction of increased arousal. This arousal pattern will reveal which response is most reactive.

At the Applied Biofeedback Institute, we have found it useful to use EMG as the initial feedback type. Training with EMG proceeds until the patient can maintain EMG levels below $3\mu V$ over the frontalis and the forearm extensor. When the patient has learned to meet these criteria, feedback of another type is employed if necessary. Criteria for these other responses are evolving as well; for example, we also train patients to develop and maintain skin temperatures of 90° F or more on the hands. In view of the observation of Lader and Mathews[10] that a relaxed individual will exhibit from one to three spontaneous GSR responses per minute, perhaps a maximum of two per minute could be used as a GSR criterion. Cool, damp hands are a common condition in chronically anxious individuals. A high rate of spontaneous GSR activity and decreased hand temperature are reflective of sympathetic arousal. The biofeedback training for individuals with chronic anxiety is thus designed to decrease general arousal, thereby promoting an autonomic, cortical, and skeletal motor profile characteristic of relaxed, and therefore, unanxious patients.

At this stage of training the patient is encouraged to try out his newly developed skills in real-life situations. The confidence to do this can be strengthened by means of several procedures. Systematic desensitization of relevant anxiety hierarchies (see Budzynski and Stoyva[2,3] and Wickramasekera[20]), role rehearsal, and assertive training are some of the behavior therapy approaches that can be employed. One procedure that appears to be of value involves the visualization of anxiety-arousing situations until the anxiety is definitely felt. With well-trained patients, the visualized anxiety situations must be grossly exaggerated in order to produce feelings of anxiety. The patient is receiving feedback of EMG, GSR, or temperature at this time, and is thus aware of the physiologic effects of the anxiety. He then attempts to recover from the heightened arousal by lowering the feedback indicators. We have found that a patient learns to do this in the space of one or two training sessions. Convinced that he can recover successfully with feedback, the patient then practices without feedback. "Recovery training" of this sort provides the patient with the confidence that even if he should begin to experience anxiety outside the clinic, he can bring himself under control. Armed with this knowledge, the patient is less likely to avoid situations that were formerly anxiety-provoking in nature. Hence, he has a greater probability of undergoing in vivo desensitization on his own.

Sleep-onset Insomnia

The process of falling asleep involves a lowering of arousal that is indicated by decreasing muscle tonus and heart rate, as well as a decrease in brain wave frequencies. Typically, the relaxed, eyes-closed alpha rhythm begins to slow and diminish in amplitude as theta (4-7 Hz) begins to increase. We felt, therefore, that a useful program for sleep-onset problems would involve muscle relaxation followed by the shaping of drowsy brain wave rhythms.

Thus far, we have trained 11 sleep-onset insomnia (SOI) patients with EMG feedback and theta EEG feedback. Six of the 11 have improved, three dramatically. Five showed no improvement for a variety of reasons.

In general, we have found that individuals with SOI show high EMG levels and an activated EEG. However, several patients could produce very low EMG levels as a result of prior training with various relaxation techniques. These individuals, however, did *not* show evidence of drowsy brain rhythms (theta EEG). Two were able to acquire control over theta by means of theta feedback, and their sleep subsequently improved. The other low EMG patient could not increase theta and did not improve.

The assumption that patients with high levels of muscle tension have difficulty producing theta rhythms was tested in an experiment by Sittenfeld et al.[18] The study compared the ability of normal subjects with high and low muscle tension to produce an increase in theta activity through biofeedback. The results clearly showed that high EMG subjects required prior EMG feedback before theta EEG training was effective. Low EMG subjects, on the other hand, were able to increase their theta activity through theta feedback without the prior EMG training.

Procedures to increase the base operant of theta other than by lowering EMG are being explored at the present time.[1]

Additional support for the application of EMG biofeedback to insomnia comes from the study by Raskin et al.[15] Five of six patients with sleep disturbances learned to put themselves to sleep without medication. This was reported to have markedly decreased their fears of insomnia, even though the patients also stated that their sleep was not as restful as the sedative-induced sleep previously experienced. It is very possible that the medication problem (withdrawal fears and physiologic reactions) with insomnia patients is similar in kind to that encountered in migraine cases. Thus, insomnia patients who regularly take medication before bedtime may benefit from a medication-withdrawal systematic desensitization prior to the actual in vivo gradual withdrawal from medication.

CONCLUDING REMARKS

An accumulating body of clinical and research evidence suggests that biofeedback represents a relatively effective technique for the shaping of self-control over certain physiologic events. These events are usually autonomous in that they tend to occur automatically and below the level of awareness. When these internal events fall outside the normal range of functioning, they constitute maladaptive behaviors that can lead to feelings of anxiety, or the appearance of such stress-related disorders as migraine and tension headaches, certain cardiovascular problems, and sleep-onset insomnia, to name a few. Through biofeedback training, patients learn to maintain their physiology within a normal range of functioning.

In addition to the alleviation or elimination of the symptoms of stress-related disorders, biofeedback training could constitute a preventive technique to enable individuals to better cope with the stress of a "future shock" environment. Furthermore, the development of self-control of internal functions at an early age might represent one of the most effective programs for the prevention of those disorders that produce the highest incidences of morbidity and mortality in our industrialized, fast-paced culture.

REFERENCES

1. Budzynski T: Some applications of biofeedback-produced twilight states. Fields Within Fields ... Within Fields 5:105, 1972. Republished in Shapiro D, et al (eds): Biofeedback and Self-Control: 1972. Chicago, Aldine-Atherton, in press

2. Budzynski T, Stoyva J: Biofeedback techniques in behavior therapy, in Birbaumer N (ed): The Mastery of Anxiety. Contribution of Neuropsychology to Anxiety Research. Reihe Fortschritte der Klinischen Psychologie, Bd. 4, München, Wien: Verlag, Urban & Schwarzenberg, 1973, in press. English version republished in Shapiro D, et al (eds): Biofeedback and Self-Control: 1972. Chicago, Aldine-Atherton, in press

3. Budzynski T, Stoyva J: EMG biofeedback and behavior therapy, in Jurjevich R (ed): Direct Psychotherapy, vol 3: International Developments. Coral Gables, Fla, University of Miami Press, in press

4. Budzynski T, Stoyva J, Adler C: Feedback-induced relaxation: Application to tension headache. J Behav Ther Exp Psychiatry 1:205, 1970

5. Budzynski T, Stoyva J, Adler C, et al: EMG biofeedback and tension headache: A controlled outcome study. Psychosom Med (in press)

6. Engel BT: Response specificity, in Greenfield N, Sternbach R (eds): Handbook of Psychophysiology. New York, Holt, Rinehart & Winston, 1972, p 571

7. Gellhorn E: Motion and emotion. Psychol Rev 71:457, 1964

8. Green E, Green A, Walters E: Voluntary control of internal states: Psychological and physiological. J Transpersonal Psychol 2:1, 1970

9. Jacobson E: Progressive Relaxation (ed 2). Chicago, Univ of Chicago Pr, 1938

10. Lader MH, Mathews AM: A physiological model of phobic anxiety and desensitization. Behav Res Ther 6:411, 1968

11. Lader MH, Wing L: Physiological Measures, Sedative Drugs, and Morbid Anxiety. London, Univ of Oxford Pr, 1966

12. Leitenberg H, Agras W, Thompson L, et al: Feedback in behavior modification: An experimental analysis in two phobic cases. J Appl Behav Anal 1:131, 1968

13. Love WA: Problems in therapeutic application of EMG feedback. Presented at the Annual Meeting of the Biofeedback Research Society, Boston, 1972, unpublished

14. Marks IM: Fears and Phobias. New York, Academic Press, 1969, p 207

15. Raskin M, Johnson G, Rondestvedt T: Chronic anxiety treated by feedback-induced muscle relaxation. Arch Gen Psychiatry 28:263, 1973

16. Sargent J, Green E, Walters E: Preliminary report on the use of autogenic feedback techniques in the treatment of migraine and tension headaches. Psychosom Med 35: 129–135, 1973

17. Schultz J, Luthe W: Autogenic Training. New York, Grune & Stratton, 1959

18. Sittenfeld P, Budzynski T, Stoyva J: Feedback control of the EEG theta rhythm. Presented at the American Psychological Association Meeting, Honolulu, 1972

19. Stoyva J, Budzynski T: Cultivated low arousal—An anti-stress response?, in DiCara LV (ed): Recent Advances in Limbic and Autonomic Nervous System Research. New York, Plenum, in press

20. Wickramasekera I: Instructions and EMG feedback in systematic desensitization: A case report. Behav Ther 3:460, 1972

Chapter 12: Furor Therapeuticus *Revisited*

Introduction

IN THIS CHAPTER, Dr. Lynch looks with a critical eye at the furor and near hysteria surrounding much of what is written and said about biofeedback and its "potential" and presents his own analysis of the psychic and sociologic forces that he believes lie behind it. He pinpoints part of the trouble as being due to the wishful-thinking, utopian dream phenomenon and historically traces the predecessors of this as far back as William James' description in 1908 of the wish for a "Mind-Cure" in *The Varieties of Religious Experience* (see page 194).

As an antidote to this, he quotes Kubie's remarks, in 1952, at a conference on cybernetics, in a paper prophetically called "The Place of Emotions in the Feedback Concept":

> In these conferences, my role is one to which the psychiatrist must often reconcile himself. He is always a troublemaker because he must insist on the complexity over which not only the laity but even fellow scientists would prefer to gloss. The layman wants these phenomena to be simple so that his pet beliefs and biases and prejudices will not be disturbed. The experimentalist wants them to be simple because otherwise the experiments which he can devise in the laboratory, his laboratory models and his mathematical formulae will be an inadequate facsimile of that which they aim to produce.

Lee Birk, M.D.

Biofeedback: Some Reflections on Modern Behavioral Science

James J. Lynch, Ph.D.

This paper reviews the current status of biofeedback research within the context of the evolution of behavioral science research in general. Some of the methodologic and conceptual problems inherent in current biofeedback research are discussed in terms of earlier conditioning theory and research. In addition to a discussion of the scientific problems inherent in biofeedback research, this paper reviews some of the reasons this work has gained such widespread popular interest. Part of the interest in biofeedback research is traced to a widespread cultural belief in the efficacy of scientific technology to deliver the mind-cure, described earlier by William James. The future implications of biofeedback research for the practice of clinical psychology and psychiatry are discussed.

OVER TWO DECADES AGO, Larry Kubie presented a paper at a conference on cybernetics entitled "The Place of Emotions in the Feedback Concept."[12] The introduction to his paper perhaps might help set the "Leitmotiv" for this essay on biofeedback.

> In these conferences, my role is one to which the psychiatrist must often reconcile himself. He is always a troublemaker because he must insist on the complexity of the phenomena of the mind, a complexity over which not only the laity but even fellow scientists would prefer to gloss. The layman wants these phenomena to be simple so that his pet beliefs and biases and prejudices will not be disturbed. The experimentalist wants them to be simple because otherwise the experiments that he can devise in the laboratory, laboratory models, and his mathematical formulae will be an inadequate facimile of that which they aim to produce (p. 48).

Echoing the sentiments expressed by Kubie, one senses that at least one statement that can be made with certainty regarding the field of biofeedback is that this field encompasses an incredible array of the most complex psychologic and neurophysiologic phenomena. And yet in spite of the obvious complexity of this field few movements in psychology have recently gained more widespread and instantaneous recognition and interest. From major review articles in *Science*,[16] *Scientific American*,[4] and *American Scientist*[1] to an annual series of edited research reports entitled "Biofeedback and Self Control"[26] all the way to a detailed report in *Playboy*,[3] this field has caught the imagination of both scientists and laymen alike with a fervor that would certainly convert any doubting Thomas. The growth of interest in this field is reminiscent of the spirit of some peculiar scientific revival meeting, with an amazing range of clinical applications being suggested and reported, from the elimination of migraine headaches, cardiovascular problems, and epilepsy, all the way to "biologically teaching people how to be happy and serene."[15] And like other revival phenomena it has a somewhat distinctive American flavor, a point we

---

Supported in part by Grant DADA17-73-C-3030 from the U.S. Army.
Reprint requests should be addressed to Dr. James J. Lynch, Institute of Psychiatry and Human Behavior, University of Maryland Medical School, Baltimore, Md. 21201.
©1973 by Grune & Stratton, Inc.

shall return to subsequently. Current applications of biofeedback techniques range from outright opportunism and charlatanism, to a rather widespread noncritical acceptance by both the public and scientific community alike of naïve explanations for the most complex psychophysiologic phenomena, all the way to some very interesting and promising clinical applications. There have been exceptions to the uncritical acceptance of this field,[7,22,23] but until recently their protests have been voices crying in a wilderness.

Given the complexity of this field, coupled with its many controversial aspects, this review will focus on those aspects of biofeedback that seem of more general concern to the field of psychiatry and psychology. No specific research areas in biofeedback will be critically assessed, however, since each of these areas would require separate detailed analyses. Our concern is not with the specific methodology of biofeedback nor any specific applications but rather with the more general philosophical direction and implications of this field.

THE EVOLUTION OF BIOFEEDBACK

At the 1967 Annual Meeting of the Pavlovian Society of North America, a most remarkable report was given by Dr. Neal Miller.[17] He presented an ingenious technique that was first worked out by Jay Trowill. Animals were immobilized with d-tubo curarine, and artificially respirated. Electrodes were placed in the "pleasure centers" of the animal's brain, and a wide variety of physiologic systems operantly conditioned with amazing ease. At that meeting, Dr. Miller reported that the paralyzed animal could learn through operant conditioning to either increase or decrease its heart rate, change blood pressure, increase or decrease kidney flow, change the vasodilation in the ears, increase or decrease gastric motility—there seemed to be few physiologic limits to what was possible. One simply had to "reward" the animal with a brief electric pulse to the "pleasure center" for behaving in a method determined by the experimenter. But the "behavior" that was being rewarded was unusual—it was any specific physiologic system that the experimenter wished to control. So response specific was this operant control over the autonomic nervous system that it was reported that heart rate could be altered while blood pressure remained unaffected. At the time of this meeting, the specificity and precision of the control seemed so remarkable that it almost appeared to defy well-established physical laws of hydraulics, let alone defy previously long-held beliefs in physiology!

I remember being so stunned by an animal "learning" to slow its own heart rate by more than 100 beats/min while paralyzed, that I asked in jest if one could teach an animal through operant rewarding techniques to slow its heart rate to the point of total cardiac arrest? That question was, however, answered quite seriously by Dr. Miller with the following statement: "Indeed many animals had shaped themselves into their own final reward." That animals could learn, through operant conditioning to kill themselves seemed too difficult to believe and too complex to understand. After reflecting on these reports, it seemed evident that if the interpretation of these laboratory data in terms of operant conditioning processes was correct, then perhaps there was something profoundly wrong with the whole notion of conditioning. This led to the comment that if rats could learn to kill themselves through operant conditioning then "through an accelerated program of successive approximation perhaps in the not too distant future cats could be 'shaped' to bark, dogs 'shaped' to meow, and rats 'shaped' to walk on water!"[13]

The reports from Miller's laboratory were both preceded and followed by an avalanche of similar findings from other laboratories, and by 1971 the Annual Series of selected papers in *Biofeedback and Self-Control* had reached 565 pages.[26]

Mixed with a growing number of reports from various laboratories of the successful operant conditioning of a wide range of autonomic nervous system functions emerged the fascinating possibility of operantly learning to control both animal and human brain wave activity.[1,10] These reports were exciting not only because of the inherent relevance these findings offered for clinical problems such as epilepsy, but also for the subjective feeling states that purportedly accompanied the control of human brain wave activity. Kamiya and others reported that humans could learn, through feedback techniques, to either turn on or block their own alpha activity and that the turning on of alpha activity was generally accompanied by positive subjective feeling states that ranged from very pleasant to sensuous.[8,10,20]

To someone unfamiliar with conditioning theory and techniques, however, the very idea of a paralyzed rat "learning" to control its heart rate, or a human "learning" to control his or her brain wave activity would have to appear both rather strange and exciting. The conditioning theory that led to these techniques will be outlined subsequently. Within the field of psychology, these findings not only set off an explosion of research activity, but the most intriguing statements began to be heard at scientific meetings and published in the literature. The following are just a sample of what was and is still being stated.

(1) There is a strong traditional belief in the inferiority of the autonomic nervous system and the visceral responses that it controls. The recent experiments disproving this belief have deep implications for theories of learning, for individual differences in autonomic responses, for the cause and cure of abnormal psychosomatic symptoms, and possibly also for the understanding of normal homeostasis[16] (p. 435).

(2) It is now biologically possible to teach people how to be happy and serene.[15]

(3) By the year 2000 all types of subjective states will be anchored to specific EEGs.[19]

(4) In general, people who tend toward a lot of alpha in their EEGs are dull, uninteresting, unimaginative, hardworking, plugging-along ordinary people. And that's the truth.[3] (Curiously, that statement was made in an article that had previously pointed out that Albert Einstein probably possessed high alpha activity).

(5) Damn the issue of mediation in Biofeedback. Who cares how people control their heart rate or brain waves. The only important thing is that they do it. (Comment made by a scientist at the 1971 Psychophysiological Meetings — name withheld.)

(6) The question of the meaning of the word Behavior is sheer nonsense. Philosophy is dead. Philosophical concerns bogged down psychological progress for centuries. Philosophical concerns never bought anybody anything. (Statement made by one of the leading Behavioral Scientists in the U.S. at a meeting in 1972 — name withheld.)

(7) Kamiya speculated that this state might be similar to Zen and Yoga meditation and suggested that operant conditioning may be a more efficient way of learning to achieve this state than the usual protracted Zen or Yoga training procedures — a method, perhaps, for attaining instant Nirvana.[1]

This sample of recent statements is presented to emphasize the central theme of this paper, and that is that the biofeedback movement encompasses not only specific techniques purported to alter physiologic processes as well as subjective feeling states, but it also reflects a general philosophic climate that appears to be dominating the "Behavioral Sciences" as our 20th century begins to ebb.

BEHAVIORAL SCIENCE AND THE SEARCH FOR THE MIND-CURE

Both the current biofeedback techniques, and the statements previously quoted have evolved out of a philosophic-scientific union that has, in this century, made heroic efforts to resolve with objective techniques the mind-body problem, and from a culture that appears to be in desparate pursuit of scientific solutions to problems of human emotions and feelings.

One must, however, look at the whole sociology of science and especially the sociology of "scientific" psychology in order to see the biofeedback movement in perspective. The very research paradigm worked out by Dr. Miller is itself of great interest. There are many aspects of this model that merit closer empirical scrutiny, and a discussion of the historical antecedents of this model will be briefly presented in a later section of this paper. However, over and above the specific empirical problems inherent in this model is a more general idea that is of great interest. If one steps back to take an overview of this research, the picture that emerges is remarkable. An animal rests completely immobilized by a drug. And yet, in spite of this condition, the most profound and precise physiologic changes occur through operant conditioning apparently without any effort. The animal does not have to work at producing profound physiologic changes; in fact the animal cannot work! The animal does not have to change or do anything, it simply lets these changes happen. The animal quite literally has no investment in the process, and is powerless to help or prevent its physiology from being rewarded into change. And flowing from the powerful impression of this empirical model is the implicit belief that if these profound changes occur in such controlled animal situations, then one need not worry about the many methodologic problems that might surround similar human operant conditioning control over physiology!

The passivity of the animal in this curare model is strikingly similar to the passivity advocated by much Eastern philosophy, and indeed many discussion of biofeedback are accompanied by references to and interest in Zen, Yoga, and other Eastern meditative techniques. As already noted in one of the quotations, "instant Nirvana" seems to be one of the ultimate goals for some of the scientists involved in biofeedback research.[1] This Nirvana will apparently be delivered through the combined efforts of science and behavioral technology. Mechanical salvation will be delivered to the masses by a new breed of psychotechnicians. By embracing the collective wisdom of psychology, psychiatry, physiology, medicine, and engineering, it would appear that these sciences are on the verge of technically delivering both health and joy to one's life; that is, they will "biologically teach people to be happy and serene."[15]

To a spectator outside the arena of the biofeedback movement, the statements made by some of its proponents might sound like lines from some tragic comedy in which the actors had a curious technical method to their madness. And yet, in spite of its complexities, it is not very difficult to understand why biofeedback research has met with such widespread interest. It would seem to have not only potential practical clinical applications but it also appears to satisfy some rather deep-rooted needs embedded in the American culture. The groundwork for something akin to biofeedback has been quietly prepared for over 100 yr.

About 70 yr ago, William James published his text on *The Varieties of Religious Experience,*[9] in which he outlined the most peculiar American propensity towards what he termed the religion of "healthy-mindedness" and its derivative, the American pursuit of the "mind-cure." In many ways, James' description of this phenomenon seems to remarkably parallel the type of philosophy currently expressed in biofeedback.

> If we were to ask the question "What is human life's chief concern?" one of the answers we should receive would be: "It is happiness . . ." But in the theory of evolution which, gathering momentum for a century, has within the past twenty-five years swept so rapidly over Europe and America, we see the ground laid for a new sort of religion of Nature, which has entirely displaced Christianity from the thought of a large part of our generation . . . We find evolutionism interpreted thus optimistically and embraced as a substitute for the religion they were born in by a multitude of our contemporaries who have either been trained scientifically, or been fond of reading popular science . . . To my mind a current far more important and interesting religiously than that which sets in from natural science towards healthy mindedness is that which recently poured over America and seems to be gathering force every day . . . and to which, for the sake of having a brief designation, I will give the title of the 'Mind-cure movement' . . . The most characteristic feature of the mind-cure movement is an inspiration much more direct. The leaders in this faith have had an intuitive belief in the all-saving power of healthy-minded attitudes as such in the conquering efficacy of courage, hope and trust, and a correlative contempt for doubt, fear, worry and all precautionary states of mind . . . The blind have been made to see, the halt to walk, lifelong invalids have had their health restored.
>
> The plain fact remains that the spread of the movement has been due to practical fruits, and the extremely practical turn of character of the American people has never been better shown than by the fact that this, their only decidedly original contribution to the systematic philosophy of life, should be so intimately knit up with concrete therapeutics (pp. 78–112).

The similarities of the biofeedback movement and the mind-cure movement described by James are striking. First, biofeedback is inextricably bound up with "concrete therapeutics" and is clearly practical in its outlook. Its philosophy is exemplified in the quotes from its proponents. Second, biofeedback is clearly rooted in the scientific theory of conditioning that derives a good deal of its cross-species validity from the theory of evolution. Third, as is implicitly suggested by animal research in which the animal is totally immobilized, the physiologic changes that do occur must take place in the brain, that is, the mind must cure the body. It would seem then that the striking parallels between the mind-cure movement and current biofeedback research might reflect some fundamental features of American culture that have had a direct influence on the evolutionary development of the behavioral sciences.

If we were to ask again, as did William James, what is life's chief concern? one of the answers we would indeed receive would be "It is happiness." But who are the modern custodians and deliverers of happiness? While the chief concern for questions dealing with human happiness were once entrusted to religion, clearly within our modern culture the custody of our happiness has been entrusted with a growing enthusiasm to science, which delivers its service through technology. Signs of the belief in the power of science and technology are everywhere. Even more than at the beginning of the 20th century when William James wrote his text, evidence of the success of scientific technology abound. One of the more recent notable technical successes was our walking on the moon. And yet, how are these impressive technical achievements going to be translated into internal, subjective improvement in our quest for happiness. Clearly again, science or at least our belief in scientific technology make it the likely choice. It seems to be widely believed that the science that put us on the moon should be able to deliver health, joy, and meaning to our lives. And what specific scientific discipline will be responsible for this latter charge? Clearly, psychiatry and psychology and its supportive scientific substratum, the behavioral sciences, will help in this endeavor, if not be totally in charge of the movement.

It does appear that at least part of the cultural legitimacy of psychiatry and psychology rests in the widespread belief that these fields are based in scientific knowledge and scientific methods. Their current leadership in the cultural search for the mind-cure rests in their implicit and explicit claims of scientific status. Every high school and college student who takes a course in psychology is ritualistically told on page one of their textbooks that *psychology is the scientific study of the behavior of organisms.* The growth and proliferation of psychology departments and psychology courses in American colleges since 1900 is nothing short of astounding. They have outstripped the growth of almost every other basic science department at a rate that might be logarithmic. It would perhaps be useful to occasionally ponder whether the substantive base of this field, compared to the other basic sciences, justifies such explosive growth. It is also most curious to observe the manner in which psychiatry departments in the United States medical schools have also included the words Behavior or Behavioral Science in their departmental titles. One can speculate as to why these additions have occurred so recently? It would appear that this reflects, at least in part, a yearning for scientific validity.

Coupled with this academic growth in psychology and psychiatry, and their concern for scientific status is the equally phenomenal cultural demand for their services. Traditional psychotherapeutic approaches with their emphasis on one-to-one patient–therapist relationships that often proceed very slowly do not seem to be able to keep pace with the cultural demand for their service. Indeed, the demand for the service seems so great that traditional one-to-one, client–therapist psychotherapeutic techniques may very well have failed to service the mind-cure needs of the culture. Is it any wonder, then, that we are now witnessing a remarkable growth in group psychotherapy techniques including group therapy, sensitivity groups, and the ultimate emergence of something called Community Mental Health Centers? The myriad of complexities inherent in all of these movements seem to be of little consequence in slowing their growth—after all, it is implicitly believed by most that they are ultimately based in scientific principles and methods. And being scientific, it should only be a matter of time before they develop the proper technology to deliver the mind-cure.

And yet mixed with this phenomenal growth in the cultural belief in science and its technology is the curious emergence of the beginnings of a belief in the opposite, a belief in, or at least a widespread fascination with, the nonrational. While this belief in the nonrational has the earmarks of a fad in many of our college campuses, and is reflected in a widespread interest in phenomena such as astrology, within science itself the collision of the rational and the nonrational take the form of a most serious debate. Indeed, it appears as if it is the very success of various scientific endeavors that is crystallizing and opening up to challenge the basic assumptions of these fields. The very "success" of biofeedback research forces one to reconsider the basic tenets of conditioning theory.

Perhaps the scientific field where these forces are colliding most directly is in molecular genetics. In little over 100 yr, this field has evolved from the quiet observations of law and order in the growth of peas to the cracking of the genetic code. But with the code now cracked, the question can be asked more precisely, what gives law and order to life? Does law and order come from chance or some kind of necessary design? The collision of the rational and the irrational in this field is perhaps best outlined by Gunther Stent in his article, "An Ode to Objectivity."[25] Stent's article is an essay on Jacques Monod's recent book entitled *Chance and Necessity,* in which he outlines the conflicting philosophic beliefs that seem to be emerging from modern evolutionism pushed to its ultimate. One of the outcomes may very well be, as Stent suggests, that the 64 elements of the genetic code may be replaced by the 64 elements of the I Ching. It is curious how Eastern philosophy creeps into discussions of molecular genetics as well as biofeedback.

As Stent summarized, "Law and order may not only be disappearing from the streets but from the universe."

While space mitigates against the elaboration of this point, the fact remains that these struggles in the basic sciences have a direct bearing on the future scientific status of psychiatry and psychology. If indeed the validity of the basic sciences is seriously questioned, then it will not take long for that debate to engulf the behavioral sciences.

To repeat a statement made earlier, it is the apparent total "success" of the operant conditioning studies that expose its central beliefs to closer scrutiny. Dr. Miller now states that neither he nor any of his colleagues can replicate any of their original findings and suggests that the earlier findings may have been due to the curare they used in their original studies.[18] It is also now apparent that the earlier reports on alpha wave feedback control had serious methodologic flaws.[14] Like so many other endeavors in the history of science, however, perhaps there are important lessons for psychiatry and psychology that will emerge from these studies. Some attention both to the historical antecedents of this work, and the philosophical beliefs implicit in this work might be useful.

In some ways the initial exuberant statements made in biofeedback research echo a theme sounded by the behaviorist John B. Watson many years earlier. He stated that if he were given suitable control of environmental factors, "he could take any normal baby and "guarantee" to "train him" to become any type of specialist I might select—doctor, lawyer, artist, merchant-chief, and yes even beggar-man and thief, regardless of his talents, penchants, tendencies, abilities, vocation and race of his ancestors." It was really only a small step to extend that type of logic to behavioristic control over physiologic processes.

Given its Watsonian-Skinnerian tradition, however, current biofeedback techniques present the most curious array of bedfellows. These techniques emerged out of the behaviorist tradition, which believed that through precise control of environmental contingencies and immediate reward following the appropriate behavior, one could "shape" and control "behavior," whether that behavior be a rat pressing a bar, or a rat learning to lower its heart rate. But as any student of history will recall, the utilization or mention of concepts such as consciousness and awareness were particularly eschewed by the early Behaviorists. In fact, Watson initiated the Behavioristic movement more or less as a direct reaction against the techniques of introspection used by psychologists during the early 20th century. The introspectionists were, at that time, wrestling with the phenomenon of consciousness and the subjective nature of man. Given this history, it is most paradoxical that in the concept of "biofeedback" mention of awareness, consciousness, and subjective feelings reappear. These trends are most apparent in the human alpha wave "conditioning" studies in which repeated references to altered "states of consciousness" and subjective mood changes are made.

The fundamental issues involved in the controversy surrounding current biofeedback research closely resemble a debate that has periodically waxed and waned since the 16th century. An exhaustive discussion of all the empirical and philosophical antecedents of this area, however, would be far beyond the scope of this paper and we refer the interested reader to other sources for an overview.[2,11,21] The central problem, however, is that two fundamental issues that have constantly plagued empirical psychology since its inception appear once more in biofeedback research: (1) the idea of a reflex; (2) the idea of a conditional reflex.

Few ideas are more central to modern physiology, psychology, and psychiatry than the idea of the existence of something called a reflex. The notion first emerged from Descartes' observations of the mechanical operations of water gardens popular in his day, which curiously also operated on the principle of feedback, hydraulic rather than biologic. "Reflection" was the mechanism for how animal spirits traveled down "Tubules" to move a small boy's foot away from a hot fire. But how did the little boy learn not to put his foot in the fire again? How did he learn? Descartes had the brilliance to extract himself from this difficult question with a leap of faith—man had a soul. Descartes believed that animals operated just like the preprogrammed water gardens, "automata," functioning under what we would now understand as cybernetic principles. But man—clearly he thought—he had a soul, and in a sense he did not conform to any simple cybernetic laws.

Subsequent to Descartes' observation an entire new way of "understanding" how a little boy moves his foot out of fire began to evolve. Today we "know" that such flexion movements are accomplished through nerves (rather than tubules) that form a reflex arc. We also "know" that he learns not to put his foot in the fire again through conditioning; that is, the little boy forms a "conditional avoidance reflex." As stated elsewhere, the older Cartesian concept, "I think, therefore, I am," has been gradually replaced by the implicit scientific belief "I think, therefore, I possess protein molecules."[13] But as Kubie suggests, perhaps we have chosen to gloss over many of the problems inherent in our modern explanations as a comfortable alternative to realizing that we simply do not understand the process. The subjective nature of man, his emotional fiber does not seem to yield to simple cybernetic formulae. While man is a reflex creature, he seems to be something more, and is at the very least the most complex of cybernetic beasts.

Descartes' idea of a reflex has evolved through a bewildering series of metamorphoses in the intervening centuries. The evolutionary additions and changes in the meaning of the word reflex have been documented in detail by Fearing in his text *Reflex Action*.[6] For the scientific status of psychiatry and psychology, a profound addition to the meaning of the word reflex came at the beginning of the 20th century when I.P. Pavlov began developing the idea of a conditional reflex. Pavlov did not concern himself with general philosophy, and never really questioned the essential meaning of the term reflex (Gantt, personal communication). Rather, he was a reflex physiologist, dealing with the reflex physiology of the gastrointestinal system. The utility of his ingenious work won him the Nobel Prize. As is well known, however, his painstaking observations on the reflex physiology of digestion, gradually were confounded by the fact that animals not only showed gastric secretions to the physical presence of food in their stomachs, but indeed if specific procedures were repeated frequently enough the animal would begin to manifest gastric secretions to the human who was bringing the food, the room in which he was fed, etc. That is inborn reflexes (unconditional reflexes) once only elicited by natural stimuli (unconditional stimuli) could now be elicited by stimuli (conditional stimuli) that previously did not elicit reactions but now did (conditional responses) through their frequent pairing with unconditional stimuli. Rather than gloss over this development Pavlov decided to explore this phenomenon in depth and the study of "higher nervous activity" began in earnest.

Watson quickly seized upon Pavlov's model as the best hope for the development of an objective psychology. But as conditioning research developed and grew in scope, the old Cartesian problem began to emerge, semi-disguised with new terminology. By the mid 1930s, bitter debates were triggered by the question: Where did conditional reflexes develop? Where in the peripheral nervous system or central nervous system did conditioning take place? The search for some new type of Cartesian pineal gland has been carried on intermittently ever since in deadly earnest, with few, however any longer willing to entertain the possibility that perhaps the formation of conditional reflexes requires a soul! Among the first uses of curare by psychologists was in conditioning research, where it was used to rule out peripheral activity as a necessary component of conditional reflex formation. It should be equally obvious why Miller used a curare derivative in his conditioning procedures. He also was attempting to rule out obvious peripheral factors that might have mediated or influenced the heart rate reactions of his rats. But as one begins to systematically rule out mediating factors in conditioning, the opposite question begins to emerge. If this, and this, and this do *not* mediate conditioning, what does?

Curiously, following Skinner's paper, "The Concept of the Reflex in the Description of Behavior,"[24] the intensity of the debate about the locus of conditioning subsided somewhat. Skinner sensed the obvious—the old definition of reflex had a number of implicit negative connotations i.e., it was *nonvoluntary, nonconscious*, etc. These terms could not be operationally defined and were obviously counterproductive to scientific progress. His solution to this dilemma was to redefine a reflex in strictly "operational" terms as nothing more and nothing less than a "correlation between a stimulus and a response." With this new definition, one could easily begin to understand "behavior" as a complex chain of simpler reflexes. For many, this solution has proven quite practical. For others this new definition of a reflex is only more confusing.[5,13] In any event, it is easy to see how the idea of biofeedback could evolve from this new operational definition of a reflex. After all, a newspaper blowing down a street in the wind could now "operationally" be called a reflex and its "behavior" understood.

Perhaps Schrödinger's observation regarding the gap between our understanding of physics and our understanding of subjective life is apropos. He observed that no objective measure of light quanta emitted from a child's eyes would equal the joy in the child's eye. Something seems to be missing in physics. In our understanding of the word "Behavior," something indeed seems to be missing.

EPILOGUE

Several months ago, a middle-aged lady called me on the telephone and told me that she was suffering from severe gastric pain. She was calling to find out if I would be willing to teach her biofeedback techniques so that she could control her stomach and therefore alleviate her pain. She said she had seen numerous physicians but they were no help. When I told her that I did not think biofeedback techniques were sufficiently advanced to help her, and that I personally was skeptical of the current therapeutic utility of this approach, she quickly said, "Even if you don't think it's any good I am certain these techniques can help me."

Similar statements of profound faith in biofeedback techniques have been heard by a large number of research personnel engaged in biofeedback research. We stated earlier that the early alpha wave feedback research had been replicated and methodologic shortcomings in the early reports had been noted. The methodologic problems are discussed in detail elsewhere.[14] One of the central issues in this work was the question of whether subjects actually learned to control alpha wave activity, or were they doing something else that was influencing alpha activity. The basic design was one in which an individual was seated in a room and his EEG recorded. Through a feedback system his EEG was linked to either a tone or a light that changed pitch or color during the presence of alpha. The subject's task was simply to keep the alpha tone or the alpha light on as much of the time as possible.

In our first group of subjects, we used visual feedback in which a light changed from red to green during the presence of alpha activity. Our first subjects did appear to be able to turn on the green light with an increased frequency with practice. All of the subjects reported that the turning on of the green light was pleasurable, the entire experience most enjoyable. We were initially very impressed with these reports and the entire phenomenon.

It took an artifact in one of our sessions to prod us into a closer empirical analysis. One day a subject came into our experiment who had virtually no naturally occurring alpha activity in his EEG. For four or five trials the feedback light remained red. Then suddenly alpha activity burst on and the green light stayed on almost continuously for the remainder of the experiment. No subject had ever demonstrated such complete success before. Rushing into the room after the experiment I asked him how did he attain such success? He looked at me with a broad smile and said, "I pinched my cheek." Then with a pause, he went on to tell me that this had been one of the more interesting experiences in his life. The young man's cheek was beet red. Then I asked him how did he come to think of pinching his cheek to perform this task? He stated he had been staring at the red light so hard and so long that tears began to run down his cheek. When he brushed one tear away he noticed the green light came on and so he began to press against his cheek. What this particular subject did was move his cheek in such a way that a muscle artifact of 10 cycles/sec at 20–30 μV was created on the mastoid reference lead, which was the precise criteria for alpha activity. Our other subjects had indeed generated alpha activity, but this event was particularly illuminating. How could pinching one's cheek in the dark for 45 min produce such joy and meaning?

We decided to run control subjects who were given false feedback, or more precisely given the median pattern of feedback that had been produced by our initial group of subjects. The subjects given false feedback also produced more alpha activity over repeated trials. But it was obvious they could not be learning anything about the alpha activity simply because they were given incorrect feedback. Nevertheless, these subjects also reported this experience to be most enjoyable. Some even stated that it was one of the more interesting experiences in their lives. The "objective reality" of the situation was that these individuals were simply seated in a room in which a red light periodically flashed green. There seemed to be an enormous gulf between our objective reality and their subjective interpretations. Not only had we directly suggested the affective reactions to them, they were implicit in the entire structure of the experiment. After all, it is not every day in the week that "scientists" take you in their laboratories and help you *control* your own brain waves!

It is of interest to reflect on the fact that the subjects who reported that a red light that occasionally and randomly flashed green provided them with one of the more meaningful experiences in their lives were not uninformed people. Rather, they were students from one of our nation's Ivy League colleges.

In this review, no specific area of biofeedback has been examined in detail, and obviously each of these areas merit individual appraisal. While the tone of this review has been critical, it is my hope that it will serve to stimulate rather than discourage additional research in this area. While, like Dr. Kubie, I find myself a troublemaker insisting on the complexity of the mind, it is only because I find the complexity of the mind exhilarating. Indeed, no cybernetic computer employing feedback principles ever found joy and meaning in pinching its cheek!

ACKNOWLEDGMENT

Many thanks are due to Aaron Katcher, M.D., Larry Kubie, M.D. and David A. Paskewitz, Ph.D. for providing some of the ideas presented in this paper. A special debt is also due to a group of medical students who have during a luncheon seminar over a 2-yr period struggled with me to understand the Behavioral Sciences. They have helped crystallize the philosophical point of view expressed in this paper.

REFERENCES

1. Black A: The direct control of neural processes by reward and punishment. Am Sci 59:236–245, 1971
2. Boring EG: A History of Experimental Psychology. New York, Appleton-Century-Crofts, 1957
3. Brown B: Quoted in: A heart-stopping, eye-bulging, wave-making idea. Scot Morris, Playboy, December 1972, pp 229–249
4. DiCara L: Learning in the autonomic nervous system. Sci Am 222:30–39, 1970
5. Efron R: The conditioned reflex: A meaningless concept. Perspect Biol Med 9:488–514, 1966
6. Fearing F: Reflex Action. New York, Hofner, 1964
7. Gantt WH: B.F. Skinner and his contingencies. Cond Reflex 5:63–74, 1970
8. Hart JT: Autocontrol of EEG alpha. Presented at the Seventh Annual Meeting of the Society for Psychophysiological Research, San Diego, October, 1967
9. James W: The Varieties of Religious Experience: A Study in Human Nature. London, Longmans, Green & Co., 1908
10. Kamiya J: Operant control of the EEG alpha rhythm and some of its reported effects on consciousness, in Tart CT (ed): Altered States of Consciousness. New York, Wiley, 1969
11. Klein DB: A History of Scientific Psychology. New York, Basic Books, 1970
12. Kubie L: The place of emotions in the feedback concept, in Cybernetics: Transactions of the 9th Conference: The Josiah Macy, Jr., Foundation, March 1952, pp 48–72
13. Lynch JJ: The stimulus—the ghost—the response: The carousel of conditioning. Cond Reflex 5:133–139, 1970 (editorial)
14. Lynch JJ, Paskewitz DA: On the mechanisms of the feedback control of human brain wave activity. J Nerv Ment Dis 153:205–217, 1971
15. Maslow A: Toward a humanistic biology. Am Psychol 24:724–735, 1969
16. Miller NE: Learning of visceral and glandular responses. Science 163:434–445, 1969
17. Miller NE: Paper presented at the Annual Meeting of the Pavlovian Society of North America. Cond Reflex 3:129, 1968
18. Miller NE: Comments made at the symposium: Issues in biofeedback and operant control of physiological processes. Presented at the 12th Annual Meeting of the Society for Psychophysiological Research, Boston, Nov. 9–12, 1972
19. Murphy G: Psychology in the year 2000. Am Psychol 24:523–530, 1969
20. Nowlis DP, Kamiya J: The control of electroencephalographic alpha rhythms through auditory feedback and the associated mental activity. Psychophysiology 6:476–484, 1970
21. Russell B: Wisdom of the West. London, Rathbone Books Limited, 1969
22. Schoenfeld WN: Oyepk on Mediating Mechanism of the Conditional Reflex. Cond Reflex 5: 165–170, 1970
23. Schoenfeld WN: Conditioning the Whole Organism. Cond Reflex 6:125–128, 1971 (editorial)
24. Skinner, BF: The concept of the reflex in the description of Behavior. J Gen Psychol 5:427–457, 1931
25. Stent G: An ode to objectivity: Does God play at dice? Atlantic Monthly 1972, pp 125–130
26. Stoyva J. Barber T, DiCara L, et al: Biofeedback and Self-Control. New York, Aldine, Atherton, 1971
27. Watson JB: Psychology as the behaviorist views it. Psychol Rev 20:158–177, 1913

IV. Conclusion

Chapter 13

Biofeedback—A Clinician's Overview

Lee Birk, M.D.

THE MAJOR AIM of this seminar is to present the best work now available on the clinical use of biofeedback in a variety of psychosomatic conditions, together with an account of the basic science foundations underlying these new techniques. No attempt is made to cover other new interesting and important applications like the treatment of subvocalization as a cause of slow reading[1,2] or like fertility control.[3] It also does not attempt to cover other established and legitimate uses, as in stroke rehabilitation,[4,5] or other medical applications still in the stage of early research, such as in the treatment of asthma,[6] colitis,[7] or peptic ulcer.[8]

Of the clinical applications this book does describe, the usefulness of biofeedback in the treatment of tension headache (Chapter 4) and of migraine headache (Chapter 5) seems especially well documented. Beyond question, biofeedback is of major clinical importance in the treatment of these problems, previously notorious for their resistance to definitive treatment.

The physiologic efficacy of biofeedback is also well established in cardiac arrhythmias, ranging from premature ventricular contractions (see page 79) to atrial fibrillation (see page 101) to Wolff-Parkinson-White Syndrome (see page 115). The clinical significance of these effects, however, especially in comparison with other treatment techniques, is a complicated question not yet fully answered.

Partly because other forms of treatment are so generally unsatisfactory, biofeedback should be considered seriously in the treatment of the relatively rare disorder, Raynaud's disease. Although the number of treated cases is still small, and although the optimum technique for feedback has not yet been established by comparative research, the results in these pilot cases are generally encouraging enough to consider the technique to be practically useful.

The use of biofeedback in the treatment of established essential hypertension has to date been disappointing. This is hardly surprising in view of the known irreversible pathophysiologic changes that take place in the walls of blood vessels chronically subjected to abnormally high pressures. Although clinical results with established hypertension for this reason have been predictably poor, the outlook may be better in the case of early labile hypertension without deteriorative blood vessel changes. Biofeedback for hypertension therefore remains an important area to be explored in further clinical research.

Combining a screening and early-case detection program with a biofeedback training program may yet prove to be of very great value. This is certainly worth exploring, especially in view of the seriousness and extremely high incidence of this psychosomatic condition. Such preventive possibilities, including

© *1973, by Grune & Stratton, Inc.*

perhaps the concomitant use of assertive training,* along with biofeedback, for detected early cases, should receive earnest research attention.

Biofeedback in the treatment of epilepsy is certainly at a very early stage of exploration, with only four treated cases reported in Dr. Sterman's pioneer chapter. In spite of this, the early results do appear quite promising, although the unexpected finding of a need for continued training sessions over time may mean that the technique will never reach the stage of being widely popular, and may in fact limit its practical clinical usefulness to drug-refractory cases. Of these, of course, there are many, even though they comprise a mere fraction of the overall number of patients with epilepsy. If biofeedback should in more extended study prove clinically useful to only a fraction of patients with drug-refractory seizures, that in itself would be a major contribution to medicine.

The usefulness of biofeedback procedures as an adjunctive or major element in behavior therapy seems reasonably well established, particularly for treatment-refractory insomnia and for patients with various kinds of phobias who need systematic desensitization but do not respond well to simpler methods of learning relaxation. In addition, even for other patients undergoing behavior therapy we have found EMG feedback to be a very useful monitor of the level of relaxation: some patients think they are relaxed and are not, and others are, but (as a psychoanalytic-type of resistance)† don't want to admit it!

Finally, not surprisingly for the broad-spectrum[9] or psychodynamic[10,11,12,13] behavior therapists, biofeedback procedures, like other kinds of behavior therapy, can in certain instances operate synergistically with and catalyze psychotherapy.

Let us hope that we in medicine can be open and flexible enough to continue, by further basic and clinical research, to explore, validate, and refine the various clinical uses of biofeedback, the new Behavioral Medicine, without falling into the *furor therapeuticus* that befell Benjamin Rush.

REFERENCES

1. Hardyck CD, Petinovich LF, Ellsworth DW: Feedback of speech muscle activity during silent reading: rapid extenction Science 154 (3755)1467–1468, 1966

2. Hardyck CDS, Petinovich FR: Treatment of subvocal speech during reading. J Reading 12:361–368, 1969

3. Fievch DS, Lieb CS, Fancion SL, et al: Self induced scrotal hypothermia in man: a preliminary report. Paper presented at the Biofeedback Research Society Meeting, Boston, Mass, November, 1972

4. Marinacci AA: Applied Electromyography. Philadelphia, Lea & Febiger, 1968

5. Johnson HE, Garton UN: A practical method of muscle reduction in hemipligion: Electromyographic facilitation and conditioning. Unpublished manuscript, Casa Colina Hospital for Rehabilitation Medicine, Pomona, Calif

6. Vachon L: Cited in: Biofeedback in action. Medical World News, March 9, 1973

7. Peper, E.: Personal communication

8. Gorman P, Kamiga S: Voluntary control of stomach pH. Research note presented at the Biofeedback Research Society Meeting, Boston, Mass, November, 1972

9. Lazarus A: Behavior Therapy and Beyond. New York, McGraw-Hill, 1971

---

*Hypertensive patients are often angry in a suppressed way due partially to an inability to be effectively assertive.

†This may happen because learning to relax is often the first stage of many behavioral treatment plans; if the patient can remain in this first stage, he can avoid facing later and dreaded stages.

10. Birk L: Behavior therapy-integration with dynamic psychiatry. Behav Ther 1:522-26, 1970

11. Birk L: Intensive group therapy: An effective behavioral-psychoanalytic method. Invited paper presented at the joint meeting of the American Academy of Psychoanalysis and the American Psychiatric Association, Honolulu, May 9, 1973. Am J Psychiatry (in press)

12. Feather BU, Rhoads JM: Psychodynamic behavior therapy: I. Theory and rationale. Arch Gen Psychiatry 26:496-502, 1970

13. Birk L: Psychoanalysis and behavioral analysis: a natural resonance and complementarity. Int J Psychiatry 11, 1973

Index

Aggression, reduction in hypertension through control of, 140–141
Agoraphobia, reduction of arousal levels in, 184
Alpha activity
  degree of learning in, 147
  methodological problems in study of control of, 200–201
  "passive volition" in control of, 29
  positive subjective feeling state related to, 193
Analgesic drugs, migraine treatment with, 52, 53
Anger
  headache syndromes through supression of, 35–36, 52
  hypertension and, 140
Animal learning, instrumental conditioning of, 5–13, 21, 192–193
Anxiety
  hypertension and, 140
  reduction of arousal levels in, 183–185
Arousal levels in phobias, desensitization of, 183–185
Arrhythmias, operant conditioning techniques for control of, 173–178
Atrial fibrillation (AF), ventricular rate (VR) control of, 101, 114
Atropine
  premature ventricular control (PVC) and, 81, 84–85, 86, 91
  ventricular rate (VR) control in atrial fibrillation (AF) and, 103, 107, 108, 111
  Wolff–Parkinson–White syndrome and, 116, 118, 119
Autogenic training
  hypertension reduction through, 140
  migraine reduction through, 57–59, 67
  transfer of control and, 178
Autonomic conditioning
  animal learning experiments with, 5–6, 9–13, 21
  human vasomotor control through, 124–125
Autonomic drugs
  premature ventricular control (PVC) and usage of, 81, 86–87, 91
  ventricular rate (VR), control and usage of, 103, 107–108, 110, 111
  Wolff–Parkinson–White syndrome and usage of, 116–117, 117–118

Behavioral sciences, biofeedback and conflicting philosophies in, 194–200
Biofeedback, definition of, 2–3

Blood pressure
  hypertension control through self-regulation of, 131–143
  instrumental conditioning of, in animals, 11–12, 13
Brain
  electric impulse stimulation of pleasure centers in, 192
  epilepsy control through reduction in seizure activity in, 145–165
  migraines through vasodilatation of arteries in, 53, 56

Cardiac rates
  electric impulse stimulation and control of, in animal studies, 192–193
  instrumental conditioning changes in, in rats, 9–11, 13
  operant conditioning control of arrhythmia of, 73–78
Clinics, biofeedback procedures in, 177–188
Control strategies, transfer from clinic to "real life" of, 178–179
Curare agents, animal autonomic conditioning experiments and, 21, 194

Diastolic blood pressure. *See* Blood pressure
Drug usage
  migraine headaches and, 52–53, 55, 57, 182–183
  placebo effect in, 22
  sleep-onset insomnia and, 186
  tension headaches and, 45–46, 48
  ventricular rate (VR) control and, 103, 107, 110, 111
  See also Autonomic drugs

Eastern philosophy, influence of, 194, 197
Edrophonium
  premature ventricular control (PVC) and, 81, 86–87, 91
  ventricular rate (VR) control in atrial fibrillation (AF) and, 103, 107, 108, 111, 113
EEG activity
  epilepsy control through production of sensorimotor rhythm (SMR) and, 145, 147–164
  "passive volition" in, 29–30
  variations in subjects' mood reports and, 22–24

Electromyogram (EMG) feedback techniques
    anxiety arousal level reduction through, 185
    sleep-onset insomnia and, 186
    tension headache treatment through, 35–51, 66–67, 180–182
Epilepsy, reduction in seizure activity for control of, 145–165
Ergotamine tartrate, migraine treatment with, 52, 55, 56, 57
Expectancy factors, placebo effect and, 24–28, 31, 177

Frontalis muscles
    headaches through tension in, 2–3, 35–37, 41, 139, 181
    lowering anxiety arousal levels in, 184–185
    specific effects of EMG on, 29

Generalized anxiety, reduction of arousal levels for control of, 184
Glandular response changes in animals, instrumental conditioning of, 12

Hand-warming techniques
    migraine reduction through, 53, 58–66, 182, 183
    Raynaud's disease control through, 121–122, 125–127
Headaches. *See* Migraine headaches; Tension headaches
Heart rates. *See* Cardiac rates
Home practice of relaxation techniques, 40, 48, 178–179
Hypertension, self-regulation of blood pressure for control of, 131–143
Hypothalamic dysfunction, migraine and, 56–57

Insomnia
    EMG reduction in arousal levels in, 49, 186
    psychotherapeutic progress and elimination of, 157, 171–173
    relaxation techniques for, 49
    treatment-refractory, 183
Instrumental conditioning, visceral and autonomic functions in animals and, 5–13
Intestinal contractions, instrumental conditioning of, in rats, 10, 12
Isoproterenol
    premature ventricular control (PVC) and usage of, 81, 85, 86, 91
    ventricular rate (VR) control in atrial fibrillation (AF) and, 103, 107, 108, 110, 111
    Wolff–Parkinson–White syndrome and, 116, 118–119

Meditation, reduction of hypertension through, 140–141
Menstrual cycle migraine headaches, medication during, 183
Methysergide maleate (Sansert), migraine treatment with, 51, 52–53, 56
Migraine headaches
    hand-warming techniques for reduction of, 51–69, 182–183
    psychotherapeutic progress through elimination of, 167, 169–171
Mind-cure movement, biofeedback similarities to, 189, 195–196
Minnesota Multiphasic Personality Inventory (MMPI), measurement of tension headache reduction through, 44–45
Monomethylhydrazine, sensorimotor rhythm (SMR) feedback and, 151
Motivation
    cardiac arrhythmia control and, 70, 77
    as crucial variable in success of therapy, 128
    hypertension control and, 138–139
Motor activity, sensorimotor rhythm (SMR) and levels of, 162–163
Muscle contraction headaches, EMG feedback lessening of, 35–51, 66–67

Occipitalis muscle tension, headaches and, 2–3, 35, 36

Phentolamine, premature ventricular control (PVC) and usage of, 81, 91
Phenylephrine
    premature ventricular control (PVC) and usage of, 81, 91
    Wolff–Parkinson–White syndrome and, 116, 117–118
Phobias, arousal level reduction in control of, 49, 183–184
Placebo effect
    biofeedback procedures and, 17–24, 31–32
    expectancy factors in, 24–28, 31, 177
    PATI model for evaluation of, 24–31
    prediction of effectiveness of procedure and, 30–31
Premature ventricular contractions (PVCs), operant conditioning control of, 75, 79–80
Primary reinforcement, in instrumental conditioning of animals, 6, 7
Propranolol
    premature ventricular control (PVC) and usage of, 81, 86–87, 91
    ventricular rate (VR) control in atrial fibrillation (AF) and usage of, 103, 107, 108, 110, 111
    Wolff–Parkinson–White syndrome and, 116, 118

Psychosomatic disorders, psychotherapeutic treatment of, 141–142
Psychotherapy
  biofeedback success and progress in, 167–173
  migraine headache treatment through, 52
  psychosomatic disorders and, 141–142

Raynaud's disease, blood flow control in, 121–130
Reflexes, evolution of theories of, 190–200
Relaxation techniques
  electromyogram (EMG) feedback and. See Electromyogram (EMG) feedback techniques
  evaluation of Transcendental Meditation (TM) techniques for, 30–31
  hypertension control through, 140–141
  phobia arousal level reduction through, 183–184
  taping of exercises in, 178, 180
  tension headache reduction through, 40, 44, 47–49, 66–67, 180–181

Seizure activity, epilepsy control through reduction in, 145–165
Sensorimotor rhythm (SMR), epilepsy control through production of, 145, 149–164
Serotonin, migraine headaches and levels of, 51, 52, 56, 121
Skeletal muscle activity
  instrumental conditioning of animal learning and, 9, 10, 11
  tension headaches and, 35
Skin temperature measurements. See Hand-warming techniques
Sleep studies
  sensorimotor rhythm (SMR) feedback and, 151, 162
  See also Insomnia
Social phobias, arousal level reduction for control of, 183–184
Somato-motor activity, interrelationship of autonomic-visceral activity to, 10, 13

Stress
  migraine headache syndrome and, 51
  tension headache as expression of, 35–36, 47–48, 181–182
Success of therapy
  elimination of symptoms through biofeedback and, 167–173
  patient's self-perception of, 179
  PATI model for evaluation of, 24–31
Sympathectomy, Raynaud's disease treatment through, 481, 485, 489, 121, 125, 129
Systolic blood pressure. See Blood pressure

Tachyarrhythmia, operant conditioning control of, 75–76, 77
Tension headache, EMG feedback lessening of, 35–51, 66–67, 180–182
Theta activity
  "passive volition" in control of, 29
  sleep-onset insomnia and increase in, 186
Transcendental Meditation (TM)
  PATI model applied to, 30–31
  as relaxation technique, 140–141

Ultimate placebo, biofeedback as, 20, 21

Vasodilatation of cranial arteries, migraine and, 53, 56
Ventricular rate (VR) control
  atrial fibrillation (AF) and, 101–114
  cardiac arrhythmia and, 73–78
  premature ventricular contractions (PVCs) and, 75, 79–100
  Wolff–Parkinson–White syndrome and, 76, 77, 115–118
Visceral functions in animals, autonomic conditioning of, 5–13

Wolff–Parkinson–White syndrome, cardiac rate control learning in, 71, 76, 77, 115–119

Yoga
  autonomic control through, 19, 57
  relaxation techniques in, 140

FAMILY PRACTICE LIBRARY

FAMILY MEDICAL CENTER
1700 West 13th Street
Little Rock, Ar. 72202